START A REVOLUTION

Nine World-Changing Strategies for Single Adults

STEPHEN FELTS

LifeWay Press
Nashville, Tennessee

© Copyright 1996 • LifeWay Press
Reprinted 1997, 1999

ISBN 0-8054-9823-0

Dewey Decimal Classification Number: 248.84
Subject Heading: SINGLE PEOPLE–RELIGIOUS LIFE

*For information on adult discipleship and family resources, training, and events, visit our Web site at
www.lifeway.com/discipleplus or contact Customer Service Center, MSN 113; 127 Ninth Avenue, North;
Nashville, TN 37234-0113; FAX (615) 251-5933; email customerservice@lifeway.com*

Printed in the United States of America

LifeWay Press
127 Ninth Avenue, North
Nashville, Tennessee 37234

As God works through us …
*We will help people and churches know Jesus Christ and seek His Kingdom by providing
biblical solutions that spiritually transform individuals and cultures.*

Contents

The Author

stephen **felts**

Stephen Felts is former editor-in-chief of the award-winning *Christian Single* magazine and a popular conference speaker. He presently serves as minister with single adults at First Baptist Church, Franklin, Tennessee. A never-married single adult, Stephen has been a leader among single adults for more than 20 years.

Previously Stephen pastored churches and served on church staffs in the Seattle, Kansas City, Orlando, and Nashville areas for eight years. Stephen is a graduate of William Jennings Bryan College and of Dallas Theological Seminary.

Preface

A crisis of leadership exists today among single adults in America. By leadership I do not mean simply having a title that connotes leadership. I mean the kind of leadership that motivates single men and women of God to recognize needs in their world and take initiative to address those needs in Christ's name to bring glory to Him. This vacuum exists not because single adults lack the desire to lead but because many simply do not know how to begin influencing their world for Christ. Giving single adults those practical skills is the purpose of this book.

Leadership is lacking both in the church among single adults and in the world where single adults live every day. Excellent leaders exist. But alarmingly, few single adults are actively pursuing positions of Christian leadership. Recently, one of the largest Protestant denominations in the country surveyed its churches and found that in their single-adult ministries only 7 percent of the single adults were involved in any form of leadership. The other 93 percent of single adults were following the leadership of married persons.

Christian single adults need to hold in high regard the married leaders who minister with them. Many early leaders in single-adult ministry were married persons with a burden for single adults who did not know Christ. Without their love, devotion, and burden many single-adult ministries in America would not exist.

This book is not a call to expel the married leaders God has led to work with single adults in the church. And it is not a call for single adults to lead only in single-adult church work. It is a call for single adults, as peer adults, to join the rest of the body of Christ in spreading the gospel. It calls single adults to take steps that will intentionally integrate their faith into their world—at church, at work, or at school.

Jesus said, " 'Let your light shine before men, that they may see your good deeds and praise your Father in heaven' " (Matt. 5:16). The very fabric of our society needs that light. The world will not come to the church. The church must go to the world. To do that, you need a strategy. *Start a Revolution* provides practical help for getting started.

Single adults are, first of all, adults. According to the government, a person becomes an adult at a certain age, usually 18 or 21. But in Christian ministry adulthood is defined not by biological age but by maturity and character. Have you ever known an adult who was childish in his ways? This person was physically mature yet still had not become an adult. Although immaturity is likely present in any single-adult group, churches also have thousands of Christian single adults who are mature. They are stable in their lifestyles, committed to living godly lives, and consistent in Christian growth. However, many of these single adults are passive about Christian leadership.

Often, in some churches single adults are limited in Christian leadership because others have misunderstandings and misperceptions about single adults. Some churches, for instance, assume that all single adults are immature and thus disqualify them from ministry leadership. It is true that immaturity has no place in leadership. But it is not true that all single adults are immature.

Some single adults do not pursue leadership roles in ministry because they have been conditioned to be passive. If a church believes that single adults are simply overgrown youth who will get married someday if they ever get their lives together, then single adults are prohibited from pursuing serious leadership roles. Such single-adult ministries often follow the pattern of a youth ministry, with chaperones—older, married leaders—and an authoritarian ministry style. Single adults are told what their programs, events, ministries, and plans will be. They are then expected to follow the leaders who are there to watch over them.

This approach is unfair to the thousands of godly, mature single adults who are capable of reflecting Christ's character in leadership roles. Such a pattern encourages passivity toward leaders and instills an unwillingness in single adults ever to emerge as true leaders in ministry.

Other single adults are overlooked for leadership positions because some churches believe that church growth comes only by focusing on young married couples with 2.4 kids. Since single adults don't fit the stereotypical church-growth equations, these churches allow single adults to participate in their ministries, but they focus most of their energy on married couples. The unwritten and nonverbal message is: You need not apply for leadership positions until you are married. Are single adults selected as deacons or elders? Do sermons include illustrations of single adults along with those about husbands and wives, children, youth, and the elderly? Subtle messages teach single adults to listen and absorb—but not to contribute. Consequently, these messages stifle their desire to become godly leaders.

Unfortunately, many times it is not just the church that limits single adults from leadership. It is single adults themselves. Many do not perceive themselves as leaders. A leader, by definition, is a person who assumes a position in front of a group, not to be in the limelight but to set direction and purpose, to achieve a specific goal. Today's single adults must realize that they are gifted and must recognize the responsibility and accountability that accompany their gifts.

I believe there is no group with greater potential to radically influence the world for Christ than single adults. Single-adult ministry has come of age. The U.S. Census Bureau states that presently, single adults are the fastest-growing segment in American society. By the year 2000 more than 50 percent of the adult population will be single. It's time! It's time for single adults to be proactive rather than passive. It's time for single adults to take the initiative to reach the world around them. It's time for them to do what no other group on earth can do exactly like them.

Someone once said: "Don't follow the path to see where it may take you. Instead, go where there is no path and leave a trail for others to follow." That is the definition of leadership. Just because a single adult lacks a role model or a functioning program in which to participate does not mean that person's dream for ministry cannot become a reality. It simply means that, by default, the single adult has received the opportunity to act as the principal person, the initiator, the pioneer in the church or single-adult group to begin a particular ministry—to start a revolution. This book is written for single adults who know they have received gifts and talents from God and who recognize their responsibility to use them in service; for those whose heart's desire is to be useful in God's kingdom but don't know what direction their ministry should take; and finally, for those who have a passion for a particular ministry but don't know the beginning steps.

When single adults begin to recognize their potential and to understand how God can use them to make a difference, they will view the world through new eyes and will discover the most amazing opportunities. It's not a road of ease but one of great adventure in Christ. To those who choose to travel this road with me, I say, Come, let's change the world together and give the glory to God!

Introduction

A common scenario occurs every week in the lives of single adults across this nation. The following illustration may sound familiar to you.

Bill had been a Christian for about 18 months. Accepting Christ during his senior year in college radically altered his lifestyle. His spiritual growth was a sterling example to his family, his friends, and his church.

Before becoming a Christian, Bill lived in an apartment complex noted for promiscuity, and he partied often. But now as a Christian, he viewed his friends and neighbors in the complex as persons looking for what he had found. Concerned about their spiritual condition, he wanted to make a difference.

Bill approached the associate pastor at his church. "I'd like to reach the persons in an apartment complex for Christ," Bill told him. "Can you tell me what I can do?" Bill's burden was genuine. He had a passion for Christ and a burning desire to tell others that Jesus was available to them, as well.

The answer Bill received was also very genuine, but as is often the case, it was insufficient. "Bill," the associate pastor said, "Why don't you take our evangelism course here at the church. I'll lend you some of my books, and you can begin a neighborhood Bible study in the complex. Invite some of the other single adults in our church to attend." It sounded like a good plan to Bill. So armed with this advice, he was on his way.

There are several problems with the advice Bill received. First, Bill was led to believe that the primary key to leadership is academic education. "Take this course; read these books" is sometimes the bulk of advice to Christians seeking to lead out in reaching others for Christ. But academics does not make a person a leader. It makes him only an educated novice. Jesus' disciples were not brilliant. In fact, the intellectuals of Jesus' day were amazed that His followers were common, everyday citizens. In Acts 4 Peter and John were brought before the high priest and the teachers and rulers of Israel who were in Jerusalem. "When they saw the courage of Peter and John and realized that they were unschooled, ordinary men, they were astonished and they took note that these men had been with Jesus" (Acts 4:13).

The apostle Paul, on the other hand, was a highly educated man, but he did not consider his education automatic grounds for leadership status. He wrote to the Corinthian church: "When I came to you, brothers, I did not come with eloquence or superior wisdom as I proclaimed to you the testimony about God. For I resolved to know nothing while I was with you except Jesus Christ and him crucified. I came to you in weakness and fear, and with much trembling. My message and my preaching were not with wise and persuasive words, but with a demonstration of the Spirit's power, so that your faith might not rest on men's wisdom, but on God's power" (1 Cor. 2:1-5). Paul did not mean that education is insignificant; he meant that education alone will not make you a leader. The same is true today.

Bill's second oversight was his own personality. Bill was an extrovert and a visionary. He could sell sand in the middle of a desert. But he was not a detail person. Any new Christian work or ministry involves countless details. Bill's might include—

- locating a place for the group to meet;
- deciding on a topic for the Bible study;
- selecting a day and a time;
- securing funds for printing the invitations;
- designing and printing the invitations;
- acquiring the apartment manager's permission to distribute the invitations;
- devising a plan for distributing the invitations;
- contacting those who respond to the invitations.

These are only a few of the details involved in beginning a ministry. However, Bill refused to consider them, even though they were vital to success, because they drained him emotionally and drove him up a wall. Bill's dream was clear to him, but the details were blurry.

The third major consideration Bill overlooked before beginning this ministry was the biblical approach to building leaders and beginning ministries. It is what we commonly call discipleship. In 2 Timothy 2:2 the apostle Paul said to Timothy, "The things you have heard me say in the presence of many witnesses entrust to reliable men who will also be qualified to teach others." This verse is the heart of modern-day discipleship. Please do not confuse Paul's command to teach others with today's academic practices. Paul taught Timothy, but he didn't do it in a classroom. His university was the marketplace. As Timothy traveled with Paul, he learned Paul's values and priorities. He observed first-hand how Paul lived his values every day. This was how Paul taught others, and it was how he encouraged Timothy to teach others. It was also how Jesus taught His disciples and how they taught their disciples. But it's a practice frequently lost in today's mobile society and especially in churches that employ an academic educational model.

Paul stressed the idea of relationship because he understood that all great leaders are born and nurtured by relationship. For the apostle Paul it was the great leader Gamaliel. For Timothy it was the apostle Paul. Paul told Timothy to pass on the relationship, for relationship builds great leaders. Henry Cloud, the codirector of the Minirth-Meier Clinic West in California, states: "Because we live in a fallen world, we are not born into connection. It has to be gained, and it is an arduous, developmental process. Without going through that process of bonding, we are doomed to alienation and isolation. Not only do we not grow, we deteriorate."[1]

Paul also talked about character. Entrust, Paul said, "to reliable men." Someone once said, "Reputation is what others think about you, but character is what you are in the dark." Without godly character, faithfulness is sporadic. And without faithfulness, leadership is impossible.

Finally, Paul spoke to Timothy about responsibility and a teachable spirit. He was instructed to entrust to reliable men "who will also be qualified to teach others." The ability to teach requires the ability to be taught. Teaching is easy when you know something well. The more you understand something, the easier it is to explain it to someone else. Good leaders possess both a teachable spirit and an understanding that what they learn, they must pass on to others. But what is learned in the context of life cannot be taught in the context of a classroom; it must be taught in life.

This is the biblical model for building leaders. It is not primarily academic, although it involves learning. It is not primarily organizational, although it involves various levels of organization. It is primarily the outgrowth of a relationship. Without strong core relationships, a leader in the making loses heart, becomes discouraged and confused, and eventually quits.

That is what happened to Bill. He completed the evangelism course and learned volumes. It helped him with his personal evangelism, and he was grateful. But when he began to implement the apartment ministry, he encountered those details he hadn't expected. The more they grew, the more overwhelmed he became. The more he attempted to deal with them, the more emotionally drained he became. After a while, since he had no experienced leader to follow and no core group to help him, Bill gave up in frustration, deciding that he must not be cut out for ministry. Someone else could make a difference, but apparently, he could not.

The next time Bill's church asked him for help in an area of ministry, he remembered his earlier experience and responded: "No thanks. I don't think I have what it takes for that." Another potentially good leader remained untapped. More importantly, because of Bill's self-perception, any area of need he discovered in the future would go unheeded because he had convinced himself that he didn't have what it takes to be leader.

The Purpose of This Book

In spite of the obstacles single adults face, I believe they can radically change the world for Jesus Christ. Given the tools and understanding, single adults are capable of more than we can possibly imagine. Equipping single adults is the purpose of this book. John Wesley, the founder of the Methodist Church, once said, "Give me one hundred men who fear nothing but God, hate nothing but sin, and are determined to know nothing among men but Jesus Christ and Him crucified, and I will set the world on fire with them." A bold statement—but John Wesley proved he was right and did just that.

John Wesley is gone, but opportunities to set the world on fire are still available. I truly believe that God has placed single adults, more than anyone else on this planet, in the strategic position of setting the world on fire with the radical message of Christ. The question is not, Can the world be set on fire? The question is, Who will do it? No group has greater potential to lead the way in a revolution of the gospel than single men and women of God who carry that fire of personal devotion in their hearts, just as John Wesley's followers did in the 19th century.

Desire is not lacking. Devotion is not lacking. The missing ingredient is the practical knowledge for beginning a revolution. What principles can help make godly single adults' dreams of influencing their world for Christ become a reality? Many of those principles are here in *Start a Revolution*.

I have worked alongside single adults in ministry for more than 20 years. I have experienced success and failure. I have learned what will work and what will not. I am convinced that God has placed single adults in strategic places to revolutionize their world.

Given the climate of today's culture, single adults cannot approach their world the way John Wesley did his. The needs of people have not changed, but the methods for reaching them have. Many methods that were highly successful in the past no longer work. Although people readily acknowledge that Wesley's culture and today's culture are vastly different, many fail to recognize that our culture today is vastly different from just 20 years ago. Failure to adapt to that change has left many well-meaning Christians unequipped to reach the world for Christ.

For that reason *Start a Revolution* begins by addressing the need to revolutionize our own thinking. The world has changed! The gospel is the same as when Jesus gave it to us, but society demands that our approach be as fluid as that society. Today no one rides a horse from community to community preaching along the way. In Wesley's day that approach revolutionized the world. What do you think would happen if you tried that now?

Of course, the natural question is, What approach works today? The answer is too involved to offer a simple response. Our culture is amazingly diverse. For example, at one time most of society adhered to the same philosophical premises. In America most members of society were at least nominally Christian. If they were not committed believers, they at least agreed with the basic premises of Christianity. But today no such assumption can be made.

A diverse culture requires a diverse approach to bring about positive change—change that will bring glory to God. But diverse approaches cannot be mass-produced in a canned, step-by-step instruction manual. What would work in one setting might be a total failure in another.

We need a foundational set of principles that provides a framework, a set of parameters that leaves room for creative, pragmatic thinking by individuals, each in a unique situation. When individuals assess their personal strengths and weaknesses, devise a unique plan to influence their world for Christ, and then implement that plan, others can duplicate the process, devising practical steps for their own situations.

This new way of thinking is the basis of *Start a Revolution*. It may not be the answer for everyone, but for many single adults, it can so empower them that their world and their lives will never be the same.

How to Use This Book

This book is not to be read passively. It is a strategy book designed to revolutionize your life and, in so doing, to revolutionize the world in which you live. This book is not for single adults who want to be spoon-fed throughout their adult lives. It is for single adults who have a grasp of their faith in Christ, an awareness that God has an enormous plan for their lives, and a desire and willingness to pursue that plan.

Start a Revolution introduces nine strategies for changing the world:

Strategy 1, "Acquire Integrity: The Principle of Character," explains the need for a better understanding of your abilities and limitations before you attempt to change the world. You need to know not only what you can do but also what you cannot do. You can use this knowledge to make wiser decisions, not only in your career and relationships but also in areas of Christian ministry—which ones to consider, which ones to avoid, and the specific areas of a particular ministry for which you are best suited.

Strategy 2, "Know Yourself: The Principle of Wisdom," provides an opportunity to understand yourself better by completing a unique set of inventories. Mels Carbonell's combination of a personality test and a spiritual-gifts inventory can help you find ways to meld your personality temperament and spiritual gifts into a fulfilling ministry for Christ.

Strategy 3, "Reengineer Ministry: The Principle of Initiative," emphasizes the necessity of developing what the corporate world calls a self-directed work team. Currently, most churches do not capitalize on this ministry style, and most are virtually ineffective in influencing their communities with the message of Christ, especially when communicating with younger single adults. Developing a ministry team to begin doing ministry in a new way can revolutionize an individual, a team, and even an entire church.

Strategy 4, "Start a Company: The Principle of Integration," advocates a ministry-team approach and illustrates the functions of such a team.

Strategy 5, "Unite the Team: The Principle of United Effort," provides practical ways to unite the team as it learns to think and act as a unit. In addition, this strategy discusses several common problems that occur in ministry teams and ways to avoid them.

Strategy 6, "Define Your Vision: The Principle of Clarity," identifies the ingredients needed to succeed; discusses the value of goals; and explains how to set clear, attainable ministry goals.

Strategy 7, "Find a Place to Start: The Principle of Details," emphasizes the importance of details that are often overlooked or considered insignificant. It reveals the value God places on details and guides you to establish measurable objectives for the ministry team.

Strategy 8, "Be Flexible: The Principle of Innovation and Dynamics," helps you understand the patterns that emerge whenever you introduce change into your world. Understanding these patterns allows you to remain flexible and to be creative in overcoming obstacles to arrive at a workable solution.

Strategy 9, "Set Limits and Replace Yourself: The Principle of Duplication," defines the parameters that will help you recognize when it is time to step down and turn over your leadership to another. In doing so, you become free to begin again with a new vision. In addition, this strategy discusses the need for limits on the individual and the team to prevent burnout.

"Ideas for Ministry," beginning on page 235, lists dozens of areas in which an individual or a team can minister. Prayerfully consider these ideas as you seek God's will for your role in ministry.

Making a significant impact for Christ in your world is possible if you have the desire and the willingness to pursue that desire. But it can't be done in ignorance or isolation. It must be accomplished with forethought, careful placement of persons and personalities, and teamwork toward a common goal. With the tools provided here, any single adult can start a revolution!

----

[1]Henry Cloud, *Changes That Heal* (Grand Rapids: Zondervan, 1992), 50.

.a c q u i r.e
integrity

the principle of character

We know what we are, but know not what we may be.[1]

—William Shakespeare

Often, when a person speaks of integrity, morality is a major focus. Certainly, integrity involves being forthright in your personal morals. But integrity goes beyond morality. It includes being totally honest with yourself and with others about both the positive and negative areas of your life, as well as living a lifestyle true to your beliefs and identity.

Let's begin by defining the term. Webster's dictionary defines *integrity* as "the quality or state of being complete or undivided: completeness. Synonym: honesty."[2] If I say that the cloth hanging around a window in the dining room is a curtain, then at the same time I am saying that the four-legged, wooden structure beneath it is not a curtain. When you know what something is, you also know what it is not.

When you apply this principle to yourself, you develop total integrity–an understanding of who you are and who you are not and an honesty in all areas of your life: your strengths and weaknesses, your personal relationships, your occupational goals in life, your dreams, and much more. Integrity is also clearly understanding who God is, having a relationship with Christ, and knowing your reason for existence on this earth. By understanding and accepting these realities, you have the focus you need to make a major difference in life.

To start a revolution, you need total integrity. By *total* I don't mean that you must reach a state of perfection. I mean that you admit your shortcomings and attempt to overcome them. You also admit your strengths without being boastful or proud, and you search for ways to use them for God's glory. When you are doing these things in each area of your life, you are living with total integrity.

Many Christian single adults sell themselves short, especially when it comes to being used by God. They fail to recognize the great things God wants to accomplish through them—things He has equipped them to do if they only believe He can work through them. Often, the reason they fail to recognize their potential is that they cannot accept and believe that God truly has great plans for them. What they need is total integrity—the ability to be honest with themselves, including their positive attributes. Only when persons are honest with themselves can they be honest with God. And when they are honest with God, He brings about the character changes that allow Him to use them mightily!

But honesty is not always easy to accept, even in yourself. One of my many jobs while a college student was working as a security guard. Every hour I made my rounds. I checked each door on campus and registered the time on the security clock I carried with me. After finishing each round, which took about 30 minutes, I would return to the administration building and wait until time for my next round.

One night as I made my rounds, I was angry with God. After mulling over the situation, I said, "Oh, well, praise the Lord anyway!" Right then the Lord spoke to me in a somewhat humorous tone: "Whom are you kidding?" At that moment I realized that God saw my heart! There in the middle of the campus I began talking out loud to Him. If others had heard me, they would have thought I had lost my mind. Out of a dead silence they would have heard a one-sided, very loud, and very intense conversation that began with "All right! All right! Yeah, I'm mad! And you want to know why? Well, I'll tell you why I'm mad." And I unloaded all the anger toward God I had been concealing. But as I talked, I also listened to myself. The more I talked, the sillier it all sounded. I was being pretty childish. Before I could finish, I began to laugh at myself. I was trying to convince myself that I was right, but the more I listened to my own words, the more ridiculous I sounded, even to myself! At the same time, I realized that God was not shocked by my outburst. He was actually waiting for it. Of course, in my laughter I realized that the problem was not God; it was me. When I laughed, I could sense that God was laughing with me.

When the laughing stopped, God opened my eyes to see a principle, which He taught me in the form of an illustration. God respects your decisions. If you choose to play games and hide what you're feeling or thinking, He will not tear it from your heart. (You really can't hide anything from God. You can only fool yourself into thinking He doesn't see.) But if you ever want God to remove something from your heart or mind, you have to take whatever is there and hold it out to Him. When you take what's inside, place it in the palm of your hand, and hold it out to God, then He will take it from you—and only then. That's being honest with yourself and with God.

That's what He did with my anger that night. But it happened only because I decided to be honest with myself and with Him. I believed I wasn't supposed to be mad at God. He's God! So I tried to tell myself that all was fine with me. But it really wasn't. I was angry. It didn't seem theologically correct, but it was real. When I honestly told God how I felt, He removed it. And in doing so, He strengthened my character. That's the value of personal honesty. That's personal integrity.

Total integrity means that you are honest with yourself, with God, and with others about your strengths and your weaknesses. And the outgrowth of that honesty is observed in the character of your lifestyle. For example, Jesus said that He had come not for the righteous but for sinners: " 'It is not the healthy who need a doctor, but the sick' " (Matt. 9:12). He was not implying that persons existed who were healthy, or righteous, apart from Him. He was identifying those who were honest with themselves and with Him about their spiritual, emotional, or physical states. Those who were honest enough to admit their shortcomings were in a position to receive healing from Jesus. God honors that kind of personal, total integrity that accepts and acts on the truth rather than hides from it. Jesus said to His disciples in John 8:32, " 'You will know the truth, and the truth will set you free.' " Persons with total integrity know their strengths and admit their weaknesses. They know their likes and their dislikes. In every facet of life they strive to be forthright and honest with themselves, with God, and with others.

Do not misunderstand this concept. Total integrity does not mean looking

John 15:2,8

for all of your faults and denigrating yourself. If you focus on your faults and deny your strengths, your self-confidence wanes, and depression may set in. On the other hand, if you focus on your strengths and deny your faults, you can become arrogant and unteachable. Total integrity means evaluating yourself honestly. You have some amazing strengths, some things you can do well, even though all of them may not be fully developed. But the potential is there, and if you are honest with yourself, you will come to see that potential. When you admit your faults and your strengths and act accordingly, you combine self-respect and total integrity in living. If you are going to start a revolution, make a commitment to personal, total integrity.

The Results of Total Integrity

The more you understand your abilities and inabilities, the more you can focus your energies and increase your impact in society for God's glory. Total integrity leads you to such an understanding.

God designs every person to pursue a certain course in life. I am referring not to occupation but to purpose. You are on this planet for a reason. That reason, once discovered, gives you direction for your life. Without knowing your reason for being here, you can drift along like a ship without a rudder. Any wind that comes along might carry you off course. Ephesians 4:14 uses this same analogy to describe maturity or immaturity: "We will no longer be infants, tossed back and forth by the waves, and blown here and there by every wind of teaching and by the cunning and craftiness of men in their deceitful scheming." When you are mature, you have spiritually and emotionally grown to a point at which you know the truth and follow it instead of misguided persons' deceitful schemes. Children go with the flow. Mature believers set a course in accordance with God's will and follow it.

A Christian's primary purpose is to bring glory to God. But even Christians have different sets of values by which they live in order to bring glory to God. Some Christians value recognition and visibility in order to reach more persons for Christ. Others choose to make an impact by developing deep relationships with only a few persons. One is not right and the other wrong. They operate with different sets of values that govern their perspectives and priorities as Christians. Many ways exist for you to fulfill your goals in life.

God's design for your life is not restricted to the spiritual dimension. You were born with or developed certain capabilities that cause you to be better at doing some things. Try to find a niche that allows you to work from your strengths and to downplay your weaknesses. The more you are able to do so, the more effective and personally fulfilled you will be.

Identifying Your Purpose in Life

Because you were created in God's image, when you develop a personal relationship with Him through salvation and spiritual growth, you can recognize His character traits in your life. Identify which traits you need to develop and which are already strong. His indwelling presence gives you the capacity to develop and strengthen His character traits within you.

All learning begins with a point of reference. When you learn what green is, you know what is not green. The same is true about learning who you are. Society in general is egocentric; its point of reference for learning is humanity itself. But if you begin with the wrong point of reference, you arrive at the wrong conclusion—a basic problem in today's world. When people believe that humanity is basically good, then they also believe that they have no need of a Savior. The gospel of Christ calls people to change their point of reference about themselves and, therefore, about Christ.

A Christian's point of reference is not himself or herself; it is God. When you recognize that God willingly gives His compassion and forgiveness to those who don't deserve them, you also realize your need to develop or nurture those same character traits. Some find it easier than others to develop compassion and forgiveness, but no one is exempt from the need to possess these qualities. They are part of God's character, and because you are made in His image, you should reflect these traits, as well. But you don't develop them naturally. You recognize your need for them when you discover that they are characteristics of God Himself.

The Westminster Catechism, a Presbyterian statement of faith, reads, "The chief end of man is to know God and to enjoy Him forever." Socrates said, "Know thyself." These ideologies seem to oppose each other, but they need not. When you have a clear understanding of who God is, you have an even clearer frame of reference for discovering who you are as His child. Your well-being vitally depends on having a firm grasp of your identity in Christ and His ways of moving in the affairs on earth.

Likewise, to discover God's purpose for you on earth, you need to know your personal strengths and weaknesses. For example, you may think that you are very sensitive. But what do your friends think? If they are honest with you and question that area as one of your strengths, then you probably need to work not only on your sensitivity but also on your self-perception. To gain a better understanding of yourself, get feedback from those who know you best: your friends and family.

Deepen your understanding of who God is—His person, His character, His ways on earth. But also strive to understand how God designed you. Purposely notice your personality traits and identify your spiritual gifts. As you learn more about yourself, you more accurately define your reason for existence.

Certainly, every Christian's goal is to bring glory to God. Part of this important goal is to discover and be who He created you to be through His unconditional love and acceptance. Scripture calls this spiritual maturity. Romans 12:3 says, "Do not think of yourself more highly than you ought, but rather think of yourself with sober judgment, in accordance with the measure of faith God has given you." Such maturity comes when you realize, through Christ's power, all He has called you to be and can set aside all that would restrain you from following Him. At this point you can discover what God has equipped you to do and what others can do better than you.

The apostle Paul spoke of this freedom: "It is for freedom that Christ has set us free. Stand firm, then, and do not let yourselves be burdened again by a yoke of slavery" (Gal. 5:1). The freedom Christ gives you is the freedom to follow Him unrestrained. It is a freedom to discover who you are and what God's design is for your life.

Identify Early Clues

Part of the answer to the question, What is your purpose in life? lies in recognizing your innate abilities and interests. God provides parents to help their children discover their purposes in life. Not long ago parents went too far in guiding their children's directions in life, even arbitrarily choosing the occupations their children would enter. Their decisions were based on their own desires rather than on those of their children. That was not God's design.

Perhaps as a reaction to the practices of earlier generations, the teaching of parental laissez-faire became popular through such theorists as Benjamin Spock. Dr. Spock taught parents that any guidance or restriction would inhibit a child's creative ability to find his own way. Many parents accepted this concept and gave their children virtually no guidance. This teaching was also wrong. Many single adults today received such an upbringing, making it difficult for them to find direction in life. For example, 10 years after graduating from college, most adults are in occupations that do not relate to their academic majors.

God's design was for children to identify their strengths and weaknesses very early in life. With proper guidance and instruction they would live their lives with a clear understanding of God's expectations. One Scripture passage supporting this idea is Proverbs 22:6:

> Train a child in the way he should go,
> and when he is old he will not turn from it.

Many parents have suffered unnecessary guilt after rearing their children according to God's truths, only to see them rebel against God when they gained their independence. These parents believed that their children would return, as Proverbs 22:6 promises. However, many children did not return to God, even when they were older. *Is God's Word reliable?* the parents wondered.

Many well-meaning Christians have claimed Proverbs 22:6 as a spiritual promise. Perhaps more accurately, it is a statement of God's purpose for a person's life. The origin of the Hebrew word for *train* comes from a Hebrew cultural practice. When a woman gave birth, a midwife would receive the baby, wet her own little finger, then rub the pallet of the baby's mouth. This would encourage the innate sucking desire in the baby. The desire already existed in the baby; it needed only to be prodded. Awaking that desire enabled the baby to breathe.

"Train a child" in Proverbs 22:6, then, does not mean teaching guidelines, rules, and values the child will never discard, although these certainly play a vital role in a child's upbringing. This verse is not a prescription for guaranteed spiritual success in child rearing. It does emphasize that parents should encourage the child's natural, God-given abilities that complement his personality. The verse continues to say, "in the way he should go," not "in the way you want him to go." In addition to teaching moral absolutes based on biblical revelation, it is the parents' responsibility to guide their children to discover and pursue their natural abilities and to help them recognize those abilities as God's gifts to be used for His purposes and for His glory.

If parents observe how their children spend their free time, they can begin to understand the patterns, habits, and activities toward which their children gravitate. If parents guide their children in social, occupational, and educational paths that agree with those earlier patterns, the children will pursue them naturally and with an internal motivation. They will enjoy what they do, feel personally fulfilled, and be content.

For example, if a young child takes toys apart rather than playing with them intact, constantly disassembles doorknobs, and is fascinated with moveable parts, the child may have the makings of a great mechanic or engineer. How do you distinguish between a mechanic and an engineer? You also study personality traits. Is she introverted or extroverted? Does she enjoy playing with other children or playing alone? If such information is learned early in life and those traits are nurtured, life is smoother and more productive as the child grows and makes decisions.

Commit to Accountability

How do you learn who God created you to be if you did not receive direction as you grew up? One practical step toward personal understanding is to surround yourself with a select group of persons who commit to being accountable for one another. Single adults need such groups, because without life mates, many do not share deep relationships that reveal and meet character-development needs and promote healing.

In today's mobile society many single adults depend too much on themselves. In asserting an almost defiant independence, some single persons deprive themselves of valuable relationships. This is one advantage of participating in a healthy single-adult group in a church. It may take some time and effort to find a group that meets your needs and shares your desire to influence the world for Christ, but the satisfaction that results from being a part of such a group is worth the search.

Here are some characteristics of a healthy single-adult group.

- Possesses a strong commitment to the integrity and inspiration of the Bible.
- Accepts all persons who enter.
- Is led by mature, godly persons who provide direction for the entire ministry. The more single adults who exhibit maturity, the healthier the group.
- Fits your particular life stage. For example, if you're 25 years old, look for a group of single adults near your age; bonding will be easier.

Do this exercise with a friend to demonstrate the importance of accountability. Sit down facing each other. As your friend watches you, position the center of the palm of your right hand on the tip of your nose. Now try to bring all of your fingers into clear focus. Unless you are unusually gifted, your eyes will cross, and you will see multiple fingers and thumbs. But your friend will see the back of your hand very clearly. Similarly, when an issue is very close to your heart, you may not clearly see the whole picture, certainly not as clearly as a good friend can see it. That's the value of an accountability group. Trusted friends can see things in you that you may not see in yourself. You may even say at times, "I just don't see what you're saying about me." That statement may be entirely correct from your perspective, but it doesn't mean that what they see isn't there.

An accountability group can teach you more about yourself and can allow you to do the same for others.

Listen to Your Heart

Another way to find out who you are is to identify the things you most enjoy doing. Today most success-seminar leaders and motivational speakers promote this as a primary rule: to succeed in life, you must love what you do! When you love your work, it is not perceived as drudgery; it is enjoyable. If God created you as a person who thrives on being with people, consider a ministry that involves a high degree of personal interaction. Your fulfillment will be greater if there is consistency between who you are and what you do.

Occasionally, you hear of CEOs in their mid-50s who leave their positions with six-figure-incomes to open bakeries or flower shops. They learned to be honest enough with themselves to admit that they were unhappy in their careers. Although they had always loved baking or gardening, society had convinced them that success awaited only atop the corporate or professional ladder. They had climbed to the top, but they hadn't liked what they found. These highly successful people had been driven or had driven themselves in the wrong direction. Finally, they had decided to be true to who they were and to do the things they loved to do. In short, they had discovered who they were.

Scripture tells us that God directs us in this manner. Psalm 37:4 says,

> Delight yourself in the Lord
> and he will give you the desires of your heart.

This verse does not mean that when you place God first in your life, He gives you anything you want. Rather, as you grow in your knowledge of and love for God, He places godly desires in your heart, and through those desires He can lead you through life.

God used this approach to lead me into Christian ministry. In changing my heart's desires, He also changed my self-perception. I used to be shy and withdrawn, exhibiting little initiative. As God led me to grow, I learned to stop looking at my limited resources and to focus on His unlimited ones. Today through Him I've overcome my shyness and lack of initiative. Now my desire is to change the world for Christ.

In college I was still a fairly immature Christian. I had accepted Christ at age 10 but had not grown significantly. When I recommitted my life to Christ at age 19, a minister-of-music friend took me under his wing, and I began to mature. I joined the church's music ministry, sang in the choir, and traveled with an ensemble.

As I shared my faith at college, often someone would ask, "Are you some kind of a preacher or something?" "No," I would say, "I'm just a Christian who loves the Lord." Whenever that conversation took place, I later prayed: "God, I'm so glad You haven't called me to preach. Maybe some of these people will come to understand that preachers aren't the only people who love You."

Imagine my surprise when God placed in my heart a desire to preach! A few times during church services I actually imagined myself preaching. When I caught myself, I mentally scolded myself for being what I believed to be sacrilegious: *What pride I must have! What arrogance! Besides,* I reminded myself, *God hasn't called me to preach.*

Then came instances when God began pointing out specific Scriptures during my personal times of prayer and Bible study with Him. When He directed me to a passage related to preaching, I quickly told myself that He simply wanted me to be a more vocal witness. After all, ... you know. As He rearranged the desires of my heart, however, I took steps in a direction I would never have gone if He had not changed me. The desires God placed in my heart have helped me overcome my shyness to speak before thousands of people.

Listen to the Holy Spirit

One role of the Holy Spirit is to guide you along life's path so that you bring glory to God the Father. A part of that process is discovering who you are, with all of your wonderful gifts, talents, and potential.

Many Christians balk at obeying God's leadership in their lives because the challenge God lays before them does not fit their self-image. In the Old Testament Gideon, at first, didn't see himself as a prophetic leader of Israel. But God did. When the angel of the Lord first addressed Gideon, he called out, " 'The Lord is with you, mighty warrior!' " (Judg. 6:12). Part of my battle was coming to believe what God told me I had the ability to do rather than what I told myself I would never be able to do.

Learning to listen to the Holy Spirit involves learning to accept what He says about you even if you initially find it hard to believe. God's plans for you may even exceed what you think He can do through you. They certainly may exceed your self-imposed limitations or the limitations others have placed on you. Learn to listen to the Holy Spirit. He knows you better than you know yourself; trust His judgment.

This is part of what Paul meant in Romans 12:2: "Do not conform any longer to the pattern of this world, but be transformed by the renewing of your mind. Then you will be able to test and approve what God's will is—his good, pleasing and perfect will." When your mind is transformed, your perspective of God and of yourself also changes. You begin to think as He thinks, not only about the world but also about yourself.

How do you listen to the Holy Spirit? Be sensitive to the still, small voice and to the vision God places in your heart. Read God's Word. The Holy Spirit inspired it and will illuminate your reading. Because He will not lead you contrary to His Word, reading and obeying the Scriptures ensures that the direction you take is guided by the Holy Spirit.

Responding to Paradigm Shifts

As you seek God's purpose and as He works in your life, be ready to recognize the changes He brings in your circumstances and in your character so that you remain open to His ongoing activity. You need to be open to paradigm shifts. A paradigm shift is a radical change in perspective. In *The Seven Habits of Highly Effective People* author Stephen R. Covey writes:

> The term *paradigm shift* was introduced by Thomas Kuhn in his highly influential landmark book, *The Structure of Scientific Revolutions*. Kuhn shows how almost every significant breakthrough in the field of scientific endeavor is first a break with tradition, with old ways of thinking, with old paradigms.
>
> For Ptolemy, the great Egyptian astronomer, the earth was the center of the universe. But Copernicus created a paradigm shift, and a great deal of resistance and persecution as well, by placing the sun at the center. Suddenly, everything took on a different interpretation.[3]

A paradigm shift changes your point of reference and, in doing so, alters your perspective. Here is an example of the way a paradigm shift occurs.

Suppose you have a roommate who borrows your car to go to a party across town. You specifically tell your roommate that your only stipulation is that the car is returned, with gas in the tank, no later than midnight.

Midnight comes and goes—still no roommate. At first your reaction is mild anger. How could he be so disrespectful and inconsiderate? This is the beginning of a paradigm shift: your thoughts shift from trust to anger.

One o'clock in the morning comes and goes with no sign of your roommate. Your anger is boiling, but suddenly another set of thoughts bombards your mind. Perhaps he has had an accident. Perhaps he is in the hospital fighting for his life. Has something serious happened? After all, he has to work tomorrow, too; it's not like him to stay out this late. Finally, you sleep. At 3:00 a.m. you awake to find that he's still not home.

Now you have encountered another paradigm shift. What began as anger is now genuine worry over the well-being of your friend and roommate. You call some of the local hospitals looking for your roommate; you hope he's not there. Immediately after you call the third hospital, your phone rings, and it's your roommate. The tone of his voice indicates that he is not hurt, and instantly your mind undergoes another paradigm shift, returning to anger over his abuse of your generosity.

But your roommate tells you that he was on the way home when he observed a terrible accident. He stopped to help, administering life-saving CPR to a little girl who was thrown from a vehicle. Your roommate stayed with the other family members, ministering to them in Christ's name and praying with them that God would spare their little girl's life. This was his first opportunity to call.

Now what thoughts and emotions might you have toward your roommate? Anger? Disgust? Disrespect? No, you would experience another paradigm shift. You would feel admiration, pride, and love for a friend who demonstrated Christ's love and character to someone in a moment of great need.

Had circumstances changed for the roommate with the car? No, his actual circumstances remained the same. He was ministering to persons in need. The change occurred in your perspective—four times, in fact. At first your perspective changed because of perceived information: your roommate was taking advantage of your generosity. But as other information became available, your perspective changed. This is an example of a paradigm shift. You received data, processed it, and then used it to begin a different thought pattern.

What happens when you fail to make a paradigm shift? Here's a classic example. At one time a Swiss watch epitomized quality in the watch industry. If you wanted an exquisite watch, you had to purchase one with Swiss movement. At the height of their success, Swiss watch owners controlled more than 75 percent of the world's watch market.

But then someone invented a new movement; it was called quartz. Of course, it was introduced to the giants in the watch industry, the Swiss watch makers. But the Swiss watch makers forgot they were in the watch-making business. They thought they were in the business of making Swiss movements. They were wrong. Even though they owned 75 percent of the world's market at that time, their world was not secure.

Failing to make a paradigm shift, the Swiss watch makers rejected the quartz technology. The Japanese learned about it, capitalized on it, and captured 60 percent of the Swiss watch market. Today the Swiss hold only 17 percent of the market, most of which is contributed by a quartz watch called the Swatch. By the way, do you know who invented the quartz movement? The Swiss! They ignored their own innovators; failed to make a paradigm shift; and as a result, lost the bulk of their own market.

Sometimes spiritual growth occurs in your life only when you encounter and accept paradigm shifts. God may bring these into your life through commands He wants you to obey, directions He wants you to take, or circumstances He engineers. But to obey means that you must choose either to believe what God knows you can do or to retreat into your old way of thinking about yourself. When you retreat, you bypass an opportunity for a paradigm shift. In doing so, you fail to learn something very valuable and insightful about yourself. In a sense, you remain in darkness.

Moses is a great example of someone who had to discover who he was before he could be used by God. Because of his impatience and quick temper as a young single adult, he killed a man and was forced to flee Egypt for 40 years. Tending sheep for many years gave Moses ample time to develop a paradigm shift. He changed from Moses the self-reliant savior of the Israelites to Moses the humble shepherd.

When God approached Moses through the burning bush, He already knew that Moses was a leader of leaders. But Moses didn't know it. He would have to experience yet another paradigm shift. After Moses acknowledged God's authority in his life, God brought about this second shift in thinking by using Moses' own shepherd staff. A shepherd staff was a valuable tool in the skillful hand of an expert. With it he fought off wild animals, balanced himself while climbing, rested against it, and used it to guide and prod his sheep. Moses' very life depended on his staff.

When Moses obeyed God and threw down his staff, it turned into a serpent. Then Moses encountered a paradigm shift. No longer could his staff save his life; instead, it could kill him. One minute Moses was calm and complacent; the next he was fearful, and his heart was pounding.

But God wasn't finished yet. He commanded Moses to pick up the serpent. He told him exactly where to pick it up—not behind the head, where you would normally grab a snake, but by the tail. Why the tail? Because God wanted Moses to experience a paradigm shift. Peter Lord once said, "In the Christian life sometimes your greatest assets can become your greatest liabilities." When you possess personal strength that you have not yielded to God, you may sometimes attempt to do His will using only that personal strength. Here's the truth God wanted Moses to learn. Gripping the snake by the tail, he knew that his life would be spared only if God worked through the snake. God did. And when Moses obeyed in spite of his fear, the serpent turned back into a staff. From that point on, the staff was no longer called Moses' staff; it was called the staff of God (see Ex. 4:20). When Moses encountered Pharaoh, the staff of God accomplished things the staff of Moses never could have.

The same is true of your skills and abilities today. Single adults across this nation are gifted with phenomenal talents and abilities, but many have limited views of themselves and of what God can do through them. Until they undergo a paradigm shift in thinking about their talents and abilities, they will function below their capabilities and will be only mildly effective for God's kingdom. When Moses accepted God's commands for him and allowed God to alter his thinking, he found new opportunities to bring glory to God. So can you!

[1] William Shakespeare, *Hamlet*, act 4, sc. 5, as quoted by John Bartlett in *Familiar Quotations* (Boston: Little, Brown and Co., 1942), 96.
[2] *Webster's Ninth New Collegiate Dictionary* (Springfield, Mass.: Merriam-Webster, 1991), 628.
[3] Stephen R. Covey, *The Seven Habits of Highly Effective People* (New York: Simon & Schuster, 1989), 29.

strategy ②

k n o w
yourself

the principle of wisdom   Psalm 139

Knowledge comes, but wisdom lingers.[1]

—Alfred, Lord Tennyson

Fulfilling your dreams involves finding out why God created you and discovering the unique contributions you can make to this world. It is believing that you are not an accident, that in the incredible intricacies of human interaction you play an integral part and hold a meaningful place. And although your unique expression of this meaning may at times be obscure, the nucleus of your purpose is actually quite clear: in all you do, you are called to demonstrate God's love, compassion, and power to the world around you. How you do that is based on your personality type, your spiritual gifts, and the opportunities God gives you.

The purpose of this strategy is to give you a better understanding of yourself. When you know your strengths, you also know your weaknesses. A wise person devotes energy to his strengths and seeks to improve his weaknesses. He does not consider or accept a position that requires maximal performance in an area of weakness. Instead, a humble yet wise person responds: "What this task requires is not my strength. I would rather help in an area that better suits my abilities."

For example, you may have the spiritual gift of evangelism but the personality of an introvert. To attempt to practice evangelism that is confrontational or that requires a lot of personal interaction would be disquieting to you, even though God gave you the gift of evangelism. How you do evangelism needs to be based on your personality style. A number of approaches can be used to share the gospel. Some persons have no problem standing on a street corner or on a university campus and openly proclaiming the gospel. These extroverts are energized by confrontation. If someone opposes or challenges them, their adrenaline flows with excitement and enthusiasm at every opportunity for direct interchange. But for an introvert a direct confrontation is terribly intimidating. The best way for this person to practice the gift of evangelism might be to send cards and letters to visitors at church or to write messages for extroverts who have difficulty clarifying their thoughts. An introvert with the spiritual gift of evangelism and the desire to do evangelism needs to cultivate her own style rather than to assume that the extrovert's methods are the only ways to evangelize.

Knowing your spiritual gifts, then, is not enough. You need to know your personality type, as well. When you blend your spiritual gifts with your personality type and find a niche in God's kingdom that utilizes both, you will have found a fulfilling place of ministry that energizes and challenges you. The inventories that compose the remainder of this strategy will help you discover and integrate your spiritual gifts with your personality type. I have selected inventories developed by Mels Carbonell, who conducts seminars on this subject.[2] This material is copyrighted, so please do not duplicate it. Other inventories may also be used, but be sure they assess both your spiritual gifts and your personality traits.

The following pages may look complicated, but I encourage you to invest the time and effort required to complete them. Discovering your unique blend of personality traits and spiritual gifts is an essential step in understanding who you are and how you can start a revolution for Christ.

---

[1] Alfred, Lord Tennyson, *Locksley Hall*, l. 141, as quoted by James Bartlett in *Familiar Quotations* (Boston: Little, Brown and Co., 1942), 464.
[2] The inventories in this strategy are the work of Mels Carbonell, who conducts seminars and personal consultations in a more expanded version than is provided here. For a more thorough personal analysis of your personality type and spiritual gifts or for information on bringing this seminar to your church or area, contact Mels Carbonell at P.O. Box 1826; Fayetteville, GA 30214; (770) 461-4243; fax (770) 460-0885. This section of the book is from *Uniquely You*, © copyright 1995 by Mels Carbonell. All rights reserved. Used by permission. Unauthorized duplication is prohibited by law.

Personality Profile

In each group of words decide which sets of words are most (*M*) like you and which sets of words are least (*L*) like you. Do not choose what you want to be or what you want others to think you are. Choose what you are really like under pressure. In each group place an *X* in only one box representing *M* or *L*.

Example:

M L

[X] [ ] Kind, nice, caring
[ ] [ ] Proper, formal
[ ] [ ] Demanding, asserting
[ ] [X] Outgoing, active

M L

1. [ ] [X] Kind, nice, caring
2. [ ] [ ] Proper, formal
3. [X] [ ] Demanding, asserting
4. [ ] [ ] Outgoing, active

5. [ ] [X] Playful, fun-loving
6. [ ] [ ] Firm, strong
7. [X] [ ] Law-abiding, conscientious
8. [ ] [ ] Gentle, soft, humble

9. [ ] [X] Bold, daring
10. [ ] [ ] Delightful, pleasant
11. [ ] [ ] Loyal, true blue
12. [X] [ ] Calculating, analytical

M L

13. [ ] [ ] Conservative, inflexible
14. [ ] [ ] Trusting, gullible, open
15. [X] [ ] Peaceful, calm
16. [ ] [X] Convincing, cocky

17. [ ] [ ] Decisive, sure, certain
18. [ ] [ ] Friendly, cordial, popular
19. [X] [ ] Careful, cautious
20. [ ] [X] Obedient, submissive

21. [ ] [ ] Promoting, encouraging
22. [X] [ ] Straight, conforming
23. [ ] [X] Risk-taking, courageous
24. [ ] [ ] Pleasing, good-natured

M L

25. ❑ ❑ Considerate, thoughtful
26. ❑ ❑ Forceful, strong-willed
27. ❑ ☒ Hyper, energetic
28. ☒ ❑ Perfectionist, precise

29. ❑ ❑ Contented, satisfied
30. ☒ ❑ Compliant, go by book
31. ❑ ☒ Brave, adventurous
32. ❑ ❑ Enthusiastic, influencing

33. ❑ ☒ Smooth talker, articulate
34. ❑ ❑ Loving, sincere, honest
35. ❑ ❑ Persistent, restless, relentless
36. ☒ ❑ Right, correct

37. ❑ ❑ Positive, optimistic
38. ❑ ☒ Entertaining, clowning
39. ❑ ❑ Shy, mild
40. ☒ ❑ Competent, do right

41. ☒ ❑ Contemplative, thinker
42. ❑ ❑ Diplomatic, peacemaking
43. ❑ ☒ Admirable, elegant
44. ❑ ❑ Winner, competitive

45. ❑ ❑ Joyful, jovial
46. ❑ ❑ Flexible, adaptable, agreeable
47. ❑ ☒ Ambitious, go for it
48. ☒ ❑ Deep, intense

M L

49. ❑ ❑ Steady, dependable
50. ❑ ❑ Talkative, verbal
51. ❑ ☒ Challenging, motivating
52. ☒ ❑ Accurate, exact

53. ☒ ❑ Stable, balanced
54. ❑ ❑ Confident, self-reliant
55. ❑ ☒ Perspective, see clearly
56. ❑ ❑ Animated, expressive

57. ☒ ❑ Controlling, taking charge
58. ❑ ☒ Merciful, sensitive
59. ❑ ❑ Pondering, wondering
60. ❑ ❑ Persuading, convincing

61. ❑ ☒ Sociable, interactive
62. ❑ ❑ Serious, unwavering
63. ❑ ❑ Sweet, tender, compassionate
64. ☒ ❑ Guarded, masked, protective

65. ❑ ❑ Powerful, unconquerable
66. ❑ ☒ Merry, cheerful
67. ❑ ❑ Generous, giving
68. ☒ ❑ Preparing, researching

69. ❑ ❑ Timid, soft-spoken
70. ❑ ❑ Systematic, follow plan
71. ❑ ☒ Industrious, hard-working
72. ☒ ❑ Smiling, happy

start a revolution

M L

73. ☒☐ Inquisitive, questioning
74. ☐☒ Tolerant, patient
75. ☐☐ Driving, determined
76. ☐☐ Dynamic, impressing

77. ☐☐ Serving, sacrificing
78. ☐☐ Sharp, appealing
79. ☒☐ Direct, to the point
80. ☐☒ Original, creative

81. ☐☒ Peppy, playful
82. ☐☐ Devoted, dedicated
83. ☐☐ Courteous, polite
84. ☒☐ Strict, unbending

M L

85. ☒☐ Outspoken, opinionated
86. ☐☐ Inducing, charming
87. ☐☐ Inventive, imaginative
88. ☐☒ Hospitable, enjoy company

89. ☐☐ Zealous, eager
90. ☒☐ Quiet, reserved
91. ☐☐ Organized, orderly
92. ☐☒ Exciting, spirited

93. ☐☐ Faithful, consistent
94. ☐☐ Responsive, reacting
95. ☐☒ Helpful, assisting
96. ☒☐ Bottom line, straightforward

Marking Sheet

Identify your *M* and *L* for each group of words on "Personality Profile" as *D, I, S, C,* or *B.*

M L

1. S ☒☒ S
2. B ☐☐ C
3. D ☒☒ D   M 3   L 31
4. B ☐☐ I

5. B ☐☒ I
6. B ☐☐ D   M 7   L 5
7. C ☒☐ B
8. S ☐☐ S

M L

9. B ☐☒ D
10. I ☐☐ I
11. S ☐☐ S   M 12   L 9
12. C ☒☐ C

13. C ☐☐ B
14. B ☐☐ B   M 15   L 16
15. S ☒☐ S
16. D ☐☒ D

	M	L			M	L
17. D ☐☐ D				45. B ☐☐ I		
18. I ☐☐ I	M	L		46. S ☐☐ B	M	L
19. C ☒☐ C	19	20		47. D ☐☒ D	48	47
20. S ☐☒ B				48. B ☒☐ B		
21. I ☐☐ I				49. S ☐☐ S		
22. C ☒☐ B	M	L		50. I ☐☐ I	M	L
23. D ☐☒ D	22	23		51. D ☐☒ B	52	51
24. B ☐☐ S				52. C ☒☐ B		
25. S ☐☐ B				53. S ☒☐ S		
26. D ☐☐ D	M	L		54. D ☐☐ B	M	L
27. I ☐☒ I	28	27		55. B ☐☒ C	53	55
28. C ☒☐ C				56. B ☐☐ I		
29. S ☐☐ S				57. D ☒☐ D		
30. B ☒☐ C	M	L		58. S ☐☒ S	M	L
31. D ☐☒ D	30	31		59. C ☐☐ C	57	58
32. B ☐☐ I				60. I ☐☐ B		
33. B ☐☒ I				61. I ☐☒ I		
34. S ☐☐ S	M	L		62. D ☐☐ D	M	L
35. D ☐☐ D	36	33		63. B ☐☐ S	64	61
36. C ☒☐ C				64. C ☒☐ B		
37. D ☐☐ D				65. D ☐☐ D		
38. I ☐☒ I	M	L		66. I ☐☒ B	M	L
39. B ☐☐ S	40	38		67. S ☐☐ B	68	66
40. B ☒☐ B				68. C ☒☐ C		
41. C ☒☐ C				69. B ☐☐ S		
42. S ☐☐ B	M	L		70. B ☐☐ C	M	L
43. I ☐☒ B	41	43		71. D ☐☒ D	72	71
44. B ☐☐ D				72. I ☒☐ I		

start a revolution

M L

73. C ☒☐ C
74. S ☐☒ S   M   L
75. D ☐☐ D   73   74
76. I ☐☐ I

77. S ☐☐ S
78. I ☐☐ I   M   L
79. D ☒☐ D   79   80
80. B ☐☒ C

81. I ☐☒ I
82. B ☐☐ B   M   L
83. S ☐☐ S   84   81
84. C ☒☐ C

M L

85. D ☒☐ D
86. I ☐☐ I   M   L
87. B ☐☐ C   85   88
88. S ☐☒ S

89. D ☐☐ D
90. B ☒☐ B   M   L
91. C ☐☐ C   90   92
92. I ☐☒ I

93. B ☐☐ C
94. I ☐☐ I   M   L
95. S ☐☒ S   96   95
96. D ☒☐ D

Counting Instructions

1. Use "Marking Sheet" to identify your *M* and *L* for each group of words on "Personality Profile" as *D, I, S, C,* or *B.*
2. Count all *D's* marked as *M's* on "Marking Sheet." Record the total *D's* counted in the appropriate total box on the next page. Then count all of the *I's* marked as *M's* and record them in the appropriate total box on the next page. Do the same with the total *S's, C's,* and *B's* on "Marking Sheet."
3. Count all of the *D's* marked as *L's* on "Marking Sheet." Record the total *D's* counted in the appropriate total box on the next page. Then count all of the *I's* marked as *L's* and record them in the appropriate total box on the next page. Do the same with the total *S's, C's,* and *B's* on "Marking Sheet."
4. Add the total number of *D's, I's, S's, C's,* and *B's* in the total boxes on the next page to make sure they total 24. If not, recount and place a check mark beside each one as you count it.

Totals

M	D	I	S	C	B	
	5	1	2	12	4	=24
L	6	7	54	3	4	=24

After recording the total number of *D*'s, *I*'s, *S*'s and *C*'s in the total boxes, use those numbers to plot the *M* and *L* graphs on the next page. You will not use the *B*'s from this point on.

Example:

Totals

D	I	S	C
0	10	11	3

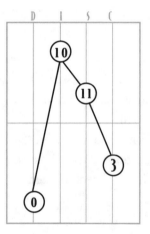

M Graph   L Graph

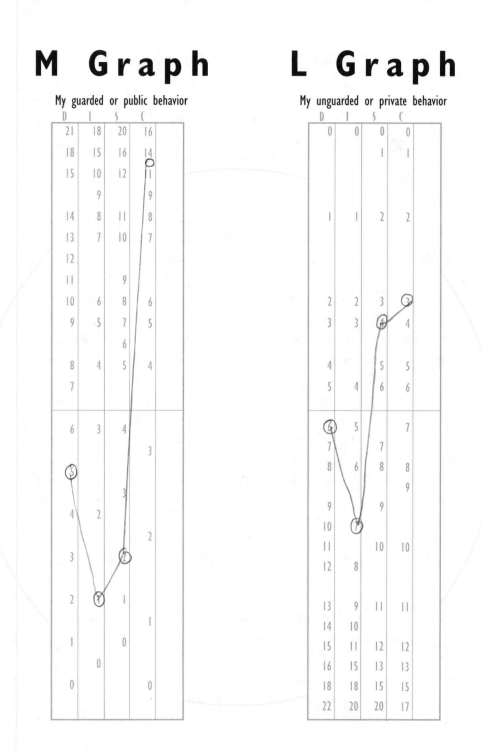

My guarded or public behavior   My unguarded or private behavior

How to Read Your Graphs

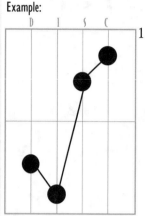

1. Look at each graph and find your highest plotting position. The higher the plotting position, the greater the intensity of that specific type of behavior. The lower the plotting position, the less the intensity of that specific type of behavior. Every point above the midline is considered high. Every point below the midline is considered low. Focus on the high or low position rather than on the number. Notice in the example that the highest point is *C* and that the next highest point is *S*. This profile is a *C/S* personality.

2. From this point on, do not think of *M* and *L* as *most* and *least*. Your *M* and *L* graphs do not represent what is most and least like you. Rather, both graphs reflect your behavior in different situations. Your *M* graph is your response to how you think people expect you to behave. It's your normally guarded and masked behavior. Your *L* graph is your response to how you feel and think under pressure—how you really feel and think inside. It's your normally unguarded and unmasked behavior. Compare your two graphs. If the *M* and *L* graphs are alike, understanding your personality will be easier. If the two graphs are different, you may be struggling with your attitude about what is expected of you and how you really want to behave. However, a difference between the graphs can also mean that you are flexible in adapting your behavior to a variety of situations.

3. Read the section of "Interpretation," beginning on page 41, that corresponds to your highest plotting positions. Personalize this information by understanding the phrases that accurately describe you and by ignoring the phrases that don't apply. From the information in "Interpretation" we learn, for example, that *C/S* individuals are cautious and steady. They like to do one thing at a time and to do it right the first time. They also like stable, secure surroundings. They don't like to take risks or to cause trouble. *C/S*'s need to be more outgoing and positive. Their behavioral blend is competent/specialist. See "Discovering Your Behavioral Blend," beginning on page 50, to identify your specific composite behavioral type.

4. Also notice your lowest plotting positions. The example shows *I* as the lowest point, meaning that this person doesn't enjoy inspiring others or interacting with large groups of people. He or she tends to be shy and calculating and is more reserved than outgoing. He or she likes people on an individual basis. The low *I* is not bad. It merely indicates a low interest in enthusiastic and carefree behavior.

5. Read the other sections to overview the general differences among the *D, I, S,* and *C* tendencies.

Remember, there is no bad personality. Everyone doesn't think, feel, or act the same way. We need to accept the way we and others naturally respond as unique traits. When we understand our differences, we are more comfortable and effective with ourselves and others.

Interpretation

You have a predictable pattern of behavior because you have a specific personality. Four basic personality types, also known as temperaments, blend to determine your unique personality. To help you understand why you often feel, think, and act as you do, the following illustration summarizes the four-temperament model of human behavior.

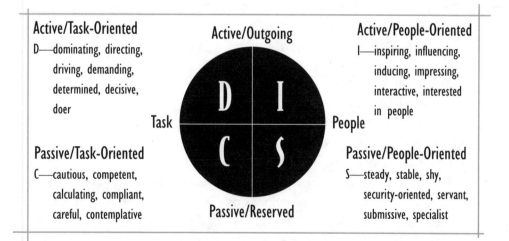

Active/Task-Oriented
D—dominating, directing, driving, demanding, determined, decisive, doer

Active/Outgoing

Active/People-Oriented
I—inspiring, influencing, inducing, impressing, interactive, interested in people

Task

People

Passive/Task-Oriented
C—cautious, competent, calculating, compliant, careful, contemplative

Passive/Reserved

Passive/People-Oriented
S—steady, stable, shy, security-oriented, servant, submissive, specialist

D Personality

Active/task-oriented, known as choleric

Biblical example: Paul

Described as—

- dominant;
- direct;
- demanding;
- decisive.

Basic motivation: challenge and control

Desires—

- freedom from control;
- authority;
- varied activities;
- difficult assignments;
- opportunities for advancement;
- choices rather than ultimatums.

Responds best to leader who—

- provides direct answers;
- sticks to task;
- gets to the point;
- provides pressure;
- allows freedom for personal accomplishments.

Needs to learn—

- you need people;
- relaxation is not a crime;
- some controls are needed;
- everyone has a boss;
- self-control is most important;
- to focus on finishing well;
- more sensitivity to people's feelings.

Biblical advice: Be gentle, not bossy: "Wisdom ... from above is ... gentle" (Jas. 3:17, KJV). Control your feelings and actions: "In your anger do not sin" (Eph. 4:26). Focus on one thing at a time: "One thing I do" (Phil. 3:13). Have a servant attitude: "Serve one another in love" (Gal. 5:13).

C Personality

Passive/task-oriented, known as melancholy

Biblical example: Thomas

Described as–

- competent;
- compliant;
- cautious;
- calculating.

Basic motivation: quality and correctness

Desires–

- clearly defined tasks;
- details;
- limited risks;
- assignments that require precision and planning;
- time to think.

Responds best to leader who–

- provides reassurance;
- spells out detailed operating procedures;
- provides resources to do task correctly;
- listens to suggestions.

Needs to learn–

- total support is not always possible;
- thorough explanation is not everything;
- deadlines must be met;
- to be more optimistic.

Biblical advice: Be more positive: "If anything is excellent or praiseworthy–think about such things" (Phil. 4:8). Avoid a bitter and critical spirit: "Get rid of all bitterness" (Eph. 4:31). Be joyful: "The fruit of the Spirit is ... joy" (Gal. 5:22). Don't worry: "Do not fret" (Ps. 37:1).

I Personality

Active/people-oriented, known as sanguine

Biblical example: Peter

Described as—
- inspiring;
- influencing;
- impressing;
- inducing.

Basic motivation: recognition and approval
Desires—
- prestige;
- friendly relationships;
- freedom from details;
- opportunities to help others;
- opportunities to motivate others;
- chance to verbalize ideas.

Responds best to leader who—
- is fair and is also a friend;
- provides social involvement;
- recognizes abilities;
- offers rewards for risk taking.

Needs to learn—
- time management;
- importance of deadlines;
- danger of being overly optimistic;
- responsibility is more important than popularity;
- how to listen better.

Biblical advice: Be humble/avoid pride: "Humble yourselves before the Lord" (Jas. 4:10). Control your speech: "Be quick to listen, slow to speak" (Jas. 1:19). Be more organized: "Everything should be done in a fitting and orderly way" (1 Cor. 14:40). Be patient: "The fruit of the Spirit is ... self-control" (Gal. 5:23).

S Personality

Passive/people-oriented, known as phlegmatic
Biblical example: Moses
Described as—
- submissive;

- steady;
- stable;
- security-oriented.

Basic motivation: stability and support

Desires—
- an area of specialization;
- identification with a group;
- established work patterns;
- secure situation;
- consistent and familiar environment.

Responds best to leader who—
- is relaxed and friendly;
- allows time to adjust to changes;
- allows to work at own pace;
- gives personal support.

Needs to learn—
- change provides opportunity;
- friendship isn't everything;
- discipline is good;
- boldness;
- taking risks is sometimes necessary.

Biblical advice: Be bold and strong: " 'Be strong and courageous' " (Josh. 1:6). Be confident and fearless: "God has not given us a spirit of fear" (2 Tim. 1:7, NKJV). Be more enthusiastic: "Whatever you do, do it heartily, as to the Lord" (Col. 3:23, NKJV).

Biblical Examples of Personality Types

The Bible is full of examples of unique personalities. Some individuals were aggressive and outgoing, while others were withdrawn and quiet. One type is not better than the others. Biblical behavior is balanced and mature.

Scripture demands both quiet and assertive behaviors of us. Mark 16:15 tells us, " 'Go into all the world and preach the good news.' " Psalm 46:10 encourages us to " 'be still, and know ... God.' " These Scriptures describe different behaviors; yet both verses are commands.

Mary and Martha are good examples of opposite types. Martha was active and task-oriented, while her sister, Mary, was passive and people-oriented. Martha demonstrated *D* behavior, while Mary showed *S* behavior (see John 11:20). When Lazarus, their brother, died, both said the same thing to Jesus (see John 11:21,32), but Jesus responded differently to each one. We should respond to persons according to their personalities, not ours. We should be all things to all persons, so that we might by all means save some (see 1 Cor. 9:22).

Individual *DISC* behavior is illustrated in the Scriptures. God uses all types of personalities to complete His plan and purpose. The most important lesson is not to let your personality control you but instead to let God control your personality. Let God fill (control) you with His Holy Spirit (see Eph. 5:18).

The apostle Paul was definitely a *D* type. He was left for dead, imprisoned, stoned, forsaken, and forgotten; yet he pressed on toward God's high calling. He didn't worry about what anyone thought of him, except God. Yet he also learned obedience and submission after God crushed him on the road to Damascus.

Peter demonstrated *I* behavior every time he spoke up for the disciples. He was often very dramatic. One moment Peter promised, in front of a crowd, never to forsake Christ. Shortly after that, he denied the Lord, when no one was watching, to a young maiden. Yet God used Peter in a great way at Pentecost.

Moses seemed to show *S* behavior when God told him to lead the children of Israel out of Egypt. Moses was unsure of himself and even tried to get Aaron to be the leader. *S* personalities don't like to be out front telling everyone what to do, but God sometimes calls persons to do great things in spite of their personality types.

Thomas exhibited *C* behavior when he doubted Christ's resurrection. *C*'s need proof and answers to questions. Jesus didn't belittle Thomas but gave him the evidence he needed to serve the Lord in a great way. Historians record that Thomas became an extremely effective missionary to India.

Practical Application

High *D*'s

- They need challenges and choices.
- They don't like to be told what to do. They want to be their own bosses.

- Controlling themselves is most important. Desiring to control others, *D*'s need to guard their feelings.
- Since *D*'s test and challenge authority, they need to learn that everyone has a boss. If not, they will push others to the limit.

Instead of telling *D*'s to complete a task immediately, let them choose between completing the task now or by a certain time. They will usually choose the latter, but at least they have the choice.

High C's

- They like to do things right. Finishing a project halfway or half right is unacceptable to them.
- Give them time and resources to do their best.
- Don't push them always to do better. They may get frustrated and give up.
- Encourage *C*'s to improve their people skills. They need to learn to be more sociable.
- Answer their questions and explain the whys of life.

Provide these types happy and positive atmospheres. They tend to be naturally pessimistic and moody. Joyful and uplifting music around the home or office can be very encouraging. Avoid being constantly negative and critical with these personality types.

High I's

- They need lots of recognition and approval.
- They like to talk and get attention. Being quiet is difficult for them.
- Give them opportunities to express themselves.
- Don't put them down for their desire to entertain.
- Encourage them to control their excitement and to share the limelight with others.

I's need to learn that they will have more friends when they make others look good. Praise them when they do well. Emphasize that their poor behavior makes them look bad when they underachieve. They especially need to guard against trying to please everyone.

High S's

- They desire steady and stable environments. Change is difficult. Give them time to adjust.
- Don't expect them to accept risks or try new things. They prefer traditional roles.
- Difficult assignments and enthusiastic challenges are not effective. Friendly, sweet appeals are best.
- Encourage them to be more outgoing and assertive so that they are not taken advantage of.

S's' natural submission causes others to take advantage of them. S's need to learn how to control their reluctance to be bold and assertive. Saying no can be frightening yet powerful. Taking chances and risks to take charge can be very rewarding.

Leadership Insights

Almost everyone responds to life's challenges and choices according to his or her personality. Therefore, individuals who relate to others must be personality-wise. For example, high S leaders should not engage high D followers in small talk. D's prefer leaders who get to the point. They want bottom-line answers. They respond best to those who do not waste their time.

On the other hand, high S followers feel comfortable with leaders who are systematic, slow, and steady in their approaches. S's don't like fast-talking, quick-paced responses. S's respond best to stable and sensitive leaders.

Leader Styles

People tend to lead according to their personalities rather than adapt to the styles of others. Here are descriptions of various leadership styles.

D Leaders

D's like to take control and be in charge. They don't like for others to tell them what to do. D leaders can be too pushy and forceful. They need to control their direct and demanding approach to management. They make better leaders when they learn to slow down, be gentle, and demand less of others.

I Leaders

I's are inspiring and enthusiastic. They love to lead and influence others. Naturally great presenters, they tend to talk too much. *I* leaders need to listen more and to be less sensitive to rejection. They are the most impressive and positive leaders. *I*'s love crowds but need to take an interest in individuals.

S Leaders

S's are the sweet, steady, and stable leaders. They seldom demand anything. They are friendly and loyal but tend to be too nice. They need to be more aggressive and assertive. Overly sensitive to their shortcomings, *S*'s need to be more confident. They hate to take risks. They often miss opportunities because of their caution. They are reliable, relaxed, and reserved.

C Leaders

C's are competent and compliant. They go by the book and want to do everything just right. They are thorough and detailed-oriented but tend to be too informative. *C*'s need to be more positive and enthusiastic. They answer questions people aren't asking. When optimistic, *C*'s are extremely influential. They should concentrate not on problems but on potentials.

Follower Styles

People also follow according to their personalities. Leaders are more effective when they can identify individual followers' styles.

D Followers

D's respect strong leaders. They want to be part of a winning team. They follow with power and authority in mind. They wonder, *Will this action make me more respected and/or get the job done?* D followers need choices rather than get-in-or-get-out ultimatums. They need opportunities to carry out projects their way.

I Followers

I's follow with their hearts and tend to be impulsive followers. They want opportunities that will make them look good. *I* followers talk a lot. They make great first impressions. Their high egos and ability to persuade often turn them into leaders who rise to the top. Sometimes you don't know who is leading whom.

S Followers

S followers don't make quick decisions. They like leaders who are understanding and gentle. They want to establish a relationship with a leader who will be around for a long time. S's are concerned about service and stability. When it comes to sensible and slow judgment, S followers feel right at home. They like familiar and low-key environments.

C Followers

C's analyze each decision. They love research and development. C's are quality-oriented followers. They don't like quick or costly decisions. Picky and precise, they follow with their minds rather than with their hearts. C's seldom respond positively at first. They often want time to think about their decisions. Once convinced, they follow best.

Discovering Your Behavioral Blend

Four basic personality types known as D, I, S, and C characterize human behavior. Almost everyone is a blend or combination of these four temperaments.

To discover your specific behavioral style, choose the one or two profiles that most closely resemble your M and L graphs and read the corresponding descriptions. You probably combine two specific profiles, although you may have some characteristics of other types.

No one has a bad personality. The most important factor is what you do with your personality. Every personality has strengths and weaknesses. One person's weakness may be another person's strength. To be more successful and improve your relationships, you must learn how to control your strengths and avoid your weaknesses. Also be aware that under pressure you lean toward your strengths. The overuse of a strength becomes an abuse, and your best trait can become your worst. Don't let your personality control you. Instead, learn how to control your personality.

D: Determined Doers

D's are dominant and demanding. They win at all costs. They do not care as much about what people think as about getting the job done. Their insensitivity to feelings makes them too strong. They are great at developing projects, but they need to improve their ability to do them correctly. Their strong will should be disciplined to prepare and think more accurately about what they are doing. They are motivated by serious challenges to accomplish tasks.

I: Inspirational Influencers

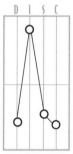

I's are impressive people. They are extremely active and excited individuals. Approval is important to them. They can have lots of friends if they do not overdo their need for attention. They can be sensitive and emotional. They need to be more interested in others and more willing to listen. They do not like research unless it makes them look good. Because they are entertainers, they often do things to please the crowd. They need to control their feelings and to think more logically. They often outshine others and are motivated by recognition.

S: Steady Specialists

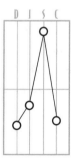

S's are stable and shy types. They do not like changes. They enjoy pleasing others and can consistently do the same job. Secure, non-threatening surroundings are important to them. They make the best friends because they are so forgiving. Other persons sometimes take advantage of them. They need to be stronger and learn how to say no to a friend who wants them to do wrong. Talking in front of large crowds is difficult for them. They are motivated by sweet and sincere opportunities to help others.

C: Cautious, Competent Types

C's are logical and analytical. Their predominant drive is careful, calculating, compliant, and correct behavior. When frustrated, they can overdo this behavior or can be the exact opposite. They need answers and opportunities to reach their potential. They tend not to care about others' feelings. They can be critical and crabby. They prefer quality and reject phoniness in others. They are motivated by explanations and projects that stimulate their thinking.

I/D/S: Inspiring, Driving, Submissive Types

I/D/S's are impressing, demanding, and stabilizing at the same time. They are not as cautious and calculating as those with more *C* tendencies. They are more active than passive. But they are also sensitive and steady. They may seem to be more people-oriented but can be dominant and decisive in their task-orientation. They need to be more contemplative and conservative. Details don't seem as important as taking charge and working with people.

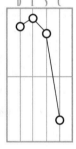

D/I: Driving Influencers

D/I's are bottom-line people. They are much like dynamic influencers. They are a little more determined and less inspirational, but they are strong doers and are able to induce others to follow. They need to be more cautious and careful, as well as more steady and stable. They get involved in a lot of projects at the same time. They need to slow down and focus on one thing at a time. They are motivated by opportunities to accomplish great tasks through a lot of people.

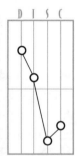

I/D: Inspirational Doers

I/D's are super salespersons. They love large groups. They are impressive and can easily influence persons to do things. They need a lot of recognition. They exaggerate and often talk too much. They jump into things without thinking them through. They need to be more studious and still. They should also be more careful and cautious. They are motivated by exciting opportunities to do difficult things. If not careful, they do things to please the crowd and, in the process, get themselves in trouble. They make inspiring leaders and determined individuals.

S/I: Steady Influencers

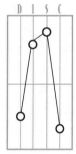

S/I's are sensitive and inspirational. They accept and represent others well. They have lots of friends because they are tolerant and forgiving. They do not hurt others' feelings and can be very influential. They need to be more task-oriented. They must learn to finish their work and do it well. They like to talk but should pay more attention to instructions. They would be more influential if they were more aggressive and careful. They are kind and considerate. Motivated by opportunities to share and shine, they induce others to follow.

C/S: Competent Specialists

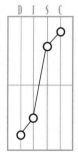

C/S's tend always to be right. They like to do one thing at a time and to do it right the first time. Their steady, stable approach makes them sensitive. They tend to be reserved and cautious. They are consistent and careful, seldom taking risks or trying new pursuits. They do not like speaking to large crowds but work hard behind the scenes to help groups stay on track. They are motivated by opportunities to serve others and to do things correctly.

D/I/C: Dominant, Inspiring, Cautious Types

D/I/C's are demanding, impressing, and competent. They tend to be more task-oriented but can be people-oriented before crowds. They need to increase their sensitivity and softness. They don't mind change. Active and outgoing, they are also compliant and cautious. They like to do things correctly, while driving and influencing others to follow. Their verbal skills combine with their determination and competence to achieve. Security is not as important as accomplishing tasks and looking good.

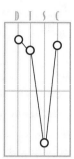

D/I: Dynamic Influencers

D/I's are impressive, demanding types. They get excited about accomplishing tasks and looking good. Determined and driven, they influence large crowds best. They can be too strong and concerned about what others think. They have good communication skills and are interested in people. They need to be more sensitive about and patient with others' feelings. Learning to slow down and think through projects is crucial for them. They are motivated by opportunities to control and impress.

I/S: Inspirational Specialists

I/S's are influential and stable. They love people, and people love them. They like to please and serve others. They do not like time controls or difficult tasks. They want to look good and encourage others, but they often lack organizational skills. They follow directions and do what they are told. They should be more concerned about what to do than with whom to do it. They are motivated by interactive and sincere opportunities to help others. Regardless of being up front or behind the scenes, they influence and support others. They make good friends and obedient workers.

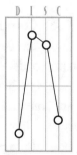

start a revolution

S/D: Steady Doers

S/D's get the job done. They prefer stable surroundings and are determined to accomplish tasks. As quiet leaders, they relate best to small groups. They do not like to talk in front of large crowds but want to control them. They enjoy secure relationships but often dominate them. They can be soft and hard at the same time. They are motivated by sincere challenges that allow them systematically to do great things. They prefer sure things rather than shallow recognition. They make good friends while driving to succeed.

C/I/S: Competent, Influencing Specialists

C/I/S's like to do things right, impress others, and stabilize situations. They are not aggressive or pushy. They enjoy large and small crowds. They are good with people and prefer quality. They are sensitive to what others think about them and their work. They need to be more determined and dominant. They can do tasks well but are poor at making quick decisions. They are capable of great accomplishments through people but need to be more self-motivated and assertive. They are stimulated by sincere, enthusiastic approval and logical explanations.

Straight Midline

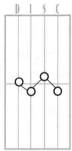

A straight-midline blend occurs when all four plotting positions are close together near the middle of the graph. This may indicate that the person is trying to please everyone. Striving to be "all things to all men" may indicate a mature response to pressure. Or it may confirm frustration over the intensity of differences under pressure. The person may be saying, "I don't know what my *D, I, S,* or *C* behavior is or should be." The person may want to complete another profile at a later time to discern any changes.

D/C: Driving, Competent Types

D/C types are determined students or defiant critics. They want to be in charge while collecting information to accomplish tasks. They care more about getting a job done and about doing it right than what others think or feel. They drive themselves and others. They are dominant and caustic. Improving their people skills is important, since they need to be more sensitive and understanding. They are motivated by choices and challenges to do well.

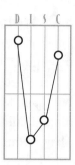

I/C: Inspirational, Competent Types

I/C types are inspiring yet cautious. They assess situations and comply with the rules in order to look good. They are good at figuring ways to do jobs better through a lot of people. They can be too persuasive and too concerned about winning. They are often impatient and critical. They need to be more sensitive to individual feelings but are often more concerned about what others think. They do not like breaking the rules; neither do they enjoy taking risks. They need to try new things and sometimes to go against the crowd. They are careful communicators who think things through.

S/C: Steady, Competent Types

S/C types are stable and contemplative. They like to search for and discover the facts. They like to weigh the evidence and proceed slowly to a logical conclusion. They enjoy small groups of people and do not like speaking in front of large crowds. They are systematic and sensitive to others' needs but can be critical and caustic. They are loyal friends but can be too concerned with finding faults. They need to improve their enthusiasm and optimism. They are motivated by kind, conscientious opportunities to perform jobs slowly and correctly.

C/S/D: Competent, Steady Doers

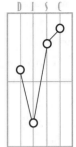

C/S/D's combine cautious, stable, and determined types. They are more task-oriented but care about persons on an individual basis. They don't like to speak in front of crowds. They prefer to get the job done and to do it right through small groups rather than through large groups. They tend to be serious. Often misunderstood by others as being insensitive, *C/S/D* types care for people but don't show it openly. They need to be more positive and enthusiastic. Natural achievers, they need to be more friendly and less critical.

Above Midline/Below Midline

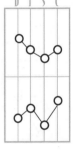

Some patterns indicate unique struggles individuals may have:

- An above-midline blend occurs when all four plotting points are above the midline. This may indicate a strong desire to overachieve.
- A below-midline blend occurs when all four plotting points are below the midline. This may indicate that the person is not sure how to respond to challenges.

Controlling Your Behavioral Blend

People often say, "I just want to be me." They want to find themselves. The problem is that when you find yourself, you often don't like what you find. You might be so dictatorial, self-seeking, insecure, or critical that God seems powerless in your life. The so-called real or natural you may be the opposite of what God wants you to be. You should not seek to be normal but spiritual, not natural but supernatural—to do what you do through God's power in your life, to be what God wants you to be through a personal relationship with Him by faith in Jesus Christ as your Savior and Lord (see Eph. 2:8-10). The bottom line is allowing the Holy Spirit to control your personality so that you can be conformed to the image of Christ.

After you discover your behavioral blend, you can clearly recognize the areas God wants to work on. The Bible, "useful for teaching, rebuking, correcting and training in righteousness" (2 Tim. 3:16), is the best source of admonitions and challenges to help you become more like Christ. Ask God to use the following Scriptures to encourage and empower you. Don't let them discourage you. The Word of God is quick and powerful, sharper than any two-edged sword. It can discern and deliver you from a self-centered attitude. Seek to grow spiritually to the point that others can't identify a particular personality in you. Balance and maturity should be your goal. Learn to be so controlled by the Holy Spirit that God is glorified in all you say and do (see Eph. 5:18).

D: **Determined Doers**

- Be careful not to offend when you take charge: "The Lord's servant must not quarrel [be pushy]; instead, he must be kind" (2 Tim. 2:24).
- Anger is normal but must be controlled: "In your anger do not sin" (Eph. 4:26).
- Be motivated to purity and peace: "Wisdom that comes from heaven is first of all pure; then peace-loving" (Jas. 3:17).
- Focus on doing one thing well: "One thing I do" (Phil. 3:13).
- Always remember that God is the Master of your fate: "The fear of the Lord is the beginning of knowledge" (Prov. 1:7).

I: **Inspirational Influencers**

- Don't exalt yourself: "Humble yourselves before the Lord, and he will lift you up" (Jas. 4:10).
- Be sure to listen more: "quick to hear, slow to speak" (Jas. 1:19).
- Work at being organized: "Everything should be done in a fitting and orderly way" (1 Cor. 14:40).
- Concentrate on doing what is most important: "Not everything is beneficial" (1 Cor. 10:23).

start a revolution

- Prepare more: "Prepare yourselves" (2 Chron. 35:4).
- Be careful what you desire: "Trust in the Lord" (Prov. 3:5).
- Don't be overconfident. Beware of what you promise: Peter claimed that he would never deny Christ (see Mark 14:31).

S: Steady Specialists

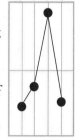

- Increase your confidence in Christ: "I can do everything through him who gives me strength" (Phil. 4:13).
- God is your "rock, ... fortress and ... deliverer" (Ps. 18:2).
- Fearfulness is not from God: "God did not give us a spirit of timidity" (2 Tim. 1:7).
- Speak out more often: "Let the redeemed of the Lord say so" (Ps. 107:2, KJV).
- Be more outgoing and less inhibited: "Christ has set us free" (Gal. 5:1).
- Be more assertive. Moses confronted Pharaoh with " 'Let my people go' " (Ex. 5:1).
- Security is possible: " 'You will be secure, because there is hope' " (Job 11:18).

C: Cautious, Competent Types

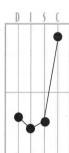

- Be more patient in correcting others: "Rebuke and encourage—with great patience" (2 Tim. 4:2).
- Correct in love: "speaking the truth in love" (Eph. 4:15).
- Be more positive: "Rejoice in the Lord always" (Phil. 4:4).
- Hope in God, not circumstances: "Be joyful in hope" (Rom. 12:12).
- The most logical thing you can do is to serve God: "Offer your bodies as living sacrifices, ... this is your spiritual act of worship" (Rom. 12:1).
- Find happiness in God: "Delight yourself in the Lord" (Ps. 37:4).

I/D/S: Inspiring, Driving, Submitting Types

- Be more calculating and careful, thinking before you act: " 'First sit down and estimate the cost' " (Luke 14:28).
- Attempt to be more organized: "Everything should be done in a fitting and orderly way" (1 Cor. 14:40).
- Be careful what you promise: " 'Let your "Yes" be "Yes," and your "No," "No" ' " (Matt. 5:37).
- Give God the glory for all you do: "Give unto the Lord glory" (Ps. 29:1-2, KJV).
- Be humble and share the glory: "Humble yourselves before the Lord, and he will lift you up" (Jas. 4:10).

D/I: Driving Influencers

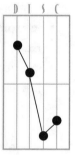

- Though naturally fearless and able, you need to respect God's power over you: "Fear God and give him glory" (Rev. 14:7).
- Guard the overuse of strength and be kind: "by the meekness and gentleness of Christ" (2 Cor. 10:1).
- Making peace is a greater challenge than winning a fight: "Blessed are the peacemakers" (Matt. 5:9).
- Choose words carefully: "A gentle answer turns away wrath" (Prov. 15:1).
- Let God control your feelings: "The fruit of the Spirit is ... self-control" (Gal. 5:22-23).

I/D: Inspirational Doers

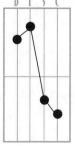

- Guard the power of your words: "The tongue ... is a fire" (Jas. 3:6).
- Don't be like those who "by smooth talk and flattery ... deceive" (Rom. 16:18).
- Always tell the truth: "speaking the truth in love" (Eph. 4:15).
- Remember who has blessed you: " 'He [Jesus] must become greater; I must become less' " (John 3:30).

- Give God the glory for all you do: "Ascribe to the Lord glory" (Ps. 29:1-2).
- Put God first in your life: " 'Seek first his [God's] kingdom' " (Matt. 6:33).
- Beware of the "lust of the flesh, … and the pride of life" (1 John 2:16, KJV). They will ultimately destroy your talents.

S/I: Steady Influencers

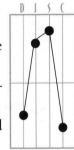

- Speak out, "bold to speak … without fear" (Phil. 1:14, KJV).
- Take stands: "Stand firm in the Lord" (Phil. 4:1).
- The Spirit of God can help you tell others about Christ: "The Spirit of the Sovereign Lord is on me" (Isa. 61:1).
- Guard against fearfulness: " 'Do not let your hearts be troubled and do not be afraid' " (John 14:27).
- You don't need people to encourage you: "David found strength in the Lord his God" (1 Sam. 30:6).
- Always do right and don't fear people: "Fear of man will prove to be a snare [trap]" (Prov. 29:25).

C/S: Competent Specialists

- Think more positively: "Whatever is pure, … whatever is admirable … think about such things" (Phil. 4:8-9).
- Guard against the fear of failure. God promises, " 'Do not be afraid, for I am with you' " (Isa. 43:5).
- Focus on the possible: " 'With God all things are possible' " (Matt. 19:26).
- Be cheerful: "The fruit of the Spirit is … joy" (Gal. 5:22).
- When everything goes wrong, God is all you need: "Our competence comes from God" (2 Cor. 3:5).
- Think like Christ: "Let this mind be in you, which was also in Christ" (Phil. 4:8, KJV).

D/I/C: Dominant, Inspiring, Cautious Types

- Be sure to listen more: "quick to listen, slow to speak" (Jas. 1:19).
- Be more sensitive to individuals' feelings: "The Lord's servant must not quarrel; instead, he must be kind" (2 Tim. 2:24).
- Be more of a peacemaker: " 'Blessed are the peacemakers' " (Matt. 5:9).
- Be more steady and don't get sidetracked: "Stand firm. ... Always give yourselves fully to the work of the Lord" (1 Cor. 15:58).
- Don't be judgmental: "If someone is caught in a sin, ... restore him gently" (Gal. 6:1).

D/I: Dynamic Influencers

- Concentrate on humility and obedience. Christ "humbled himself and became obedient" (Phil. 2:8).
- Everyone has a boss, even you. Jesus said, " 'I myself am a man under authority' " (Matt. 8:9).
- Avoid rebellion: "Rebellion is as the sin of witchcraft" (1 Sam. 15:23, KJV).
- Winning is not always most important: " 'The first will be last' " (Matt. 19:30).
- Be patient with others: "The fruit of the Spirit is ... patience" (Gal. 5:22).
- Learn to relax in the Lord, not in your ability to make things happen: "Rest in the Lord" (Ps. 37:7, KJV).

I/S: Inspirational Specialists

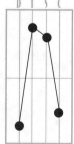

- Do everything for the Lord: "Whatever you do, work at it with all your heart, as working for the Lord, not for men" (Col. 3:23).
- Beware of seeking humans' approval: "not with eyeservice, as men pleasers" (Eph. 6:6, KJV).
- Seek to please God rather than others: " 'I always do what pleases him [God]' " (John 8:29).

- Be more task-oriented: " 'First … estimate the cost' " (Luke 14:28).
- Don't be lazy: "Never lacking in zeal" (Rom. 12:11).
- Work hard: "Each one should test his own actions" (Gal. 6:4).
- Don't just talk about what you want: "bearing fruit in every good work" (Col. 1:10).
- Be industrious: " 'Night is coming, when no one can work' " (John 9:4).

S/D: Steady Doers

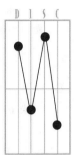

- God wants to empower what you think is weakness: "I will boast all the more gladly about my weaknesses, so that Christ's power may rest on me." God's grace—the power and ability to do what God wants—is enough for whatever you need: "My grace is sufficient for you." You are often strongest in weakness, as you trust in God and not yourself: "My power is made perfect in weakness" (2 Cor. 12:9).
- Encourage and help others daily: "Encourage one another daily" (Heb. 3:13).
- God invites you to reason with Him: " 'Come now, let us reason together' " (Isa. 1:18).

C/I/S: Competent, Influencing Specialists

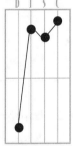

- Guard against being judgmental: " 'Do not judge, or you too will be judged' " (Matt. 7:1). "Who are you to judge?" (Jas. 4:12).
- Avoid bitterness and resentment, "that no bitter root grows up to cause trouble and defile many" (Heb. 12:15).
- God will meet your needs: "My God will meet all your needs according to His glorious riches in Christ Jesus" (Phil. 4:19).
- Be thankful in everything: "Give thanks in all circumstances" (1 Thess. 5:18).
- Let God's Word affect you: "Let the word of Christ dwell in you richly … with all wisdom" (Col. 3:16).
- Do whatever you do for God's glory: "Do it all in the name of the Lord Jesus" (Col. 3:17).

Straight Midline

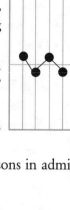

You may be trying to be all things to all persons, which is good, but it can be frustrating at times. The farther apart your plotting positions, the easier it is to read the profile.

- Recognize your identity in Christ: "I have been crucified with Christ and I no longer live, but Christ lives in me" (Gal. 2:20).
- Relax in the Lord: " 'Come to me, all you who are weary and burdened, and I will give you rest' " (Matt. 11:28).
- You cannot please everyone all the time, "having men's persons in admiration" (Jude 16, KJV).

D/C: Driving, Competent Types

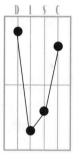

- Seek to get along with everyone: "Live at peace with everyone" (Rom. 12:18).
- Be kind and loving: "Be devoted to one another in brotherly love" (Rom. 12:10).
- Show more love: "Love one another" (1 John 4:7).
- Seek to serve, not to be served. Be "like slaves of Christ" (Eph. 6:6).
- Meekness is not weakness. Control your desire to have power over others. Be Christlike: "by the meekness and gentleness of Christ" (2 Cor. 10:1).
- Take time to be still and commune with God: " 'Be still, and know that I am God' " (Ps. 46:10).

I/C: Inspirational, Competent Types

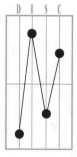

- Be careful not to think too highly of yourself: "God opposes the proud but gives grace to the humble" (1 Pet. 5:5).
- Seek to please God more than others: "When a man's ways are pleasing to the Lord, he makes even his enemies live at peace with him" (Prov. 16:7).
- Be a good example: "Set an example for the believers" (1 Tim. 4:12).

- Care more about how you look to God: " 'Man looks at the outward appearance, but the Lord looks at the heart' " (1 Sam. 16:7).
- Be bold and confident in Christ: "In him and through faith in him we may approach God with freedom and confidence" (Eph. 3:12).
- Guard statements and judgments: "The Lord hates ... a lying tongue" (Prov. 16-17).
- Don't flatter yourself: "In his own eyes he flatters himself too much to detect or hate his sin" (Ps. 36:2).

S/C: Steady, Competent Types

- Be assertive and stronger: " 'Be strong and courageous' " (Josh. 1:6).
- Be more enthusiastic: "Whatever you do, work at it with all your heart" (Col. 3:23).
- Enjoy relationships rather than endure them. Christ said, " 'I have come that they may have life ... to the full' " (John 10:10).
- Peace and happiness do not come from security and safety: " 'Peace I leave with you; my peace I give you' " (John 14:27).
- Divine peace is knowing that God's ways are beyond ours: "The peace of God, which transcends all understanding, will guard your hearts and your minds in Christ Jesus" (Phil 4:7).
- Be fearless in Christ: "I will fear no evil" (Ps. 23:4).

C/S/D: Competent, Steady Doers

- Be more enthusiastic: "Whatever you do, work at it with all your heart" (Col. 3:23).
- Don't worry so much about problems: " 'Do not let your hearts be troubled' " (John 14:27).
- Be more positive: "Whatever is pure, ... if anything is excellent or praiseworthy—think about such things" (Phil. 4:8).
- Let your sensitivity be more evident: "Be devoted to one another in brotherly love" (Rom. 12:10).
- Don't be like Moses when he was reluctant to lead because of his poor ver-

bal skills (see Ex. 4:10-16).

- Be more outwardly optimistic and encouraging to others: "Encourage one another daily" (Heb. 3:13).

Above Midline/Below Midline

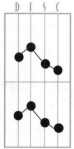

- An above-midline blend may mean that you try to over-achieve: "It is God who works in you to will and to act according to his good purpose" (Phil. 2:13). You may think too highly of what is expected of you or the real you. Remember Peter.
- A below-midline blend may indicate that you are not sure how to respond to challenges: "I can do everything through him who gives me strength" (Phil. 4:13). Think more positively about yourself: "I am fearfully and wonderfully made" (Ps. 139:14).

Spiritual-Gifts Profile

Every Christian has one or more spiritual gifts to use in ministry to others and to strengthen the body of Christ. These motivational gifts are specific ways we think, feel, and act from a spiritual perspective.

You can identify your spiritual gifts by completing and scoring this profile of 108 statements. As you read each statement, choose one of the following responses and write the corresponding number in the blank beside the statement.

5 = always true
4 = often true
3 = sometimes true
2 = seldom true
1 = never true

Avoid choosing 3 as much as possible. Don't hesitate choosing 5 or 1 from a desire to be humble or not to exaggerate. Try to be as honest and accurate as possible.

Example: __ I love to hear evangelistic messages.

Is this statement always, often, sometimes, seldom, or never true about you? Try to choose 5, 4, 2, or 1. Avoid choosing 3. Write the appropriate number in the blank beside the statement.

1. __4__ I love to hear evangelistic messages.
2. __4__ I tend to be irritated when people sin.
3. __5__ Education is very important to me.
4. __2__ Teaching without practical application is inadequate.
5. __2__ I tend to get frustrated when the church is not growing.
6. __3__ I tend to be supersensitive to sad stories.
7. __4__ I do the little things no one else wants to do.
8. __1__ Material blessings and success go hand in hand.
9. __1__ I tend to motivate others to get involved.
10. __4__ Leading persons to Christ is exciting.
11. __4__ I tend to be tough when it comes to sin.
12. __4__ Preparation to speak or teach is absolutely necessary.
13. __5__ I like to share practical steps of action.
14. __2__ I tend to be overprotective of my Christian friends.
15. __1__ I spend a lot of time helping others feel better.
16. __4__ I would rather do something than talk about helping others.
17. __3__ I don't like giving cheap gifts.
18. __1__ I can do a lot of things at once.
19. __5__ I am very concerned about lost souls.
20. __1__ I tend to be bold in public.
21. __1__ I tend to use biblical illustrations to explain things.
22. __1__ I teach topical, rather than verse-by-verse, lessons.
23. __1__ I like to guide others on a spiritual journey.
24. __2__ I identify with persons who are hurting.
25. __4__ Working behind the scenes gives me much pleasure.
26. __5__ People misunderstand my financial interests.
27. __4__ I do my best work under pressure.
28. __5__ Worldwide evangelism really excites me.
29. __2__ I like to proclaim truth I have received from God.
30. __4__ I like to explain why something is true.
31. __4__ Solving problems is my main concern.
32. __1__ I often seek to help individuals grow in Christ.
33. __1__ Some persons think I'm too sensitive.
34. __1__ I tend to take a lot of opportunities to serve others.
35. __5__ Financial accountability is extremely important.

36. __3__ I enjoy designing programs that put people to work.
37. __2__ Sharing the gospel is my passion.
38. __5__ People think I am too hard on others.
39. __1__ I prefer using my materials rather than someone else's.
40. __4__ I enjoy encouraging others.
41. __5__ I am interested in the overall ministry of the church.
42. __3__ I try to come across as loving and caring.
43. __5__ I don't like being up front or leading a group.
44. __5__ I tend to discern true financial needs.
45. __2__ I like to organize persons to accomplish great tasks.
46. __1__ I tend to be focused when witnessing.
47. __1__ I tend to know why people do what they do.
48. __5__ I can be critical of poor teaching.
49. __4__ I seem to sense when persons are discouraged.
50. __2__ Leading groups to spiritual maturity is appealing.
51. __4__ I tend to be ruled by my emotions.
52. __4__ I prefer doing manual tasks no one else will do.
53. __5__ Financial giving is a private matter to me.
54. __1__ I like impossible challenges.
55. __2__ I can share the gospel with total strangers.
56. __4__ I prefer challenging a person's status quo.
57. __4__ I like to study the Bible for long periods.
58. __5__ I often feel compelled to share advice.
59. __1__ Persons seek me out to become spiritually stronger.
60. __3__ I tend to volunteer often to help the less fortunate.
61. __4__ I would rather do a job myself than delegate it.
62. __5__ I'm concerned about meeting financial/physical needs.
63. __4__ I see the big picture of what needs to be done.
64. __2__ Sharing my faith is most important to me.
65. __2__ I discern that something is evil before others do.
66. __4__ I search for new insights as I study.
67. __1__ I believe that a plan exists to solve every problem.
68. __2__ I feel compelled to guard against evil's entering a group.
69. __2__ I am very concerned about how a person feels.
70. __2__ It is difficult for me to say no when asked for help.

start a revolution

71. _4_ I judge maturity by how money is handled.
72. _1_ I often delegate responsibilities to accomplish tasks.
73. _2_ I understand the gospel and can relate it to others.
74. _1_ Confronting someone with sin in his or her life is not hard for me.
75. _3_ Studying the Scriptures is my passion.
76. _5_ I like to help persons solve problems in logical ways.
77. _1_ I like to help others get involved in ministry.
78. _2_ When others hurt, I feel compelled to help.
79. _1_ I tend to do much more than I'm told to do.
80. _4_ I like to take care of financial needs in a timely manner.
81. _4_ I enjoy long-range planning.
82. _1_ I like to lead persons to Christ with my testimony.
83. _1_ I would rather speak out than to let something pass.
84. _4_ I tend to prepare too much material.
85. _4_ Practical application is what teaching is all about.
86. _1_ I prefer being a spiritual leader.
87. _2_ I really feel for persons who suffer.
88. _3_ I prefer serving others rather than being served.
89. _4_ I tend to give money freely where needed most.
90. _4_ I tend to take charge when no one else does.
91. _2_ I have non-Christian friends I witness to.
92. _5_ I can be stubborn and difficult to convince.
93. _5_ It bothers me to hear incorrect statements.
94. _4_ I really enjoy counseling others.
95. _2_ I seem to look for spiritual lessons in whatever happens.
96. _2_ I am sensitive to the underprivileged and handicapped.
97. _2_ I enjoy hearing messages about serving.
98. _4_ Being slothful, lazy, in business is a sin.
99. _3_ When I decide to act, I don't like to change my mind.
100. _1_ I enjoy asking persons to make decisions for Christ.
101. _4_ I research to share truth rather than just to study.
102. _5_ I am very concerned about accuracy.
103. _4_ I like giving detailed "road maps" when helping others.
104. _1_ I enjoy leading discipleship studies.
105. _4_ I can't say no to legitimate needs.

106. _5_ I believe that I show my faith best by my works.

107. _4_ I tend to make wise investments.

108. _1_ I like to organize projects to get the job done.

Spiritual-Gifts Graph

Below is a grid for recording your numerical ratings. Score your inventory by transferring your choice of 5, 4, 3, 2, or 1 to the corresponding numbered box on the grid "Numerical Ratings." Then total each vertical column in the boxes marked *A–I*.

Scoring example:

1	2	3	4
4	5	1	2

Numerical Ratings

1	2	3	4	5	6	7	8	9
4	4	5	2	2	3	4	1	1
10 4	11 4	12 4	13 5	14 2	15 1	16 4	17 3	18 1
19 5	20 1	21 1	22 1	23 1	24 2	25 4	26 5	27 4
28 5	29 2	30 4	31 4	32 1	33 1	34 1	35 5	36 3
37 2	38 5	39 1	40 4	41 5	42 3	43 5	44 5	45 2
46 1	47 1	48 5	49 4	50 2	51 4	52 4	53 5	54 1
55 2	56 4	57 4	58 5	59 1	60 3	61 4	62 5	63 4
64 2	65 2	66 4	67 1	68 2	69 2	70 2	71 4	72 1
73 2	74 1	75 3	76 5	77 1	78 2	79 1	80 4	81 4
82 1	83 1	84 4	85 4	86 1	87 2	88 3	89 4	90 4
91 2	92 5	93 5	94 4	95 2	96 2	97 2	98 4	99 3
100 1	101 4	102 5	103 4	104 1	105 4	106 5	107 4	108 1
A 31	B 34	C 45	D 43	E 21	F 29	G 39	H 49	I 29

To plot your spiritual-gifts profile, turn to page 72 and circle the numbers on the graph that are closest to your totals on the grid "Numerical Ratings."

Example:

A	B
51	28

A	B
60	60
59	59
58	58
57	57
56	56
55	55
54	54
53	53
52	52
(51)	51
50	50
49	49
48	48
47	47
46	46
45	45
44	44
43	43
42	42
41	41
40	40
39	39
38	38
37	37
36	36
35	35
34	34
33	33
32	32
31	31
30	30
29	29
28	(28)
27	27
26	26

Evangelism	Prophecy	Teaching	Exhortation	Pastoring/ Shepherding	Mercy	Ministry/ Serving	Giving	Administration
A	B	C	D	E	F	G	H	I
60	60	60	60	60	60	60	60	60
59	59	59	59	59	59	59	59	59
58	58	58	58	58	58	58	58	58
57	57	57	57	57	57	57	57	57
56	56	56	56	56	56	56	56	56
55	55	55	55	55	55	55	55	55
54	54	54	54	54	54	54	54	54
53	53	53	53	53	53	53	53	53
52	52	52	52	52	52	52	52	52
51	51	51	51	51	51	51	51	51
50	50	50	50	50	50	50	50	50
49	49	49	49	49	49	49	49	49
48	48	48	48	48	48	48	48	48
47	47	47	47	47	47	47	47	47
46	46	46	46	46	46	46	46	46
45	45	45	45	45	45	45	45	45
44	44	44	44	44	44	44	44	44
43	43	43	43	43	43	43	43	43
42	42	42	42	42	42	42	42	42
41	41	41	41	41	41	41	41	41
40	40	40	40	40	40	40	40	40
39	39	39	39	39	39	39	39	39
38	38	38	38	38	38	38	38	38
37	37	37	37	37	37	37	37	37
36	36	36	36	36	36	36	36	36
35	35	35	35	35	35	35	35	35
34	34	34	34	34	34	34	34	34
33	33	33	33	33	33	33	33	33
32	32	32	32	32	32	32	32	32
31	31	31	31	31	31	31	31	31
30	30	30	30	30	30	30	30	30
29	29	29	29	29	29	29	29	29
28	28	28	28	28	28	28	28	28
27	27	27	27	27	27	27	27	27
26	26	26	26	26	26	26	26	26
25	25	25	25	25	25	25	25	25
24	24	24	24	24	24	24	24	24
23	23	23	23	23	23	23	23	23
22	22	22	22	22	22	22	22	22
21	21	21	21	21	21	21	21	21
20	20	20	20	20	20	20	20	20
19	19	19	19	19	19	19	19	19
18	18	18	18	18	18	18	18	18
17	17	17	17	17	17	17	17	17
16	16	16	16	16	16	16	16	16
15	15	15	15	15	15	15	15	15
14	14	14	14	14	14	14	14	14
13	13	13	13	13	13	13	13	13
12	12	12	12	12	12	12	12	12
11	11	11	11	11	11	11	11	11
10	10	10	10	10	10	10	10	10
9	9	9	9	9	9	9	9	9

Now connect the circles on the graph. The higher the circle on the graph, the more intensely that gift describes you. Also notice your other strong gifts, as well as your weakest tendencies.

What are your three strongest spiritual gifts?

Giving

Teaching

Exhortation

Spiritual-Gifts Descriptions

Spiritual gifts are supernatural motivations that God gives to every believer. Everyone doesn't receive the same gift. As many parts of the human body work together as one, various spiritual gifts are given to members of the body of Christ to serve as one.

The purpose of spiritual gifts is to encourage and mature Christians for more effective ministry. As many as 21 spiritual gifts can be identified in the Scriptures. We have chosen to focus on the 9 that are most frequently seen functioning today. The following gifts are named in Romans 12:3-8 and Ephesians 4:11-12. Their descriptions are based on their functional and practical uses.

Evangelism

Christians with the gift of evangelism feel compelled to win souls. They seem to have the ability to communicate the gospel effectively. Their concern for witnessing to a lost and dying world is evident. They desire to be involved in ministries to reach people for Christ. The gift of evangelism motivates them to want nearly every message they hear to include the gospel and an invitation to trust Christ. Missions and outreach are important to them, and always being ready to witness to every person is their goal. Conversations often seem to turn toward eternal values. The worth of souls and the task of evangelism are most important to the evangelist's motivation.

- In a word: dynamic
- Overuse: zeal
- Goal: Build disciples, not statistics.

Teaching

Christians with the gift of teaching like to explain why things are true. While the prophet declares truth, the teacher explains the reasons it is true. Interested in research, those with the gift of teaching like to dig into seemingly insignificant details. They enjoy presenting what they discover. Often negligent of other needs, they press toward a deeper understanding. They love to study. Searching patiently and persistently, they may miss the obvious. They stretch the limits of learning, setting high standards of education.

- In a word: in-depth
- Overuse: digs too deep
- Goal: Reveal truth; don't exhaust it.

Pastoring/Shepherding

Pastors/shepherds enjoy leading others to serve the Lord. Unlike the gift of ministry, this gift involves the motivation to lead. Pastors/shepherds are compelled to encourage others to work together for the body's sake. Influencing others to work together is important. Stressing a need for team participation, they emphasize harmony. Untrained laypersons can also have the gift of pastoring/shepherding. They see their service as one of maturing others. With a motivation to unite the ministry, they feel strong about spiritual health.

- In a word: leader
- Overuse: takes advantage of others' trust
- Goal: Cultivate strong leadership; don't manipulate the flock.

Ministry/Serving

When you think of Christians who faithfully serve behind the scenes, you think of those with the gift of ministry/serving. To serve the Lord, they want to help others, and they love doing so. Motivated by a strong sense of need, they feel that someone has to do it. Caring and concerned for others, they find themselves doing what no one else likes to do. They tend to do whatever is called for. They are flexible, adapting to many challenges. They simply enjoy helping others and meeting needs. Often truly selfless, those with the gift of ministry like to be involved.

- In a word: selfless
- Overuse: takes on too much
- Goal: Be a servant, not a martyr.

Administration

The gift of administration is seen in those who like either to organize or to delegate to others. Compelled by a strong sense of duty, they like to find things for others to do. Unlike the gift of ministry, the gift of administration focuses on team participation. Persons with this gift see the big picture and work to keep everyone on track. Not always personally organized, they prefer delegating tasks. They like to evaluate what needs to be done, then design systems or give responsibilities to those who can get the job done. They are gifted to forge forward with a group.

- In a word: initiator
- Overuse: expects too much
- Goal: Lead by example, not by manipulation.

Prophecy

Prophets today are not exactly like prophets of old. Old Testament prophets spoke the literal word of God. Today people with the gift of prophecy seem to have the same seriousness and straightforward attitude toward truth. They like to share truth, regardless of what anyone thinks. Prophets are motivated to confront anyone with what they believe is right. When controlled by the Holy Spirit, the gift of prophecy is a powerful tool for reproving, rebuking, and exhorting others. Prophets often point the way, declare a specific truth, or stand up for something significant.

- In a word: bold
- Overuse: fighter
- Goal: Declare truth; don't divide Christians.

Exhortation

Christians with the gift of exhortation encourage others. They are compelled to give advice. As counselors, they often seem to have steps of action. While prophets declare truth and teachers clarify truth, exhorters like to tell you what to do with truth. They bless others with a strong sense of concern. Often looking to encourage others, they are sought as counselors. People find exhorters friendly, understanding, and practical. They enjoy using their communication skills to share specific insights.

- In a word: encourager
- Overuse: talks too much
- Goal: Apply truth; don't create expectations.

Mercy

Christians with the gift of mercy demonstrate genuine sensitivity to suffering. They are compelled to help people reduce their pain. They are concerned more with the person than with the reason for the suffering. Focusing on the feelings of those who hurt, those with the gift of mercy desire to minister by being there when people really need them. Sympathizing and empathizing are their specialties. While others may care more about why, what, when, where, or how, those with this gift are interested in who needs tender, loving care.

- In a word: caring
- Overuse: too sensitive
- Goal: Give wise insights, not foolish responses.

Giving

Givers tend to be seriously concerned about financial matters. The gift of giving also involves the "gift" of getting. Givers are sensitive to how money is spent and saved. Those with the gift of giving don't always give to the wheel that squeaks the loudest but to the wheel that truly needs the most grease. Givers have unique financial insights. They serve especially well on boards responsible for managing budgets. They tend to be conscientious and conservative. The gift of giving may not always be evident, but a genuine interest in wise stewardship is.

- In a word: steward
- Overuse: the power of money
- Goal: Practice sincere stewardship, not financial harassment.

Combining Your Personality with Your Spiritual Gifts

The following are 36 combinations of *D, I, S,* and *C* personalities with the nine spiritual gifts that have been described. Now that you have identified your personality type and your spiritual gifts, find the descriptions of your particular combinations. You may have several combinations to identify.

Consider the insights that best describe you and disregard those that are not like you. Keep in mind that you are a blend of behaviors and gifts. Prayerfully study each description, asking God to control and use your personality and spiritual gifts for His glory. Work to discover ways God can use you in ministry. Discovering your personality and spiritual gifts should result in a desire to grow in spiritual maturity, involvement in the body of Christ, and ministry to others.

D Personality with the Gift of Evangelism

Dynamic and demanding personalities with the gift of evangelism can be extremely effective. They are self-starters with a sense of urgency. But their driving concern to win souls can make them too pushy. D-evangelists should be more gentle and patient. Determined to get the job done, they often feel that everyone should be involved in evangelism. Direct with their presentations, they like sermons that explain the gospel and offer invitations to trust Christ. D-evangelists are dedicated to making Christ known.

D Personality with the Gift of Prophecy

Demanding personalities with the gift of prophecy are fearless in standing for the truth. Determined to preserve purity, they tend to dominate others. As protectors of righteousness, they proclaim truth without concern for what anyone thinks. They often feel that they have the divine right to be pushy. D-prophets are so driving that they often offend others. They need to be gentler rather than always strive to expose error. They should be more sensitive to others' feelings. D-prophets are the most effective declarers of truth.

D Personality with the Gift of Teaching

Driving personalities with the gift of teaching are dedicated students and demanding instructors. They like to use challenging research to convince others. They tend to be too forceful. D-teachers make strong disciplinarians. Often domineering, they need to be gentler with their insights. Digging deep while getting to the point can be frustrating. They should balance dedication to teaching with more people orientation. D-teachers can effectively explain why something is true.

D Personality with the Gift of Ministry/Serving

Driving personalities with the gift of ministry stay busy for Christ. They tend to work hard behind the scenes, doing whatever needs to be done. They can be impatient with those who don't help. Determined to minister, they tend to dominate and intimidate others to serve also. D-servants are task-oriented individuals who work tirelessly. They may need to slow down, relax, and delegate. They can become demanding and offensive. D-servants are dedicated to ministering and helping others. They are self-sacrificing doers of the Word.

D Personality with the Gift of Exhortation

Decisive personalities with the gift of exhortation are persistent encouragers. They tend to dominate conversations with practical steps of action. They like to share advice. D-exhorters are driven to control the situation in order to encourage. They need to be more flexible and sensitive. People can't always do or feel what D-exhorters want. They tend to have a plan for every problem. Often impatient, they can be too pushy. Letting others share ideas, while determining to encourage others, makes them extremely effective.

D Personality with the Gift of Mercy

Determined personalities with the gift of mercy are rare but dedicated to helping others feel better. Their domineering ways tend to conflict with their desire to sympathize with others. They can be decisive while merciful and kind. D's who show mercy are unique individuals who tend to demand that everyone display a caring spirit. Their driving personalities can be misunderstood as insensitive, while mercy is their motivation. They should guard their dominance with loving hearts. They press the need to care.

D Personality with the Gift of Pastoring/Shepherding

Demanding personalities with the gift of pastoring/shepherding tend to be ministry-driven. Seeing the big picture, they are compelled to lead others. Their domineering ways can be misunderstood as dictatorial. They may be genuinely dedicated to shepherding others but may have strong feelings about what should be done. Slowly working through persons can make them more effective. Often taking charge, they seem to control others, but their concern for the flock is evident. D-pastors/shepherds make great visionaries.

D Personality with the Gift of Giving

Domineering personalities with the gift of giving are serious about financial matters. They can be very successful in business. They also have the "gift" of getting. They tend to use money to control others. Demanding how finances are used, they can be extremely picky with budgets. They seldom give to the wheel that squeaks the loudest. They are either unbending or influencing about financial decisions. They either discourage or encourage others with their money and/or advice. *D*-givers can make great financial counselors.

D Personality with the Gift of Administration

Demanding personalities with the gift of administration are strong leaders and like to tell others what to do. They often see what needs to be done and delegate the work to others but can be too bossy. *D*-administrators tend to see the big picture but lack warmth to get others to help without pressure. They can intimidate and offend if not careful. Often concerned more about tasks than people, they need to be more sensitive and loving. *D*-administrators can be gifted leaders who press forward to do great things for God.

I Personality with the Gift of Evangelism

Influencing personalities with the gift of evangelism are enthusiastic about soul-winning. They are also very contagious as cheerleaders for Christ. Interested in people, they are naturally effective witnesses. *I*-evangelists make sharing the gospel look easy. Because of their strong desire to impress, they may care equally about what others think of them and leading others to Christ. They must constantly remember that God gifted them to shine for Him, not for self. *I*-evangelists can win many souls to Christ.

I Personality with the Gift of Prophecy

Influencing personalities with the gift of prophecy make great communicators of truth. They articulate correctness with persuasion. They tend to overuse enthusiasm and emotions to convince others. Able to induce action or reaction, they need to guard against verbal abuse. Proclaiming truth, *I*-prophets should season their speech with sugar. Making great impressions, they must remember whom they represent, not what they defend. *I*-prophets are inspiring protectors of the faith.

I Personality with the Gift of Teaching

Inspiring personalities with the gift of teaching are most interesting. They tell the best stories and use clear illustrations. Their verbal skills create fascinating studies, although they tend to have lengthy classes. *I*-teachers need to be more time-conscientious. They may also stretch the text to make a point. Concerned about what others think, they often make good impressions. They can become prideful because of their tremendous ability to communicate. *I*-teachers are some of the most interesting instructors.

I Personality with the Gift of Ministry/Serving

Inspiring personalities with the gift of ministry are excited about serving. Their impressive enthusiasm makes others want to get involved. *I*-servants are extremely effective in inducing action. They can be too persuasive and impatient. They tend to oversell and manipulate. Influencing others, they should guard their verbal skills when the job needs to get done. *I*-servants tend to work longer than necessary because they talk too much. Creating an exciting atmosphere of service is their specialty.

I Personality with the Gift of Exhortation

Inspiring personalities with the gift of exhortation make enthusiastic encouragers. They impress others with advice. But they can be too optimistic, often creating high expectations. They need to be more realistic. *I*-exhorters should guard against using their verbal skills to manipulate. They may try to influence others to do more than is humanly possible. They should listen more and speak less. Interested in others, they often induce positive responses. *I*-exhorters communicate encouragement best.

I Personality with the Gift of Mercy

Inspiring personalities with the gift of mercy influence others to care more, using their verbal skills to generate excitement for the cause of demonstrating love. Interested in people, they induce strong feelings of concern. They can be too emotional. *I*'s who show mercy can overdo their influence. Some people may think their concern is all show since they like to impress others with their kindness. They may need to calm down and be more humble. *I*'s who show mercy demonstrate evident sensitivity.

I Personality with the Gift of Pastoring/Shepherding

Inspiring personalities with the gift of pastoring/shepherding are impressive. Their influence makes people enjoy working and worshiping. They can be extremely successful and must guard against pride. People look up to them. Able to persuade, they need to be more cautious about what they promote. They love to minister and encourage others to do so. Often concerned about what others think, they need to guard against using others to build their ministries. I-pastors/shepherds can be best at using their ministry to build people.

I Personality with the Gift of Giving

Impressing personalities with the gift of giving are enthusiastic about stewardship. They like to encourage everyone to be givers. They make great promoters but can kill projects because of financial concerns. I-givers, more optimistic than others, can be too positive. Their faith is evident in giving but can become prideful. They like to tell everyone how to give more. When discouraged, they may use their verbal skills and financial credibility to influence others. I-givers are most excited when finances are involved.

I Personality with the Gift of Administration

Influencing personalities with the gift of administration are optimistic leaders. Their positive enthusiasm encourages others to get involved. They can be overly excited and tend to talk persons into doing things they don't want to do. They impress others with their friendliness and verbal skills. I-administrators need to guard against manipulating. They should serve by example. They often take on more than they can handle, disappointing those who expect a lot from them. But I-administrators can accomplish much through others.

S Personality with the Gift of Evangelism

Sweet and soft personalities with the gift of evangelism are the most gentle witnesses. They steadily share the gospel. They don't like to force issues. They tend to be too nice. Scoffers often waste S-evangelists' time. Knowing that they go the extra mile, some persons take advantage of them. Avoiding confrontation, these stable types prefer relationship evangelism. But their motivation to win souls often overcomes their natural reluctance to speak out. S-evangelists enjoy bringing persons to Jesus without a lot of fanfare.

S Personality with the Gift of Prophecy

Sensitive personalities with the gift of prophecy are shy but serious about truth. They seem to be soft, but their concern makes them persuaders. Motivated to proclaim truth, they tend to be gentle but strong. S-prophets seem to struggle with their concern for individuals and their stand for correctness. This balance makes them surprisingly effective. People are often impressed when their shyness turns into firmness. They need to be careful about extremes. S-prophets are like sleeping giants when it comes to truth.

S Personality with the Gift of Teaching

Stable personalities with the gift of teaching are systematic researchers. They like to teach steadily, step-by-step. Their simple but insightful instruction often lacks excitement. They need to be more animated. S-teachers make faithful and loyal friends but often resist conflict. They should strive to be more interested in results than in relationships and revelation. Concerned about harmony and accuracy, they can be too sweet and slow to share why something is true. You can count on S-teachers for a thorough explanation.

S Personality with the Gift of Ministry/Serving

Steady personalities with the gift of ministry/serving are every church's dream—the backbone of ministry. If anything needs to be done, they faithfully serve without recognition. They are not bossy but should be more assertive. People take advantage of S-servants. They should be more aggressive in seeking help. Always being sensitive to others' feelings makes them sought out. But sometimes they solve problems for those who may need to feel the pressure of their irresponsibility. S-servants are the most stable servants.

S Personality with the Gift of Exhortation

Sensitive personalities with the gift of exhortation are sweet encouragers. They share simple and slow steps of action to help others. They are not pushy, often waiting for others to ask for advice. They love to stabilize bad situations with practical ideas. S-exhorters can be too shy, waiting instead of aggressively confronting an issue. They need to be more assertive. Because their concern for others often makes them too nice, they may need to show tough love. S-exhorters are security-oriented encouragers.

S Personality with the Gift of Mercy

Sensitive personalities with the gift of mercy are most loving. They are sweet servants who are always ready to help. They specialize in times of suffering. S's who show mercy may be so concerned that they miss opportunities to teach lessons. They can also be deceived by insincere cries for help. They may need to be more assertive with those who use their pain as excuses. They should be more demanding. They may need to share truth rather than always listen. When people hurt, S's who show mercy shine.

S Personality with the Gift of Pastoring/Shepherding

Submissive personalities with the gift of pastoring/shepherding are selfless servants. They enjoy building relationships that result in ministry. They shepherd by example, not by demand. They can be too nice. Often more caring than confrontational, they may need to be more assertive. Concerned about the ministry, they should be more enthusiastic. Shyness often hinders their leadership. People appreciate their interest in ministry, but some may want them to be more decisive. S-pastors/shepherds make gentle leaders.

S Personality with the Gift of Giving

Security-oriented personalities with the gift of giving are not risk takers. They are submissive (willing) givers. They may lack the vision necessary to tackle challenging projects. Sensitive to individual needs, they help others behind the scenes. They are private about giving. S-givers can be too helpful and can be taken advantage of. They need to balance their sincere desire to serve with a stronger determination to do what is right. They tend to be the most sacrificing. S-givers are stable financial planners who avoid financial disasters.

S Personality with the Gift of Administration

Submissive personalities with the gift of administration are concerned about getting tasks done in steady, stable ways. They need to be more assertive and aggressive. S-administrators can be too sacrificing. Faithful in whatever they do, they need to inspire others to help. They can be quiet leaders, challenging others by example, and tend to be shy. Sometimes they surprise others with their serious concern to accomplish tasks. S-administrators are achievers who like to work through small groups.

C Personality with the Gift of Evangelism

Cautious and compliant personalities with the gift of evangelism are the most thorough witnesses. They like to go point by point, convincing persons to understand every detail. They try to have an answer for every question, but they can overwhelm with too many facts. C-evangelists are often more concerned with the task than with the person in need. As competent individuals, they need to be more flexible and friendly. C-evangelists can turn doubt into a fascinating opportunity for Christ.

C Personality with the Gift of Prophecy

Calculating personalities with the gift of prophecy are cautious and competent. They tend to be conscientious. They can be too critical of those who compromise the truth. Often convincing, they tend to be confrontational. Their concern for compliance often makes them unbending. C-prophets are insightful but can be insensitive to what others feel. They would increase effectiveness with greater interest in others rather than always being right. As protectors of truth, C-prophets are able to see and share correctness.

C Personalities with the Gift of Teaching

Compliant personalities with the gift of teaching are controlled by the quest for truth. They make great researchers. Determined to discover in-depth truth, they can overdo their lessons, becoming too factual. People seem to find C-teachers competent but boring, because they can lack enthusiasm and warmth. They should focus more on practical application. As critical thinkers, C-teachers can sound sarcastic. When sensitive, excited, and patient, C-teachers make great instructors.

C Personality with the Gift of Ministry/Serving

Competent personalities with the gift of ministry are detail-oriented. They don't like loose ends. If anything needs to be done right, they are perfect for the job. C-servants can be too picky and tend to be difficult to work with. They need to be more friendly and cooperative. Often feeling that they are the only ones who do anything, they need to appreciate others more. Positive attitudes and enthusiasm are recommended but difficult for C-servants. They can be the hardest-working and most compliant servants.

C Personality with the Gift of Exhortation

Calculating personalities with the gift of exhortation are precise encouragers. They often know just what to say. Their practical steps of action tend to be concise. They make competent counselors with specific insights, though they can be too hard on people. C-exhorters can see what needs to be done but can fail at communicating love. They should be more sensitive to others' failures and less critical, since more kindness can increase their effectiveness. C-exhorters can make great problem solvers.

C Personality with the Gift of Mercy

Compliant personalities with the gift of mercy are extremely concerned about others. They see needs no one else sees. They tend to know exactly what to say. They are careful not to miss opportunities to help but can be critical of those who don't get involved. C's who show mercy may try to analyze why people hurt. Their conservative care is often appreciated. They need to be optimistic, since they often lack enthusiasm and inspiration. C's who show mercy are competent individuals who really care about people who suffer.

C Personality with the Gift of Pastoring/Shepherding

Conscientious personalities with the gift of pastoring/shepherding are methodical. They like to go by the book and don't like to take risks and venture away from what they know works. They may need to be more open to innovation. They strive for correctness. Purity in the group is important to C-pastors/shepherds. Enthusiasm can encourage more to minister. Often conservative, they tend to be picky. Detailed assignments can often be overdone. C-pastors/shepherds are competent church leaders.

C Personality with the Gift of Giving

Compliant personalities with the gift of giving are cautious. They move conservatively, seldom making quick financial decisions. They don't like pressure and may stifle vision and growth because of pessimism. Although C-givers rarely make investment mistakes, they may miss great opportunities. Often perceived as critical, they need to be more positive and friendly. Respected by others, they should use their competence to help rather than find fault. C-givers can be valuable in financial planning.

C Personality with the Gift of Administration

Cautious personalities with the gift of administration are competent taskmasters. They see a need and organize others to meet that need. They enjoy doing things completely right the first time and tend to be picky. They would increase effectiveness with more warmth and team participation. Working through persons and creating enthusiastic atmospheres can be helpful. They should avoid being critical of what others do. C-administrators are best able to get groups to do the right tasks.

How to Handle Conflicts

One of the greatest hindrances to spiritual growth is conflict. Most problems in the church today are not theological but relational—personality conflicts. Excited Christians, desiring to serve God, are often discouraged because of misunderstandings and clashes with other Christians.

This section helps you discover why people act as they do under pressure and why you may conflict with others. Scripture is clear on how to handle clashes. The problem is that many Christians are not aware of their sensitive areas. Every personality and spiritual gift has its hot button. Everyone can act like a *D* or a prophet when pushed too far.

The following describes tendencies of particular personalities and spiritual gifts under pressure. Study this material with your behavioral blend and spiritual gifts in mind to learn how you tend to respond. Also consider how you may learn to respond differently.

D Personality with Spiritual Gifts of Prophecy, Administration, and Exhortation

Under pressure becomes—
- dictatorial;
- domineering;
- demanding;
- angry;
- intense;
- forceful;
- direct;
- bossy.

Sources of irritation are—
- weakness;
- indecisiveness;
- laziness;
- lack of discipline, plan, purpose, direction, authority, control, and challenge.

Needs to—
- back off;
- seek peace;
- relax;
- think before reacting;
- control self;
- be patient, loving, friendly, loyal, kind, and sensitive.

C Personality with Spiritual Gifts of Prophecy, Administration, Teaching, and Giving

Under pressure becomes—
- moody;
- critical;
- contemplative;
- negative;
- worrisome.

Sources of irritation are—
- incompetence;
- disorganization;
- foolishness;
- dishonesty;
- inaccuracy;
- wastefulness;
- inconsistency;
- blind faith;
- false impressions.

Needs to—
- loosen up;
- communicate;

* be joyful, positive, tolerant, compromising, open, trusting, and enthusiastic.

I Personality with Spiritual Gifts of Prophecy, Exhortation, and Teaching

Under pressure becomes—
* hyper;
* overly optimistic;
* immature;
* emotional;
* irrational;
* silly;
* wordy;
* selfish.

Sources of irritation are—
* disinterest;
* slowness;
* pessimism;
* details;
* time constraints;
* antagonism;
* doubt;
* structure;
* lack of enthusiasm;
* lack of team participation.

Needs to—
* listen;
* count the cost;
* control emotions;
* be humble, strong, disciplined, punctual, careful with words, and conscientious.

S Personality with Spiritual Gifts of Mercy, Ministry, and Giving

Under pressure becomes—
* subservient;

- insecure;
- fearful;
- weak-willed;
- withdrawn;
- sympathizer;
- taken advantage of.

Sources of irritation are—
- pushiness;
- instability;
- inflexibility;
- anger;
- disloyalty;
- insensitivity;
- pride;
- discrimination;
- unfairness.

Needs to be—
- strong;
- courageous;
- challenging;
- aggressive;
- assertive;
- confrontational;
- enthusiastic;
- outgoing;
- expressive;
- cautious;
- bold.

Natural Responses to Conflict

D: Attack.
I: Expose others.
S: Support or submit.
C: Criticize.

Recommended Biblical Responses

D: Restore with love.

I: Talk to God, not others.

S: Care enough to confront.

C: Examine self first.

Involvement: Personality Perspective

This section will guide you to discover areas of ministry in which your personality can be used most effectively. In addition to considering these ideas, give God your personality to use for His glory. Also search the Scriptures for insights into ways God can use you and ask a minister or a mature Christian friend to guide you.

Never use your personality as an excuse not to do what God commands everyone to do. For example, the Bible commands you to do the work of an evangelist. *D's* and *I's* may feel comfortable talking to people about Christ, while *S's* and *C's* may not. Yet everyone should share the good news. *S's* may feel more comfortable working behind the scenes, but God may call an *S*, like Moses, to lead a group. Or God may call an *I* to work behind the scenes. Learn to be "all things to all men so that by all possible means [we] might save some" (1 Cor. 9:22). Whatever you do, do it through Christ (see Gal. 2:20).

D Personality (Active, Task-Oriented)

Abilities:

- Leading
- Taking a stand
- Confronting an issue
- Persevering
- Dictating
- Making decisions
- Controlling

Opportunities:

- Organizing needed ministry
- Chairing stewardship committee
- Heading ushers' committee

• Committing to specific challenge

Warning: You want to control everyone but must first control yourself. Remember that to have authority, you must be under authority. Be loyal to your leaders.

Reward: Follow your spiritual leaders. Allow Christ to be the Lord of your life, and God will use you in a great way to move the ministry forward.

Prayer: Dear God, control my driving, demanding, and dominant personality so that I can be a strong and peace-making leader for Your glory.

I Personality (Active, People-Oriented)

Abilities:

- Communicating
- Inspiring
- Influencing
- Making friends
- Being optimistic
- Being enthusiastic

Opportunities:

- Giving public testimony
- Performing in drama
- Serving on social committee
- Being a greeter
- Being an encourager
- Leading discussion group
- Visiting

Warning: You naturally outshine others. Don't serve purely through your personality. Also, don't allow pride and sinful lusts to destroy your testimony.

Reward: God designed you to shine for Him. When you allow Him to shine through you, He will use you in greater ways than you ever imagined.

Prayer: Dear God, keep me humble to do Your will, not mine. Help me give You and those who praise me the credit for all You have done.

S Personality (Passive, People-Oriented)

Abilities:

- Supporting

- Serving
- Specializing
- Finishing what others start
- Working behind the scenes
- Doing what needs to be done

Opportunities:
- Being on call whenever needed
- Visiting hospital patients
- Encouraging new members
- Doing office work
- Keeping records
- Telephoning
- Counseling

Warning: Shyness hinders your opportunities to do great things for God. Be more aggressive and assertive. Be careful not to let others take advantage of you.

Reward: Believing God's promise that you can do all things through Him who strengthens you, step out and try the difficult. You may be surprised what God can do.

Prayer: Dear God, I know that You use the weak to confound the mighty. I often don't feel capable of serving You, but through Your grace I will.

C Personality (Passive, Task-Oriented)

Abilities:
- Analyzing
- Improving
- Discerning
- Calculating
- Following directions
- Doing the right thing

Opportunities:
- Serving on finance committee
- Doing long-range planning
- Doing office work
- Recording information
- Researching

start a revolution

- Teaching
- Organizing
- Ordering curriculum

Warning: Due to your cautiousness, criticism comes easily. Don't always be pessimistic and hard to convince. Increase your faith in God and trust those you follow.

Reward: Ministers need competent persons to fulfill their visions. You can be a great blessing if you continually look at the possibilities rather than the impossibilities.

Prayer: Dear God, help me be optimistic in the midst of problems—a source of encouragement to those who find faith and victory difficult.

Involvement: Spiritual-Gifts Perspective

One of the best ways to grow as a Christian is to get involved. This section will guide you to discover areas of ministry in which your spiritual gifts can be used most effectively.

Prophecy

Abilities:
- Discerning right from wrong
- Declaring truth

Opportunities:
- Community/national concerns
- Finances
- Steering committee

Warning: Don't be obnoxious or opinionated.

Reward: helping others see truth clearly

Prayer: Dear God, give me the sensitivity to show love while sharing truth that may offend.

Exhortation

Ability: sharing practical steps of action
Opportunities:
- Counseling
- Crisis center

• Evangelism

Warning: Choose words wisely.

Reward: seeing persons respond to your advice and helping them through problems

Prayer: Dear God, use me to say what You want me to say, not what I feel at the moment.

Mercy

Ability: giving sympathy or empathy to the hurting

Opportunities:
- Hospital
- Benevolence
- Counseling

Warning: Don't be taken advantage of by trying to help everyone who needs you.

Reward: knowing you helped those whom no one else would help

Prayer: Dear God, use me not only to help others by showing care but also to share truth and tough love when necessary.

Giving

Ability: using stewardship to further God's kingdom

Opportunities:
- Finance committee
- Planning committee
- Office work

Warning: Don't use money to control others.

Reward: knowing that you contributed to the advancement of ministry without personal recognition

Prayer: Dear God, use my success with finances to bless the ministry and others.

Evangelism

Ability: comfortably sharing the gospel with results

Opportunities:
- Visitation

- Outreach
- Missions

Warning: Don't think everyone should be as dedicated to evangelism as you are.
Reward: knowing that leading persons to Christ glorifies God
Prayer: Dear God, increase my vision for the lost, while helping me understand why others do not share my burden.

Teaching

Ability: clarifying truth and insights into why facts are true
Opportunities:
- Teaching
- Training
- Library work

Warning: Don't neglect other responsibilities.
Reward: knowing that people are learning truth
Prayer: Dear God, help me be practical, not just impart truth.

Pastoring/Shepherding

Ability: ministering to groups needing leadership
Opportunities:
- Committee chairperson
- Visitation

Warning: Don't get discouraged with those who don't follow.
Reward: seeing the ministry improve
Prayer: Dear God, help me be patient with those who are apathetic and/or spiritually weak.

Ministry/Serving

Ability: serving behind the scenes
Opportunities:
- Nursery
- Sunday School/Bible study
- Usher

Warning: Don't become weary in well-doing.

Reward: knowing that you make a difference doing what no one else may want to do

Prayer: Dear God, thank You for appreciating my labor of love, regardless of others' failure to appreciate it.

Administration

Ability: organizing or delegating tasks

Opportunities:

- Group leader
- Office work
- Personnel

Warning: Avoid thinking everyone will get involved.

Reward: seeing people work together to accomplish difficult tasks

Prayer: Dear God, help me be tolerant to those who don't respond as I think they should.

r e e n g i n e e r
ministry

the principle of initiative

God, give us the serenity to accept what cannot be changed;
Give us the courage to change what should be changed;
Give us the wisdom to distinguish one from the other.[1]

—Reinhold Niebuhr

This strategy will help you place your newfound knowledge about your personality traits and spiritual gifts into a larger ministry context. The best way to influence your world radically and to find fulfillment in your Christian life is to blend your personality traits and spiritual gifts into a ministry that comes from your heart and dreams. Personality traits have rarely been considered in assessing individuals' roles in ministry. As a result, you may have taken a spiritual-gifts inventory before but are still uncertain how to use the gifts you discovered. For example, if you have the gift of evangelism, God has gifted you to communicate the gospel in special ways. But if your personality trait is that of an introvert—if you are shy—you will never feel comfortable standing on a college campus preaching the gospel to passersby. The gift is right, and the motive is right. But the means of implementing the gift of evangelism is wrong for your personality temperament. You need to discover your personal dreams for reaching the world for Christ and to learn how to make them become a reality.

This strategy provides a framework for beginning that process of discovery. It explains the role, value, and limitations of your church in helping you find your place in ministry. It points out the limitations of traditional approaches to leadership. Then it examines an alternative approach to ministry called the self-directed ministry team. Rather than wait for someone to invite you to begin making a difference, you can begin to do that yourself. You are an adult. You are a child of God. With other members of the body of Christ, you have all you need to turn your world upside down. By using this approach, you can implement your dreams and can multiply your ministry many times over.

You might be tempted at this stage to take your understanding of your personality traits and spiritual gifts and launch into a ministry. I encourage you to wait. As you will see, discovering your personality traits and spiritual gifts is only the beginning.

The Role of Your Church

Learning your personality traits gives you a healthy understanding of yourself. Identifying your spiritual gifts helps you see ways God wants you to minister to others and serve Him. Although personality and gifts serve different functions, God intends for them to work together. When you express your spiritual gifts in ways that incorporate your personality traits, you can work for God in areas of your strengths and desires.

Working from your strengths, however, does not mean working within your comfort zone. God may have given you strengths you don't feel comfortable with. In that case God desires to stretch you out of your comfort zone to help you see what strengths He wants to use in your life. In the process you become more in touch with your true personality.

As you seek to apply your knowledge about yourself, realize that you cannot do that alone. This understanding must be applied in the context of relationships. One of the primary places for that to occur is among your spiritual family and friends at church. It is important to understand your church's role and limitations—its strengths and weaknesses—so that you can better blend your ministry with that of your church. Just as individuals have abilities and limitations, churches also have strengths and weaknesses. Knowing your church's roles and limitations will help you better understand what it can and cannot do for you—and what you can and cannot do for your church.

Some aspects of your church life are indispensable to your growth as a Christian. You may have other needs that your church will never be able to provide. Ultimately, your growth needs are your responsibility. When the church can help, it will. When it cannot help, you can take other measures to accomplish your goal, as we shall see.

Your church has more than one role. Ultimately, every church's primary role is to bring glory to God. That's a philosophical statement of purpose or vision. From a practical perspective, Scripture explains several functions a church performs to bring glory to God.

The first church met for several purposes. According to Acts 2:42-47:

> They devoted themselves to the apostles' teaching and to the fellowship, to the breaking of bread and to prayer. Everyone was filled with awe, and many wonders and miraculous signs were done by the apostles. All the believers were together and had everything in common. Selling their possessions and goods, they gave to anyone as he had need. Every day they continued to meet together in the temple courts. They broke bread in their homes and ate together with glad and sincere hearts, praising God and enjoying the favor of all the people. And the Lord added to their number daily those who were being saved.

This passage identifies several roles of the church. The first is theological training: "They devoted themselves to the apostles' teaching." Christians need to know what the Bible says. Some churches teach doctrine in a boring way. The problem is not so much with the doctrines as with the teachers! Understanding the truths of the Bible can be very exciting, especially when you learn how to find those truths for yourself.

They also devoted themselves "to the fellowship." The church is the best place to develop relationships with persons who follow Jesus as you do. Fellowship in the first century did not mean potlucks or chip-and-dip parties. People came together to nurture hope in one another's life. The writer of the Book of Hebrews said, "Let us not give up meeting together, as some are in the habit of doing, but let us encourage one another—and all the more as you see the Day approaching" (Heb. 10:25).

A third role of the church is "the breaking of bread," that is, communion, or the Lord's Supper. According to 1 Corinthians 11, the breaking of bread refers to serving wine and unleavened bread as Jesus did just before His death. It is to be done to remember Jesus' death, His sacrifice for our sins. One of the church's roles is to meet together and remind us through this act that we all stand on common ground. Whether we are millionaires or paupers, celebrities or ordinary people, when it comes to Christian faith, everyone has only one thing in common: the blood of Christ. The Lord's Supper reminds Christians of the one element that unites us all.

A fourth role of your church is found in the words "and to prayer." As a Christian, you need to practice a personal devotion to prayer, but you also need to devote yourself to praying with other believers. Prayer is also a primary role of your church.

"Selling their possessions and goods, they gave to anyone as he had need." This verse reflects the need for a church to meet persons' material needs. Emphasizing salvation and spiritual growth, some local churches ignore persons' material needs. But this was an integral part of Christ's ministry. He met physical and emotional needs as a platform to address spiritual needs.

Some Christians neglect giving financially or materially because they consider their resources inadequate to contribute to others. When confronted with parables that deal with a rich person and a poor person, they always view themselves as the poor person. Instead of looking up the social or economic ladder and perceiving themselves as the poor person, they need to look down the ladder and realize that to others, they are the rich persons. A single adult making $20,000 a year says: "I'm not rich. People making $30,000 are doing pretty well, but not I." But a single adult making $30,000 says: "I'm not rich. Someone making $50,000 is rich." And on and on the delusion goes.

One role of the church is to encourage those who have material goods to help those who do not. Instead of thinking that you do not have enough, look down the ladder instead of up. Those who have been blessed by God have all of the rights and responsibilities the Bible passages identify for those who are materially wealthy.

A final role of the church is found in the phrase that says the people came together "with glad and sincere hearts, praising God and enjoying the favor of all the people." One role of the church is to come together to praise God in ways the members have agreed on. Praising God on an individual basis is good, but it is never to take the place of coming together with other Christians for the express purpose of praising God.

What role is your church to have in your life? You can look to your church to be a place to learn the truths of the Bible, a place where you find and give personal encouragement, a place to remember the one element that unites all

Christians. It is a place to unite for corporate prayer, a place to address one another's personal needs, and a place to offer corporate praise to God.

The Limitations of Your Church

We have looked at some of the many things your church can do for you. But there are also some things your church cannot do for you. Your church, as wonderful as it may be, has limitations. It cannot be all things to all people all the time. Learn what roles your church needs to play in your life, but also understand what roles it cannot play.

Methodology

One limitation of the church is pragmatic: How does a church teach people how to do something, such as witness and minister, that they later perform outside the walls of the church? How do you teach businesspersons how to make their faith real in their workplace when they are taught in a controlled environment far removed from their actual work? A church primarily teaches skills for individual believers to use in their everyday lives. But the skills are taught in an unrealistic environment. There is no organizational solution to this problem, for the organization cannot move into the workplace; only individuals can.

Lacking an organizational answer to this problem, the church has settled on a commonly accepted method of academic teaching used in most schools, colleges, and universities, an educational system that teaches theory and leaves the application of that theory to the individual's ingenuity. Many educational methods practiced in today's church have roots in society's academic structure. But this style of learning teaches theoretical practices from a distance, often becoming an end in itself.

When a local church settles for academics alone, it unintentionally communicates to its members that the goal of their Christian growth is to learn information. Christians are taught to memorize Scripture, to learn biblical principles and values for living, and to understand deep theological truths. But when it comes to actual day-by-day application, all many churches can do is to say, "Go do it." From the perspective of the everyday world, the church exists in a theoretical context. It can teach elements to apply in the world, but it teaches from a distance.

I am not saying that the church is irrelevant. The church is vital, it is indispensable to your faith, and it is the instrument God chose to build His kingdom. Believers need to grow in their understanding of their faith. The church is the primary place to gain much of that understanding.

But understanding is not an end in itself; it is a means to an end. The end has always been, according to Christ, for believers to " 'let your light shine before men, that they may see your good deeds and praise your Father in heaven' " (Matt. 5:16). Light was created to penetrate darkness, not to hover together with a bunch of other lights. Your goal is to apply your knowledge in the context of everyday life.

Many churches' educational styles do not lend themselves to first-century discipleship. What is missing in the equation of the growth process is a relational aspect that takes young believers in Christ, provides them a foundation in their faith through the church, then provides mentors for them—more mature believers who can show them how to integrate that knowledge about their faith into their daily world. Many godly men and women mentor new believers. But their numbers are few in comparison to the potential and the need. This missing factor impedes Christians' ability to affect their world.

Let me illustrate. New construction workers are enlisted as apprentices. They begin work with a limited knowledge of what is required of them. To increase that knowledge, they are assigned to a fully licensed expert in their field. That expert teaches them what tools they will need and how to use them in a work environment. As they work side by side, the apprentice watches, works, and learns. In time apprentices no longer need the expert's assistance; they are well on the road to becoming an expert. Had their knowledge come strictly from a classroom, they would still be unable to actually perform the work required of them.

The same approach can be employed to integrate your Christian faith with your everyday life. This one-to-one training can be accomplished by self-directed ministry teams. Such training does not replace the church's primary approach to growth in ministry through discipleship. Rather, the two complement each other. Each has its role, strengths, and weaknesses. But before examining the concept of self-directed ministry teams, we need to recognize other limitations of the church.

Purpose

The church's second limitation is a question of purpose. Church ministers, especially, who spend the bulk of their hours within the subculture of the church, sometimes become sidetracked and forget what their purpose in the church is all about. God calls pastors and teachers "to prepare God's people for works of service, so that the body of Christ may be built up" (Eph. 4:12). The role of a ministerial staff is not to do all the work of ministering to persons' needs. Their primary role is to be a resource for equipping other believers to minister. The service mentioned in Ephesians 4 refers to serving God in the context of everyday life.

But when an organization designed to teach loses sight of its purpose, most of the "service" goes into the organization itself. When that happens, it becomes self-perpetuating and self-serving. The goal stops being to teach people how to integrate their faith into their world. The goal becomes to teach people how to integrate their faith into the church's organization and programs. The church's role should not be to integrate Christians into the subculture of the church; it should be to integrate Christians into the world to be witnesses for Christ.

This point can be illustrated by considering the purpose of a football huddle. No football team can win consistently without a huddle. Each team member comes into the huddle with an understanding of his skills and his position on the team. The huddle helps coordinate the players' functions, but every player knows that the game is won or lost not in the huddle but on the front line.

Imagine that you are an offensive player on a football team. (In case you don't know, this is not an insensitive player; it's a player whose role is to help his team score. A defensive player tries to stop the other team from scoring.) When your team is on the line as the ball is about to be snapped, every player knows that he has a role to play. The success of the play is determined by how each member of the offensive team accomplishes his immediate goal. The more often players fail at their personal goals, the more often the team fails as a team.

Every player knows his specific role. The wide receiver knows that he cannot be the quarterback or the center or the tight end. And the nose guard knows that he will never be a wide receiver or a running back. The running back, though he would like to be a quarterback, knows that his talent is in his feet, not in his hands.

The ball is snapped. The play is in motion. One of the offensive guards is stunted by a defensive tackle. The offensive guard is blindsided and is thrown in the mud facedown. Several defensive players embed cleat marks in his back as they run over him on the way to the quarterback (whose eyes by now are as big as saucers).

But luckily for the team, the wide receiver breaks free from his defender, and the quarterback sees him just before being pummeled by three defensive players. The ball is hurled into the back of the end zone. The wide receiver dives for the ball. Just before he hits the ground, he grasps the ball for a touchdown.

The crowd is wild with excitement, chanting: "We're number one! We're number one!" The quarterback is ecstatic, and so is the wide receiver. They exchange high fives on the field near the original line of scrimmage.

The whole team is pumped as they come together in the huddle, but one player in the huddle is hurting. His back is bleeding from cleat marks. His side was bruised when he was blindsided. As he stands in the huddle half dazed, he pulls grass out of his helmet and mud out of his mouth.

On one side of the huddle, players are on cloud nine. The quarterback made a fantastic throw, and the wide receiver made an amazing catch. But on the other side of the huddle, a player feels that he let down his team. The physical scars seem minor compared to that feeling.

But the other players will have none of it. "Hey, Bill," the quarterback winks and says to the guard, "shake it off, man. You'll get 'em on the next play. Our next play out is going to be a running play that will key off your block. We've got confidence in you, Bill. We're with you all the way. Now let's go for it!"

That football huddle is a close analogy to a church that comes together on Sunday. There you'll find quarterbacks in business who made fantastic throws. You'll find wide receivers in sales who made amazing catches for their companies. When they come together on Sunday, they're pumped!

But others come into that huddle who have been blindsided all week. Spiritually or emotionally, they have been thrown into the dirt, stomped in the back, and shoved facedown into the mud. They are hurting. They are members of the team, but they feel that they have let down the rest of the team.

Sunday is a time for believers to huddle and share the past week's experiences. Those who have been highly successful in their spiritual journeys can celebrate, but they can also empathize with those who come in with bruises, cuts, and feelings of despair. The downtrodden can find hope, knowing that other team members did great. After all, next week is a whole new ball game.

But herein lies the problem—the ministers' game is lived inside the huddle. Their game is played there. As the huddle becomes larger and more complicated, the focus of the huddle can shift to making the huddle better organized. At that point, when a player wants to integrate his gifts into his life for God, the goal can become to integrate him into the huddle. Rather than use the huddle as a means to accomplish the game, it becomes an end in itself.

So what is the result? The influx of new Christians helps feed the huddle but does little to place new players on the front line to play the game. No game can be won if the players spend all their time in the huddle. This doesn't mean that you should abandon your church. You may be the person God uses to bring healthy change to your church or single-adult group.

Process

A church's final limitation relates to process. Every church has a style of management—how it functions as an organization. Leadership styles have always reflected the culture of their day. Today's church-organizational leadership is no different. But due to society's rapid change in mind-set, the leadership styles of even 20 years ago are no longer as effective as they once were. Let's examine the limitations of some of these styles.

Top-down management. This church-leadership style came from the industrial-management model of the early 1900s. As is often the case, culture affected the way the church conducted its business. At the turn of the century Frederick Taylor, the father of modern industrial engineering, "recommended that the best way to manage manufacturing organizations was to standardize the activity of general workers into simple, repetitive tasks and then closely supervise them. At the time, it seemed to make sense to mechanize the activity of the general work force and to leave the decision making, coordinating, and controlling to the authorities at the top of the pyramid."[2]

Corporations have commonly come to realize that this approach does not work anymore because people have changed. Much of companies' downsizing, rightsizing, restructuring, reorganizing, and reconceptualizing has attempted to create a new leadership style that incorporates the philosophy of today's society. Those who are successful at developing that philosophy are successful as a company. Those who do not are frustrated, confused, and fearful of the future.

They sense that they are being left behind—and they are right.

Just as the clothes Christians wear to church on Sunday reflect today's cultural styles, we might expect the leadership styles used in many churches to reflect the cultural style of leadership found in modern corporations. Is that the case? Most churches have an organizational structure that places the senior pastor at the top, with the associate pastor, minister of education, and music minister below him on equal levels. Below the minister of education are the youth minister, single-adult minister, children's minister, and others. Under these are listed their respective areas of responsibility—department directors first, followed by class directors, then class teachers, then class members. "Simple, repetitive tasks" define each position's role. The task of the directors, and even more so of the ministers, is to closely supervise the persons in the roles below them on the organizational chart.

This approach to ministry follows Frederick Taylor's industrial style of leadership that most cutting-edge companies are abandoning for a more effective style. Since the church is usually at least 10 years behind societal shifts, many churches' leadership styles reflect an approach that secular corporations have rejected as ineffective.

This style of leadership, commonly called top-down management, sees the organization vertically. Some organizations can function that way; many cannot. The military still functions with a top-down management style. The basic premise of top-down management is that someone with authority wishes to see something accomplished, and they want someone below them to do it. Because past cultures accepted that style of leadership, churches naturally adopted that approach, too. Perhaps no area in the church has suffered the effects of top-down management more than the educational ministry. Church members commonly describe church leadership as filling slots or pigeonholes, meaning that the minister has the agenda set, the organizational diagrams drawn, the curriculum selected, the classrooms assigned, and the other details in place to fulfill his dream. All he needs now is to find the teachers and other leaders to fill in the blank slots on his organizational map.

The goal of top-down management is to accomplish someone else's agenda. A person of authority approaches persons with less authority and coerces them into doing something that will please the higher authority, sometimes regardless of what effect it has on the lesser persons. But most people, especially single adults, are not motivated by this kind of approach. The single adults I know have dreams of their own, not just dreams of accomplishing personal goals but dreams of being used by God in magnificent ways, dreams given to them by God. Single adults are intelligent and articulate, have faith in a big God, and dream big dreams of what God may want to accomplish through them. For someone else—even a loved and respected minister—to approach those single adults and attempt to make them commit to fulfilling their minister's dream is often defeating for a single adult. Without realizing it, that minister can non-verbally communicate: "Your dreams don't count, but mine do. My dreams come first. It's your Christian duty to help me fulfill them."

I am not saying that single-adult ministers or pastors are intentionally ma-nipulating people. And I am not saying that they have no love or concern for the dreams of their people. Most single-adult ministers and pastors truly love the people they work with. But many have innocently adopted a leadership style they have seen modeled, either in other churches or in corporations, that is not as effective today as it was in previous generations.

Some signs of top-down management in a church are constant turnover of leaders, poor-quality programs, halfhearted work by leaders, leaders who are confused about what they are supposed to accomplish (because it's not their vi-sion); difficulty securing persons to fill organizational slots such as Bible-study teachers, administration leaders, and care-group facilitators; procrastination by volunteers; and a general sense of "Oh, no. Here he comes again. What does he want from me this time?" If you have felt this or if this describes a situation you have been in, you have been involved in a ministry run by top-down manage-ment. This style is not the most effective way for you to engage in ministry. A church that uses top-down management with single adults will constantly be limited in its ministry.

Lone Ranger leadership. A second leadership style that limits the church is the Lone Ranger leadership style. Some single adults, well meaning but misguided, do not consider anyone else when it comes to ministry. They discount their single-adult minister or pastor, as well as other single adults in their group. They are so convinced that God has entrusted them to handle the particular ministry that they do not need anyone else. They can handle it all by themselves, thank you very much.

But even the Lone Ranger had Tonto. Perhaps John Donne said it best:

No man is an island, entire of itself; every man is a piece of the continent, a part of the main; if a clod be washed away by the sea, Europe is the less, as well as if a promontory were, as well as if a manor of thy friends or of thine own were; any man's death diminishes me, because I am involved in mankind; and therefore never send to know for whom the bell tolls; it tolls for thee."[3]

When someone died in old England, the church bells would be rung so that the workers in the fields surrounding the village would know. People would naturally ask who had died. Donne's point is that because humanity is so entwined, whenever someone dies, your own life is diminished because you can never be influenced by that person again. Who has lost? You have.

While the position of top-down leadership is to fulfill someone else's agenda, the position of Lone Ranger leadership is to trust only yourself; you don't need anyone else. Top-down leadership styles may be more readily seen in a ministerial staff; Lone Ranger leadership styles, among single adults themselves. Ministers with a Lone Ranger leadership style seldom last long in ministry, because ministry by its very nature involves working with other persons.

This style denies the very essence of the church's body life. Yet some single adults, refusing to become part of something larger than themselves, attempt to be effective alone. Some things can be accomplished by one individual, and sometimes someone will forge a ministry path alone and make an impact. But most of the time any impact can be expanded if others are brought into the framework.

Some churches, not knowing what to do with Lone Rangers, allow them simply to do their own things. This practice can often damage the church's single-adult ministry. For a ministry to function at its fullest capacity, synergy must operate. Lone Rangers do not cultivate synergy or interdependence; they cultivate isolation and independence. You cannot revolutionize your world as a Lone Ranger. This leadership style will always be around, but it will always be limited in its long-range effectiveness. God wants to work through all believers in the body as they develop a healthy interdependence with one another that is built on a foundation of faith in God Himself. God will resist any approach that works against this process.

The cattle herd. A third leadership style that limits the church is the cattle herd. Rather than having a group of independent-minded Lone Rangers, some single-adult groups collect a large band of followers with no leaders. When leadership is needed in an area, the work is given to the group. Everyone is responsible for the project.

The position of cattle-herd management is that everyone shares the load equally; everyone has everyone's job. But in reality, if everyone has everyone's job, no one has anyone's job. When single adults come together with an honest desire to minister yet no one takes the lead, the group attempts to make decisions by consensus. Consensus rarely clarifies who is specifically responsible for what by when. "Let's just all do this" is a common phrase in cattle-herd management. It is good for single adults to work together, but a democratic approach does not always work.

It's one thing to treat everyone fairly but quite another to treat everyone equally. To treat everyone equally is to spread the workload around so that everyone can work anywhere. Have you ever been in a group when someone volunteered to do a task and you and everyone else knew that this person would never be able to do what she was volunteering for? A cattle-herd group would collectively stay quiet and allow this person to assume that role. The fear? Hurting the person's feelings. Instead, the ministry gets hurt.

In a group that treats members fairly rather than equally, everyone is treated the same in terms of personal respect, but everyone is not treated the same in ability. If you have someone in your group who couldn't sing his way out of a tone-deaf quartet convention, don't let him lead Sunday-morning singing. He may love to sing, but that is not the point. He may love leading the singing, but that is not the point. Cattle-herd management moves as a group with no individual leadership. A church that functions with this kind of leadership in its single-adult ministry will be limited by misplaced talents going in misguided directions. There is a better way.

Self-directed Ministry Teams: A Better Approach

Churches must change their leadership styles if single adults are to become a legitimate part of the church's ministry. But change does not come easily or quickly. In the meantime, single adults can lead the way, showing churches how to organize around a method of ministry that has already revolutionized the corporate world. Single adults are in a position to recognize the need for change, to adapt to change, and to implement change in their Christian ministries.

The primary change needed is to implement a concept called a self-directed ministry team, modeled after the self-directed work teams that function in many innovative corporations. A self-directed ministry team is a self-governing group of between four and nine persons who join together to accomplish a certain goal or set of goals established by the team. Fewer than four persons becomes too taxing; more than nine is too cumbersome.

By self-directed I mean that the team members set their own direction, their own goals. They are self-governing: they regulate themselves along the way. They join together by mutual consent derived from internal desire. And that desire finds common ground in the goal or set of goals they wish to accomplish.

The self-directed team has been tried and proved in corporate structures around the world. Each member is treated with dignity and respect. Each member is valued as an equal, not a subordinate. And the contributions of every member are recognized as essential to the team's development and progress in pursuing its goals.

Several common elements are often found in a self-directed team:
- Clearly defined goals
- Equal authority among the members
- Decision making by consensus
- Shared leadership
- Planning and decision-making autonomy
- Flexibility and adaptability to change
- Personal satisfaction and development
- Increased capacity for ideas and innovation
- Evaluation on the team level
- Responsibility determined by skills rather than by titles
- Mutual support for team members
- Open lines of communication among all members
- Willingness and even a healthy desire to take risks

The Growth of Self-directed Teams

To understand the concept of self-directed work teams, it will help to understand how the approach began. As was stated earlier, around the turn of the century Frederick Taylor introduced the belief that the best way to manage manufacturing organizations was to standardize the activities of general workers into simple, repetitive tasks and then to supervise them closely.[4] This occurred at a time when America had many new immigrants who spoke no English. The concept created a work force that did the labor but got its direction from the controlling authorities. Initially, the concept produced the outcome the industrial leaders wanted. But in time companies began to lose their competitive edge. It seems that employees lost motivation because they lacked personal ownership of their products.

In the 1950s a researcher named Eric Trist conducted experiments with British coal miners. Some of the miners worked as teams and were then analyzed. The result was higher productivity and higher job satisfaction. These workers also became more flexible, responding more easily to change in the market conditions.[5]

In the mid-1960s and '70s some pioneering companies began introducing the team-based concept in America. Today a great number of companies recognize the benefits of a team-based approach to productivity. This approach to working is what turned the Japanese into the major world player they are today. At one time a Japanese product was considered virtually worthless. Today, however, some of the best products on the market are made in Japan. What changed the quality of the products was the team-based approach to business.

Lee Iococca used the team approach to turn the Chrysler Corporation from the brink of bankruptcy to become a world-class competitor. When Iococca introduced this concept to the Chrysler Corporation, he participated in a class along with plant workers to learn how to incorporate the team-based approach into their company. With the team concept in place (and yes, a boost from Uncle Sam), the Chrysler Corporation became the leader in many fields of automobile manufacturing.

General Motors also used this style of leadership to launch its line of automobiles called Saturn, an enormously successful venture. It meant mentally retooling many workers who were accustomed to the traditional industrial-management style. But once on board, the Saturn employees have scored one amazing success after another. Their process? Team-based leadership.

The True Origin of Self-directed Teams

Ironically, the self-directed team approach to leadership was not invented in the corporate world of the 1950s, '60s, or '70s. It is found in Scripture, as many successful concepts in secular business have biblical roots. As early as 600 B.C. King Solomon wrote:

> Two are better than one,
>   because they have a good return for their work:
> If one falls down,
>   his friend can help him up.
> But pity the man who falls
>   and has no one to help him up! (Eccl. 4:9-10).

Solomon understood the value of teamwork. By working together toward a common goal, two can accomplish more than they could if they worked alone. Thus, even in Solomon's day, when slavery abounded and monarchies ruled the world, the value of team-based work was recognized. It was not adopted by the societies of the day, but it was recorded in Scripture as being the best approach to productivity.

The apostle Paul expressed the same concept when he drew an analogy between the church and a physical body: "The body is a unit, though it is made up of many parts; and though all its parts are many, they form one body. So it is with Christ. ... If the foot should say, 'Because I am not a hand, I do not belong to the body,' it would not for that reason cease to be part of the body" (1 Cor. 12:12-15). Paul's point was clear. Just as every element of the body is needed for the body to perform to its maximal potential, each part of the church, the collective believers in Christ, is needed. This is the foundation of the team concept. Chuck Swindoll said: "When I meet folks who bad-mouth the church or see little significance in its existence, I pity that individual rather than feel offended. I realize he or she simply doesn't understand. It's a little like attending a symphony with someone who has no understanding of or appreciation for classical music. The whole event seems a waste of time and energy when, in actuality, the problem lies within his or her own mind."[6]

Paul acknowledged that Christ is the head of and governs His body, the church. But believers are to make ministry decisions as equal members of the body. As equals, they share all of the privileges and responsibilities that accompany those decisions.

Paul also elaborated on the team concept when he discussed the role of spiritual gifts in the church: "Do not think of yourself more highly than you ought, but rather think of yourself with sober judgment, in accordance with the measure of faith God has given you. Just as each of us has one body with many members, and these members do not all have the same function, so in Christ we who are many form one body, and each member belongs to all the others. We have different gifts, according to the grace given us" (Rom. 12:3-6). Paul wrote about operating by the principles of personal humility, accurate judgment of abilities, the equality of each member in Christ's body, and mutual responsibility to one another. This is the essence of teamwork. It is not secular. It is biblical. And when a body of believers called a church decides to operate in this fashion, God can do marvelous things.

The church stands on the threshold of the future. Some churches will adapt to changing needs in society and will move forward. Others will demand that society conform to suit the church. The world is filled with empty church buildings, reminders of people who resisted change and insisted that society retain old ways of doing things. Churches that survive in the next century will find innovative ways to keep the biblical message of the gospel alive through vital, relevant methods. The platform for the turn of the century is the self-directed ministry team.

Single-adult ministries offer a wonderful opportunity for a church to see how self-directed teams work. Now that you have some understanding of this concept, the next strategy will provide practical steps for designing a team and for making it a reality.

---

[1] Reinhold Niebuhr, "The Serenity Prayer," *Familiar Quotations*, ed. Justin Kaplan (Boston: Little, Brown and Co., 1992), 684.
[2] Richard S. Wellins, William C. Byham, and Jeanne M. Wilson, *Empowered Teams: Creating Self-directed Work Groups That Improve Quality, Productivity, and Participation* (San Francisco: Jossey-Bass, 1991), 6.
[3] John Donne, "Devotions upon Emergent Occasions, Meditation 17," *Familiar Quotations*, 231.
[4] Wellins, Byham, and Wilson, *Empowered Teams*, 6.
[5] Ibid., 7–8.
[6] Charles R. Swindoll, *The Family of God: Understanding Your Role in the Body of Christ* (Nashville: Broadman, 1986), 22–23.

start a
company

the principle of integration

✳ Two are better than one,
     because they have a good return for their work:
  If one falls down,
     his friend can help him up.
  But pity the man who falls
     and has no one to help him up! (Eccl. 4:9-10).

Single adults are the fastest-growing segment in American society today, already composing more than 44 percent of the adult population. Yet very few church rolls reflect single adults as 44 percent of their adult members. Unfortunately, many churches see single adults as an optional attachment rather than as a vital target for and participant in their ministries. Consequently, they do not aggressively pursue single adults for the Kingdom.

If the growing population of single adults is to be reached for Christ, you and your friends must commit to do it personally. You cannot wait for another group to do it. If your church will help, God bless it. If not, move forward anyway. Don't settle for merely bringing together a group of single adults. Build them into a self-directed ministry team—a group of skilled, talented, committed single adults who share the vision of setting their world on fire with the message of Christ.

The Need for a Change: The Self-directed Team Concept

For the past 30 years, and especially for the past 10 years, the leadership style that has taken the business world by storm is the self-directed team concept. In contrast to top-down leadership, Lone Ranger, and cattle-herd leadership styles,

the self-directed team functions as a cohesive unit with all of the skills, responsibilities, and authority to carry an idea from conception to completion. A team
can accomplish more than an individual can because each member contributes
on an equal level as a joint partner. The differences among the various leadership styles can be seen in this illustration:

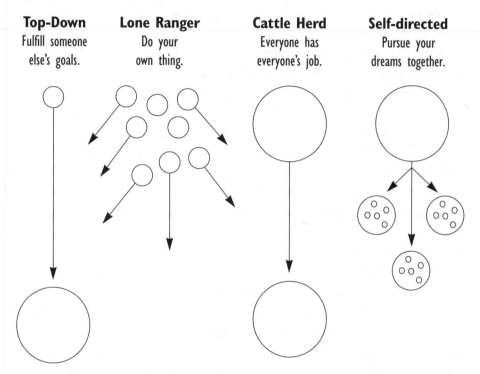

| **Top-Down** | **Lone Ranger** | **Cattle Herd** | **Self-directed** |
| Fulfill someone else's goals. | Do your own thing. | Everyone has everyone's job. | Pursue your dreams together. |

By contrasting the four styles, we can draw the following implications for
single-adult ministry.

- In top-down leadership single adults approach the group to fulfill their personal goals.
- In Lone Ranger leadership single adults splinter into nonrelated, indepen-
  dent directions.
- In cattle-herd leadership single adults can move only when the whole
  group moves together.
- In self-directed leadership single adults group themselves into teams that
  carry out commonly shared dreams for ministry.

You can understand the team concept by examining the flight dynamics of geese. You have probably seen geese flying in a beautifully symmetrical V formation. But the flight of geese is more than an art form; it is the production efficiency of a team.

Geese fly in a V formation to reduce wind drag, allowing them to fly much farther than if flying by themselves. Students of aerodynamics know that when an object moves through the air, it incurs resistance—the air itself. This resistance, called a headwind, is the reason the space shuttle is equipped with heat shields on its exterior. When it reenters the atmosphere, the air resistance builds tremendous heat. The shields protect the shuttle from burning.

The same dynamic is true of geese. The point goose breaks the headwind and absorbs the majority of the wind resistance. As the goose breaks that plane, the air is pushed outward and over its wings and back to the two geese behind it. Those two have now divided the initial air resistance between them. And the process continues through the other geese. Research shows that geese are 70 percent more efficient when flying in this manner.

Because the leader receives the bulk of the resistance, it tires sooner than the others. Therefore, geese rotate leadership. When the lead goose tires, it rotates to the back of the flock, and another assumes leadership. This way each goose has a turn at leading and following, of forging ahead and receiving much-needed rest. The responsibility of leadership is mutually shared.

If one goose becomes hurt and descends to the ground, two others break away from the flock to escort it. The escorts stay with the hurt goose to encourage it to rejoin the flock. If it cannot, the escort geese stay until they sense that the hurt goose can manage on its own before they rejoin the flock.

Finally, if some geese break away from following the lead goose, the remaining geese honk loudly to encourage the lead goose. This both reaffirms the direction of the lead goose and ensures that the flock stays together.

Parallels between the flight of geese and the team concept of ministry are striking.

1. Geese don't fly to impress people. Geese fly to accomplish clearly defined goals. Furthermore, they fly south not because their moms and dads taught them that way but to escape the cold of the north and to find adequate food and shelter to survive the winter. As they fly, they evaluate their surroundings in light of their goals. When they find a place that meets their needs for warmth, food, and shelter, they stop flying for the winter.

2. Geese organize in a V formation for increased efficiency. They organize to increase their ability to fly longer and farther. The purpose of their formation is not control but efficient productivity. If it didn't work, geese would not fly in a V formation. Their form is designed around function, not the other way around. They don't fly that way just because it's always been done that way. They don't fly that way because the head goose is an organizational freak who simply likes the way it looks. They don't fly that way because a manual said this is the way geese fly. They fly in a V formation because it works!

3. Geese share leadership. No dominant goose hoards the front slot. (Even if one tried, it would eventually burn out from exhaustion—a common phenomenon among Christians in lay and professional ministry.) The geese know that when another goose leads, their role is to follow and support the lead goose. And when their role is to lead, they lead with the same tenacity they demonstrated as followers. They recognize that every goose is a leader at different times and in different places.

4. Geese have a genuine concern for the other members of the flock. When one is hurt, they know they are diminished as a team. Their concern for the welfare of one another encourages each of them. They know that should anything happen to them, the flock will not simply desert them. It will do all it can to nurse them back to health.

5. When some geese leave the flock, the remaining geese do all they can to bolster the confidence of the lead goose. Their verbal affirmation to the lead goose encourages it to continue on course, to pursue their goals.

6. When geese break from the flock, the remaining geese are flexible enough to adapt quickly. By closing the ranks and honking, they quickly rebond to restore their unity. In doing so, they also restore efficiency and uplift the value of each remaining goose. Their honking communicates that each goose is valued and needed to accomplish the goals of the flock.

Principles for Ministry Teams

By converting the principles of geese flight dynamics into the team concept, you get a better understanding of what a self-directed ministry team is all about.

1. A ministry team consists of single adults who come together to accomplish clearly defined goals. They do not come together to accomplish someone else's goals but the goals each person wants. They do not come together be-

cause someone else pushed, told, coerced, or manipulated them. They come together because of their internal desires and motivations. Their common bond is not proximity of space; it is a shared vision. Although they may not know exactly how, when, or where their goals will be reached, they believe they will discover those answers along the way.

2. A ministry team does not organize along traditional lines of thinking. It organizes around what works best to accomplish the task. If it doesn't fit on someone's organizational charts or diagrams, it doesn't mean it's wrong. It's wrong only if it doesn't work. And if it doesn't work, the team reorganizes until it finds a way that works. A scriptural example is David's preparation for his battle with Goliath. When David first agreed to fight Goliath, King Saul put his armor on him. After all, if you're going to fight successfully, this is how it's done. Only a foolish person would go into battle without armor. But David didn't organize his battle strategy around someone else's charts and diagrams. He established a strategy that would work for him (see 1 Sam. 17:38-40). Similarly, a ministry team is not vexed by others' organizational approaches. Instead, members select their approach in light of their goals, personalities, skills, and gifts. Some basic foundational principles are common to all self-directed teams, but inherent in each team's strategy is the uniqueness that defines that team.

3. A ministry team recognizes that everyone on the team is the leader. No one person is in charge. The organization is not vertical. A ministry team shares the role of leader. At different times and in different places each person takes the reins of leadership, and the other members respect and follow the lead of that member. The other members may provide input for the person leading, but ultimately, leadership is a shared responsibility.

4. A ministry team recognizes the value of the team. Members provide one another unified support. As a football team would be significantly hurt if it went onto the field with only 10 players, a ministry team understands that when a member is unable to fulfill a role, the whole team hurts. Rather than expecting a group leader to express care and offer help, all members equally share this responsibility because they understand that there is no leader except themselves.

5. A ministry team communicates. Respect for one another's leadership is expressed both nonverbally and verbally. Each person recognizes that members

start a revolution

approach their aspects of leadership differently. Rather than attempt to conform each member to one style, each member values the others' personal contributions in leadership roles.

6. When something forces a change in its dynamic makeup, the ministry team quickly reassembles with the remaining members to bolster unity and reiterate goals. If needed, new members can be added. But if not, the remaining members fill the vacancies to allow the team to continue toward its goals.

Ministry Teams in the Church

Some ministers or church leaders may initially think that self-directed ministry teams contradict biblical teachings about the church's body life. Actually, they operate within these teachings. Passages like 1 Corinthians 12–14 and Ephesians 4 teach that a church is a body of members who exercise a variety of spiritual gifts in loving ministry and service. A major doctrine of Protestant theology is the priesthood of believers. One aspect of this doctrine is that every believer in Christ has direct access to God without going through a ministerial intermediary. This is true not only in receiving personal salvation but also in responding to God's leading in a Christian's life. Consistent with this doctrine, the ministry-team concept calls believers to listen to God's call for their lives, look for others He has given similar calls, then join together to minister in that area.

In addition, ministry teams do not undermine order in the church. Scripture explicitly identifies some of the leadership roles in the church, such as apostle, prophet, evangelist, pastor, teacher (see Eph. 4:11), overseers, deacons (see 1 Tim. 3), and elder (see Titus 1:6). Church leaders' roles are not to do all the ministry but "to prepare God's people for works of service" (Eph. 4:12). Church leaders are a resource to equip team members to accomplish the ministry goals or dreams God has given them to build His kingdom.

Those beginning ministry teams should beware of adopting the terminology of work teams while retaining their earlier style of leadership. This is sometimes done to create the illusion of being innovative. Changing the terminology doesn't change the substance of the ministry. It changes only the label.

Changing processes requires a person to learn a new way of thinking. If a single-adult leader is comfortable using top-down leadership but is convinced that ministry teams would be better, he must be willing to relinquish some of his authority over the group. That's not always easy, especially when the group begins to make decisions the former leader would have made differently. Also, a leader cannot develop a ministry team by demanding that people begin the process. That would be top-down leadership using self-directed terminology.

The best way for leaders with single adults to introduce ministry teams is to learn the leadership style, then to educate the single adults. Follow education with role-modeling the process. Finally, allow time for trial and error. The transition to ministry teams will take time and practice.

Developing a ministry-team mind-set requires time and energy on everyone's part. But in the long run it will pay handsome dividends in participants' lives. Whether you are a current single-adult leader or a committed Christian single adult who truly wants to change the world, you can develop a ministry-team leadership style.

How a Ministry Team Works

A football team illustrates the organizational makeup of a ministry team. What about the coach on the sidelines? Not truly a member of the team, he is more like an outside consultant. He does not have direct responsibilities on the field.

Each player on a football team has clearly defined roles, knows how his role relates to everyone else's role, understands that in his role he will sometimes be required to lead the way, and knows how to improve his skills to be a great team player. No member of the squad is a Lone Ranger. For every position represented on the field, other members who play the same position are waiting on the sidelines. Thus, the role of active team players is twofold: to relate to the active team in their specific roles and to relate to their same-position players in ways that allow them to sharpen each other's skills.

Every football team practices running game plans. Offensive and defensive players square off against each other to simulate actual game plays. Eleven guys are on offense and the same number on defense. There are not 11 guys on offense, plus 2 extra running backs to help them out. Plays are practiced to simulate a real game as closely as possible.

At other practice times every member of the football squad is on the field at the same time. And everyone is just as intense in this practice as when practicing game plays. But in this practice all of the kickers practice kicking skills together; all of the quarterbacks and receivers practice passing and catching skills together; all of the defensive tackles practice hits, stunts, and other maneuvers together; and all of the running backs practice specific running patterns together.

The team members on the field are specialized players who utilize their skills in the game to help the entire team accomplish its goals. The specialized groups include quarterbacks, running backs, receivers, safeties, defensive backs, and so on. If one quarterback is hurt, his responsibility is not assumed by the center. Another quarterback is brought in—a quarterback who practiced the team plays the same way the first quarterback did. If the second quarterback were hurt, the third quarterback would be brought in. The team would pull from its smaller team of quarterbacks to fulfill that specific responsibility.

This is the essence of a ministry team. Each person on the active team has a specific role. In addition to that role, the team player may also work with others who share the same responsibility. Every individual is important and valued. At different times different team members are called on to carry the ball. But no one person has the responsibility to carry the ball all the time every time.

At the same time, every team member understands and works toward the team's goals. In football the goal of the offense is to get the ball into the end zone. If the team cannot run it in or pass it in, it may try to kick it in for a field goal. But every player doesn't take turns kicking the ball. Only the kicker does that. Christian ministry works the same way. Every ministry has several responsibilities:

- Administrative—to organize, communicate, and facilitate the ministry's work
- Marketing and promotion—to convince people to participate in the ministry
- Customer service—to meet the needs of those who participate in the ministry
- Customer retention—to care for those who participate
- Facilities management—to meet the ministry's physical and logistical needs

Notice the terminology. I chose not to use the usual church terms, like *outreach* and *care groups,* to illustrate the need to use terms that are familiar to the persons with whom you are ministering. Traditional church language may not communicate what you intend and what your ministry has to offer.

No matter what you call the multiple responsibilities that exist in every area of ministry, they require multiple persons to fulfill them. A team with only one representative for each area of responsibility is like a football team with only one quarterback. Eventually, that player will be hurt, and the rest of the team will be seriously impaired. Therefore, in establishing a ministry team, you must think beyond the initial players on the team. Each player is the primary, active player in accomplishing the team's goals. But all team members need to assemble teams of their own with players who have the same responsibility as they. This not only lightens the load of the primary team member but also enables the active team to substitute a player if the need arises.

Let's say that a ministry team of single adults forms to begin a ministry to the large number of college students in their city. That team would need one person to carry out publicity, one to organize events, one to reserve meeting rooms, one to secure demographic data such as the students' names and addresses, and persons to do other jobs. Although the team may begin with only one person for each area of responsibility, each team member should seek other persons who want to work in that area to ensure the greatest creativity, innovation, and productivity.

For example, the team member who is responsible for publicity could look for someone with graphic skills, someone with computer skills, and another person with a marketing background. The four of them combine their talents to create a formidable publicity team. After considering various means of publicity, the publicity team relates those ideas to the ministry team, which evaluates them in light of the rest of the ministry team's plans. After the ministry team selects the best ideas, the publicity-team member communicates the plans to the rest of the publicity team, which then takes action to accomplish its plans.

If the publicity-team member is transferred to another city, no other member of the ministry team is asked to assume that person's responsibilities. Instead, another publicity-team member assumes the missing member's role on the ministry team. This way, the concepts, plans, directions, and actions continue moving forward. The work toward common goals continues, the team remains united, and the team's effectiveness is not diminished. Meanwhile, a new person is sought to fill the empty position on the publicity team.

Where is the coach in all this? And who is the coach? In a church's ministry the nearest person to a coach would be a single-adult minister or a pastor. This subject raises a major difference between a ministry team and a football team. On a football team the coach determines the team's plans. The coach calls the plays, and the team carries them out. On a self-directed ministry team the team members determine the team's direction and goals. That's where the dream of the ministry was born—in the hearts and minds of the team members themselves. The team was created to make the dreams a reality. While the coach (the single-adult minister or the pastor) is a great resource person to help achieve those goals, the goals and plans themselves are the sole property of the ministry-team members.

This ministry-team approach does not exclude your single-adult minister or pastor. This person may help you begin a ministry team. But he should not be a member of the team, because his positional title can be so overwhelming that he is not perceived as an equal. Matters that are debated are often referred to him for a decision. After all, he's the minister. No. You are the minister. God has gifted you. The staff member's role is to serve as a resource person, equipping you with the skills and knowledge required for ministry (see Eph. 4:11-13).

Transitional Phases of a Ministry Team

To make a ministry team work, members need to realize from the outset that there will be a lot of trial and error. The process will take time and patience. Understanding the different stages that usually occur in the formation of a ministry team will help prevent discouragement when everything doesn't meld at the very beginning. Sometimes things that are hard to accomplish in the beginning reap the greatest rewards in the end.

An enthusiastic beginning. Any project or endeavor is easy to start. It's finishing that's hard. The great football coach Vince Lombardi said, "The difference between a successful person and others is not a lack of strength, not a lack of knowledge, but rather in a lack of will."[1] When you create a ministry team, everyone will be excited. But once you begin to work, that excitement will wane. When it does, understand that this is normal. It's a common occurrence with any monumental task.

A state of confusion. Excitement gives way to confusion, which can assume various forms. It may appear as someone's passivity toward her responsibility to the team. It may suddenly surface in a meeting when someone says: "This is stupid! I don't think it'll work!" Usually, he is saying: "I don't understand. I'm confused." When this happens, do not view the member as being against the team. He is not trying to reverse the direction of the team but to move past his confusion. If each person on the team understands this phase, when confusion comes to each member (and it will), the rest of the team can help each individual member move past the confusion. This in itself helps build a team focus that will prove valuable later.

It is also common for every member to be confused at the same time. Imagine having five persons on a basketball court who have been given the task of becoming a basketball team, but none of them has ever heard of the game! You could predict a learning curve for all of them. Even after they mentally learned the elements of the game, they would experience further confusion after they began implementing what they learned. For instance, it might take some time to figure out that the person who is 6 feet, 11 inches should play center instead of guard. And the 6-foot, 1-inch player should be guard and not forward. These adjustments cannot be made studying concepts; they can be learned only while playing the game. The same is true with a ministry team. Expect confusion in the beginning, but treat it as an opportunity for everyone to learn.

A coach-centered team. Many self-directed teams have team leaders. Team leaders function as player-coaches. Perhaps they are selected as team leaders because they have grasped the concept best thus far and can relay that information to the rest of the team. The leaders are not in charge. They are not in authority. All team members share authority equally. Team leaders are simply the best persons to help the other team members understand their specific roles and to facilitate their work as a team.

For example, one dairy company operated without managers. Instead, everyone worked on a self-directed work team. When a shift reported for work, the team leader, called the communicator, met with the other shift's communicator to receive any pertinent information the rest of the team would need for their shift. This person, chosen by the team, assumed this responsibility not by rank or authority but by need.

This same transition usually occurs on a ministry team. After the enthusiasm and excitement wear off and the confusion begins to dissipate, someone in the group may exhibit skills at facilitating. Select that person to begin facilitating meetings. When others have progressed, this role can be rotated, but at this stage keep it consistent.

A conceptually tight team. With a team leader facilitating the teamwork, the other team members can focus on understanding their roles and grasping the concepts of a self-directed team. In time, and again with trial and error, every member will understand the fundamental and practical concepts of how a team functions. When this stage is reached, you have a conceptually tight team.

In the 1992 Olympics some of the best basketball players in the world played on the U.S. Dream Team. As talented and skilled as those players were and as much as they knew about playing basketball, they still had to begin by practicing together as a team. Individual expertise did not necessarily make them a team. Playing together did.

This is the equivalent of a conceptually tight ministry team. All "players" have gained the skills needed for their areas of responsibility, they understand the concepts of self-directed teams, and they know the team's goals. They are a conceptually tight team though not yet a fully functioning self-directed team.

A self-directed team. The final phase is reached when, after time, hard work, and trial and error, the team melds as one. Members know one another's strengths and weaknesses. They know each member's specific role on the team. They know what their goals are and how to measure them. And they know what works and what doesn't.

When this stage is reached, the fun begins, and the impact begins to be felt as never before. The team thinks and acts with cohesion. All team members are motivated because they are using their personalities and gifts in areas that access their strengths and because they have played roles in designing the team's goals and the strategies to achieve those goals. At this stage the amount of innovative energy created on the team can overcome even the largest obstacles. Their goals—and even more—will be accomplished.

Be aware that in the business world from one to three years are required for a company to grasp the concepts of self-directed teams. Each stage we have examined may take six months or more. Do not let this fact discourage you. Without beginning this process, you will probably still be uncertain about how or where to get involved in ministry. Begin using this approach now. It could change your life. After grasping these concepts, you may never approach Christian ministry the same.

How to Begin a Ministry Team

Subsequent strategies in this book will help you build a ministry team. But it will be helpful now for you to understand how this process develops.

Articulate your dream. A ministry team begins with a dream or a desire. Every Christian possesses not only the spiritual gifts and personality traits necessary for ministry but also a God-given desire to make a genuine difference in the world for Christ. Some may dream of being the next Billy Graham, while others may dream of being the next Cal Ripken or Margaret Thatcher. Others don't want to be in the limelight, preferring to influence the world through research, computers, or science, and are content to work behind the scenes. Although every Christian wants to make an impact in the world for Christ, many see no way to make their desires a reality. If you possess a desire, you can build a ministry team to help you pursue your dreams.

Identify your spiritual gifts and your basic personality style. With the knowledge you gained in strategy 2, you can determine the best type of ministry for you and the role within that ministry for which you are best suited.

Clarify your vision for ministry—the area in which God wants to use you. By vision I don't mean being that you awake at 2:00 a.m. when your window flies open, the curtains flap in the wind, and a voice calls from a cloud hovering above your bed. I mean that you need to set tangible, measurable goals for a ministry that appeals to you and to which God is leading you, a ministry that encompasses your personality traits and spiritual gifts.

Find other Christians who have the same dream or a similar desire. From these persons you will select your self-directed ministry team. What bonds you together is a desire to pursue a common goal in Christian ministry. This common goal is one of your team's foundation stones.

The other members of your team also need to discover their spiritual gifts and personality traits to help you decide what role each will play in fulfilling your goal. Spiritual gifts and personality alone will not determine what roles members will play, but they will reflect what team members have been designed to do well and the type of ministry for which they are suited.

For example, could a person with the spiritual gift of exhortation also work in the area of publicity? Yes. The motivation of a person with the gift of exhortation is to encourage and inspire others. Therefore, this person's publicity would consistently have a motivational slant. Someone with another spiritual gift would have another perspective. Someone with the gift of administration would handle publicity by making sure that all of the necessary details were in their proper place and were clearly understood. Efficiency would be the order of the day. Spiritual gifts affect the content of every responsibility held.

Personality style also determines the way a person ministers. An exhorter with a high-*D* personality type (see strategy 2) will be results-oriented —a real mover—but not good with details. A *C* or an *S* may be great with details but may become so bogged down with them that results are hard to achieve.

No one spiritual gift or personality temperament makes a better team worker than another. Different ministry styles are reflected in different personality traits and spiritual gifts. At different times some styles work better than others. But all are valid and necessary. Both personality types and spiritual gifts make a difference in ministry. The key is to understand the implications of each and to match them with ministry tasks that need to be accomplished.

Help team members understand the self-directed team concept. Becoming leaders in ministry requires being motivated from within. Motivation comes from realizing how team members' work directly affects their progress toward their ministry goals. If you need more information about the team concept, you might consult secular books on self-directed work teams and transfer the principles to your Christian-ministry situation.

Put your plans on paper. Clarify your goals and define the individual areas of responsibility to be addressed in this ministry. Then give all members time to decide the areas for which they want to be responsible. Remember that every member will be a leader on the team, each in a different area.

Prepare team members to assume their responsibilities. Team members should be encouraged to take these steps:

- Begin additional personal training to improve their understanding of the skills needed to accomplish their specific responsibilities.
- Find persons who would like to help in their areas of responsibility. It would be helpful for these persons to buy copies of this book and to take the personality and spiritual-gifts inventories in strategy 2.
- Clarify their specific responsibilities for the rest of the ministry team. Because team members will hold one another accountable for their areas of responsibility, expectations should be clearly and mutually understood from the start.

Plan practical ways to achieve the team's primary goal. Expect trial and error here. A successful ministry team will not be born overnight. It will take time and energy. It will require a learning curve for everyone involved. But in the end it can be tremendously successful and fulfilling.

Maintain constant communication among team members. Constant evaluation will be necessary. Always look for ways to improve. If personality issues surface, and this is normal, they are dealt with on the team level. It takes time, but a team must be able to discuss openly any problem or area of contention that affects the team. To do less not only is destructive to the team but also violates Christian principles. If Christians who are working together for common goals cannot be open and honest, the team cannot survive.

A Ministry Team in Action

The following illustration will give you a better idea of how a ministry team is formed.

Susan had wanted to get involved in a ministry for a while but wasn't sure where to begin. She volunteered in her church's preschool and children's programs but didn't really find her niche. She didn't feel qualified to lead an adult Bible-study group; she had been a Christian for only two years.

Susan learned about the self-directed ministry concept and decided to try it. By completing inventories, Susan learned that her personality temperament was primarily an *S. If* fit her. She was a people person who loved personal security and stability. She struggled with passivity but felt that she was making progress in that area. This self-directed ministry would cause her to venture out of her comfortable world.

Susan's spiritual gifts fell into the categories of exhortation and evangelism. She enjoyed intimate talks with others and liked feeling that she was able to encourage someone. She had always seemed to have an intense desire to tell others about her life in Christ. Sometimes Susan's passivity prevented her from saying anything. Witnessing was easier for her in a warm, comfortable situation, like breakfast with a college friend who did not know Christ.

Still, Susan wanted to do more, to have a greater impact. She lived in an apartment complex with many college students and single adults, but she was too shy to approach them bluntly and tell them about Christ. The self-directed ministry team seemed to be the answer. Susan began to talk with other Christians from the church and from the complex. After a while Doug, Misty, Karen, Ivy, Eric, and Judy revealed that they had the same desire to reach the apartment complex for Christ.

Together they formed a ministry team. They began by reading books and articles describing self-directed teams. After taking the personality and spiritual-gifts inventories, they had fun discussing one another's personality traits and gifts. Although Karen attended a different church than Doug, Misty, and Eric, they all knew one another from college classes. They laughed when Doug described himself according to the tests. "That's you! They read you like a book!" Ivy said as they all laughed.

It turned out that Doug was a *D* and Karen an *S* like Susan. Eric was a *C*, and Misty was an *I/S*. Every temperament would be represented on this team. That makes for a well-balanced team, but it takes time to build unity because of the initial diversity.

This is going to be fun, they thought. They were excited to find that each of them harbored a keen desire to tell others in the apartment complex about Christ. They began to meet regularly. At first ideas were popping as fast as Susan could write them down. The problem quickly became "Where do we start?"

Doug, being a take-charge kind of guy, was the first to be frustrated (a sign of confusion). He wanted results, and he wanted them tomorrow if not today. In time each began to struggle with what he or she was actually going to do. Confusion reigned for several weeks in the meetings. Finally, Misty was chosen to facilitate the meetings. She seemed to be able to calm everyone's nerves (especially Doug's) and to help make sense of all the talk.

After some time the meetings began to take on a form that made it easier to get things accomplished. Team members' goals were hammered out and written down until everyone agreed that these goals expressed their purpose for coming together. Further meetings recalled the brainstorming sessions of their earlier meetings. Now that their goals were clear, it was easier to dismiss a number of ideas that did not help accomplish their goals. The teamwork was getting easier, even though it had taken them seven months to reach this point.

By now each team member was beginning to grasp the self-directed team concept. Evaluating one another's personalities and gifts, they divided the work among them. Doug's tendency at first was to jump in and begin delegating, but he quickly remembered that this was a self-directed team. By now, after all of their discussions, each person felt comfortable talking about specific areas of the team's work that interested them. After several meetings all agreed what their responsibilities would be.

This understanding necessitated a new learning curve for the team members. Although they knew what they wanted to do and what they had agreed to do, they felt that they needed to improve their skills for carrying out their tasks. They contacted their respective single-adult ministers or pastors for training suggestions.

Eric agreed to do publicity in the complex, and the single-adult minister placed him in contact with a church member who did similar work professionally. After several meetings with this professional, Eric felt better about his responsibilities on the team as he gained knowledge and renewed his enthusiasm. The other members also received the training they needed. Four months after Misty had begun to facilitate the meetings, all members felt that they had a thorough understanding of their specific roles. The time had come to begin their ministry.

When the action plans began, things didn't go as planned. As unexpected problems surfaced, they were reported to the team, which discussed them, researched them, and brought recommendations at the next meeting. As the team members solved every problem, they became more excited. Their dream was becoming a reality, and they could see it happening right before their eyes!

Between the 11th and 13th months the team members began to turn a corner. Most major problems were falling behind them, and their ways of relating and communicating had melded. Each knew the other members well. Each believed in the others and respected them. When their ministry began to be publicized, other single adults volunteered to help and were accepted if the whole team agreed. These volunteers were not brought into the ministry team but were asked to work with team members in specific areas of responsibility.

After the ministry to the apartment complex was launched, team members began to see the fruit of their labor. Friends who lived in the complex were coming to Christ. Other Christians in the complex who had been silent witnesses began to be more visible. Eventually, that complex became a strong ministry for reaching single adults for Christ. Others asked them how they did it. Their answer? "We started a self-directed ministry team to reach our goals for Christ."

Virtual Corporations: Ministry Teams Expanded

Because of the explosion of computer technology, secular corporations are literally having to redefine who they are. No company can survive doing business as it did 10 or 15 years ago. Some may die a slower death than others, but ultimately, all will die unless they change.

One major change is called the virtual corporation. *The Futurist* magazine noted:

> Look around. The corporations you see today on the business landscape are changing rapidly in structure and function and will be, within a few decades, almost entirely new entities.
>
> What is evolving are virtual enterprises. Using integrated computer and communications technologies, corporations will increasingly be defined not by concrete walls or physical space, but by collaborative networks linking … people together.
>
> These collaborative, or consultative networks … allow businesses to form and dissolve relationships at an instant's notice and thus create new corporate ecologies. They also allow a single worker to seem like an army of workers and for work to collapse time and space.[2]

This virtual-corporation concept is becoming quite common among leading industries. It has allowed Apple Computers and IBM to collaborate on products that benefit them both. Rather than independently create products that had limitations, they worked together on certain products and overcame the limitations. Once competitors, they are now partners in selected ventures. They have formed a virtual corporation.

In Christian ministry the self-directed team concept can easily be enlarged through the virtual-corporation concept. After a ministry team has become a solid team, it can then begin to look for ways to expand its ministry. Using the virtual-corporation model, a team can pursue some ventures in ministry, though not as a long-term agreement. It could temporarily form partnerships with various entities to accomplish certain goals, then dissolve the relationships and move on.

Here's how the team that began a ministry to the apartment complex could expand its ministry with the virtual-corporation concept.

When Eric gained help from the professional in the publicity business, he also realized that if he could find help, he wouldn't have to reinvent the wheel.

Eric knew computers, but he didn't know graphic arts or publishing. And he didn't know the best ways to distribute and market. But because he was a *C,* Eric knew in detail what would be required to do an excellent job in his role. So Eric contacted several friends in the professional world. The professional publicist had already agreed to help formulate a publicity concept and strategy. Eric phoned his friend Tom, a graphic artist, who agreed to help Eric. For marketing and distribution assistance Eric E-mailed a friend. Utilizing these resources, Eric was able to create a fantastic design for publicity, a marketing strategy to go with it, and a multiple plan for distribution thorough electronic and print media. In business that process would be called a virtual corporation. After the project was completed, the network Eric created would be dissolved.

In virtual corporations every partner has something to gain. The same is true of Eric's "corporation." Since the others he contacted were professionals in their fields, Eric agreed to create a masthead on each publicity piece, giving credit to each person. The publicity generated allowed his friends to get a return on their time and involvement. It was a win-win situation for everyone involved.

Developing a ministry team is not for everyone. It's not for the impatient. It's not for someone who won't work with other persons. It's not for a person who does not have a teachable spirit. And it won't work for those who are afraid to risk and fail.

But for single adults who are willing to change their way of thinking about ministry; to try something new that will require mental retraining; and to accept the pattern of risk, failure, learning, and risk again, the ministry team can revolutionize Christian ministry among single adults.

---

[1]Vince Lombardi, as quoted in *Great Quotes from Great Leaders* (Lombard, Ill.: Celebrating Excellence, 1992), 50.
[2]Samuel E. Bleecker, "The Virtual Organization," *The Futurist,* March–April 1994, 9.

unite the team

the principle of united effort

United we stand, divided we fall.[1]

Time
Effort
Patience

—Aesop

If you were a multimillionaire and decided to enter the world of professional sports, you could buy a professional football team. You could recruit the best players money could buy. You could assemble the finest coaching staff in the league. And as soon as you had everyone on board, you could proudly announce to the world that you had a team. But in reality you would not.

A football team, like any other team, is not just an assembly of highly skilled professionals who are thrown together. In this scenario a wise owner and an intelligent coach would realize that all they had was an assembly—not a team. Teams cannot simply be orchestrated; they must be built. In football, building takes place on the practice field. Each player studies the playbooks the coaches created. They undergo intensive physical training to get their bodies in premium condition. Then they all come together on the practice field to begin the slow process of uniting as a team.

A center may be able to hike the ball perfectly, but he has to learn how to work with a new quarterback, whose style may differ from that of the previous quarterback. The quarterback must learn the receivers' timing and subtle signs that tell him exactly when they are making a move. The defensive linemen must learn how to work together to stop an opposing team. Each player must practice with the other players to perceive and adjust to their personalities, styles, mannerisms, and abilities.

The same is true for a ministry team. When you have successfully assembled a group of individuals who share your vision for ministry, you actually have an assembly; they are not yet a team. They may be highly skilled in certain areas, they may have the perfect personality types for this ministry, and their spiritual gifts may be exactly what are needed to succeed. But you do not have a team; you have an assembly of persons who are qualified to become a team.

To unite these important individuals into a team will take each team member's time, effort, and patience. Some elements will come easily, and some will be extremely difficult. But if each member is committed, a team will emerge with amazing abilities. For this to happen, certain key elements must be built into the group.

Elements That Unite a Team

Certain elements are found in well-functioning teams, whether that team manages corporations, builds cars, or plays football. The following eight principles apply to every successful team.

Common Cause

An effective team clarifies exactly what it wants to accomplish (discussed in detail in the next strategy). Each member must agree on the team's purpose. A wide variety of reasons might bring a team together, even within one ministry area. For example, scores of ministries across America attempt to reach poor people for Christ. Some perceive that they are to collect others' abundance and dispense it to those in need. Some see their mission as only spiritual, addressing the eternal needs of the poor. Others believe that their mission is to influence the government to provide greater assistance for the poor. Still others believe that they have been called to encourage the church to reclaim the responsibility of caring for the poor. A final group believes that its mission is not to provide goods and services but to provide resources to allow the poor to help themselves out of their plight.

Every group mentioned is 100 percent correct in its mission. There is not necessarily only one right or wrong way to accomplish the goal; there will always be many ways to approach ministry. Whatever the ministry team decides its mission to be, each member needs to understand clearly the team's purpose from the beginning. It must have a common cause.

Jesus identified the disciples' common cause when He said, " 'Come, follow me, … and I will make you fishers of men' " (Matt. 4:19). Jesus created a team of disciples to learn how to reach others for God's kingdom. That was their common cause. Jesus kept their purpose at the forefront of all they did. Many times His actions confused the disciples. Going into the home of Zacchaeus, the tax collector, was tantamount to treason in the eyes of many orthodox Jews in Jesus' day. Certainly, His disciples wondered why Jesus would do such a thing. But they learned that Jesus was not running for a popularity contest; He was fishing for persons, even some of the most unlikely ones. Jesus reiterated this lesson when He spoke with the Samaritan woman at the well in the middle of the day. Jesus was breaking every custom in the book. First, Jewish men didn't talk with women in public. Second, they never talked with Samaritans, especially Samaritan women. Third, they never associated with persons of questionable morals; yet this woman was quite promiscuous. And finally, even if they needed to say something to someone of questionable character, they would never do so in the bright light of the noonday sun. Jesus was socially unorthodox in the eyes of the establishment. But He was fishing. And He was teaching His disciples how to fish.

A tax collector and a Samaritan woman would not have been the kind of "fish" the disciples would have pursued if Jesus had not taught them. But Jesus was helping them see the common cause: fishing for persons. The revolution that followed attests to the fact that they got the message.

For a team to be effective, it must clarify its common cause, and each member must agree on it. You can accomplish this by holding an open forum of discussion to clarify your purpose and determine how to accomplish it. Because some personality types are not as verbally expressive as others, allow room for various ways of communicating in this process. It is vitally important to put in writing exactly what team members agree on. If members have questions or reservations about what is written, they can ask for further discussion until agreement is reached.

Common Ground

One of the most fragile times in a team's life is its beginning. When team members first begin working together, they assess every nuance of every meeting. If this period is not negotiated effectively, the tone and purpose of the team can suffer greatly.

Someone, usually the person who initiated the creation of the team, needs to function as the team leader. The team leader is not the manager or the boss. The manager mind-set is easy to fall into because of the role models of top-down management we have seen and have been taught since the Industrial Revolution. This mind-set must be avoided at all costs. A self-directed ministry team does not have a CEO.

Scripture is filled with examples of leaders who rejected the top-down management style. In the Book of Philemon the apostle Paul used a problem-solving occasion to unite his ministry team. He could have used top-down management, but he chose the wiser path.

Philemon was a wealthy slave owner whom Paul addressed in his letter. Philemon's slave Onesimus had run away. As a slave on the run, Onesimus encountered the gospel, received Christ as Savior, and ministered to Paul in prison. Paul persuaded Onesimus to return to his master, Philemon, and sent a letter on Onesimus's behalf, the book in the Bible we now call Philemon.

Paul's language in the Book of Philemon was the language of a team leader rather than that of an industrial manager. He began in verse 1 by calling Philemon a "fellow worker." Paul approached Philemon as a peer. Paul further complimented Philemon in verse 7 by telling him how much joy Philemon had brought into Paul's life by his ministry to the saints. Philemon had been working in the ministry, too, and Paul recognized his valuable work, not as a servant or follower of Paul but as a fellow worker. Paul also let him know that he had been praying for him (see v. 4).

In verse 8 Paul said that because of his unique position as an apostle of Christ he could give Philemon a directive but did not do so because of love. Paul was in a unique position as a called apostle of Christ. Like the twelve, he held a special position in the church that was not passed on after his death. His ministry continued through his converts, but his position ended with him.

What does love have to do with this situation? Why would Paul base his desire on love? Paul sought to establish a nonauthoritarian method of working, based on mutual love as equal members of the body of Christ. Therefore, he said: "I appeal to you on the basis of love. ... I appeal to you for my son Onesimus, who became my son while I was in chains. Formerly he was useless to you, but now he has become useful both to you and to me" (Philem. 9-11).

Paul lifted Philemon onto equal ground with him and appealed to him from love rather than from duty or power. Perhaps Paul used wisdom due to a mind-set Philemon might have had. As a slave owner, Philemon was accustomed to having people obey him from fear. Had Paul approached Philemon from a position of power, Philemon might have resisted, perceiving himself as a slave. So Paul approached him as an equal.

After expressing his desire to keep Onesimus with him, Paul said, "I did not want to do anything without your consent, so that any favor you do will be spontaneous and not forced" (v. 14). Paul allowed Philemon to make his own decision. And Paul would have accepted Philemon's decision, too.

In verse 17 Paul elevated Onesimus to common ground with both himself and Philemon: "If you consider me a partner, welcome him [Onesimus] as you would welcome me." Paul said to Philemon, "Just as I treat you as my equal, please treat Onesimus as your equal."

Paul understood the value of common ground. He taught it in 1 Corinthians 12, comparing the church to a physical body that has no unimportant members. He taught it when he wrote about spiritual gifts in the church (see Rom. 12; 1 Cor. 14). Paul modeled common ground in his letters and his lifestyle.

Paul was not unique in presenting this view of leadership in the church. Peter, who would naturally be prone to authoritarian leadership, wrote, "Be shepherds of God's flock that is under your care, serving as overseers—not because you must, but because you are willing, as God wants you to be; not greedy for money, but eager to serve; not lording it over those entrusted to you, but being examples to the flock" (1 Pet. 5:2-3).

When you begin a ministry team, you may need to begin as its team leader for the sake of bringing everyone together, setting up meetings, and moving the process along. But if you approach this role as an authoritarian leader, you will lose your team. Follow the examples of Paul and Peter. Operate from common ground.

Group Identity

Once you have established the common cause for the team and everyone feels like an equal partner in this venture, the team needs to choose a name. A team name serves two primary purposes. First, it galvanizes the team's identity. It lets team members know that there exist a ministry and a group to which they belong. It's not just a team; it's their team. The name helps members identify with the group and its direction. It also implies that members have personal responsibilities on this team.

You can enhance the team's identity with an item that can be easily recognized. Many companies use ball caps, T-shirts, and similar items to create team identity. If you decide to pursue such items, decide as a team rather than have one member act for the others.

Second, a team name makes others aware of what you are doing. A name that accurately describes your ministry enables people to relate to what you want to accomplish. The more you can do to help people understand your purpose, the better. They may volunteer their services, and your work force can grow. In addition, God may be leading others to get involved in the kind of ministry you are beginning, but they previously did not know how to get started.

Personal Success

Personal success in uniting a team may seem contradictory because it uplifts individual success. This element is not in conflict with group success but in agreement with it. Ministry-team members need to know that they have the freedom to excel in their areas of responsibility.

For example, the member of your team who handles data on all of the people you have targeted for ministry develops a database computer program with applications to other ministries. If that person wants to expand to include other ministries, he or she should have the freedom to do so. This could be done without merging the various ministries. If the increased work harmed the team's performance, that member would need to decide what his or her priorities should be.

Each team member needs to have room to succeed personally. If God opens other doors through this ministry, the team should support members without trying to hold them back.

Intelligent Failure

Every team of every type has to deal with failure. Your team will not be the exception. You will have failure. But failing at certain tasks does not make the team itself a failure.

I learned to downhill ski through an intensive course. My instructor taught safety first and foremost. But he also said this: "If you're never falling down, you're not improving your skiing. For if you're never falling, you're not pushing your limits; you're staying inside your comfort zone. To improve your skiing, you sometimes have to get outside your comfort zone, fall sometimes, but learn all you can accomplish."

The same is true for a ministry team. Sometimes you will fall. If you bury problems that develop, you will never learn from them. The only way to learn from them is to acknowledge them, bring them to the surface, and discuss as a team what caused the problems and the best way to solve them. The more you practice this process as a team, the wiser all members become. The learning is not happening with only one or two members; it is happening with all members. And the wiser each of you becomes, the more quickly you will be able to avoid similar situations in the future. In addition, discussing a problem as a team and learning from it build unity.

If a problem arises between two members, keep the focus of the team's discussion on the problem rather than on personalities. Otherwise, one member is bound to lose. When a solution allows both parties to win, the team remains unified.

Individual Responsibility

The best way to move an elephant is not to push it, not to pull it, but to tap into its internal motivation. An elephant pretty much moves when it decides to and not before. A ministry team is better united if each member is internally motivated to participate in the ministry. That internal motivation must then translate into an internal sense of responsibility. Each member must understand that everyone on the team is responsible for carrying out his or her tasks.

Some adults can act like children. Your team needs to consist of mature adults who take the initiative to do the work they have agreed to do. For the sake of the team, communicate this expectation at the very beginning.

If team members do not perform tasks because they were waiting for someone else to take the initiative, the team needs to challenge this wrong thinking. Irresponsibility creates additional work for others. Someone must constantly support the dysfunctional member. A ministry team is as healthy as the persons who make up that team. That's why it is important to choose members wisely. Don't just choose your friends; choose persons who share the vision and who demonstrate individual responsibility in their lives.

Individual responsibility helps unite your team because it is a character trait of Christ. The apostle Paul discussed the spiritual gifts of apostleship, prophecy, evangelism, pastoring, and teaching that God gave the church; persons in these roles are to "prepare God's people for works of service, so that the body of Christ may be built up until we all reach unity in the faith and in the knowledge of the Son of God and become mature" (Eph. 4:12). He went on to say, "From him the whole body, joined and held together by every supporting ligament, grows and builds itself up in love, as each part does its work" (4:16). Paul stressed that the way to achieve unity was for each part to do its work. For a ministry team to work, each member must pull his or her weight. Anything less disrupts unity and hurts the team.

Personal Sacrifice

Although each member needs freedom to have personal success, sometimes each member must make personal sacrifices for the good of the team. Sacrifice should be balanced. If one member is inordinately called on to make sacrifices, something may be out of place on the team. Perhaps the person needs to find someone with similar personality strengths and spiritual gifts to share the workload. But reasonable sacrifices are a normal part of a healthy team's life.

Once I was in a church ministry when I sensed God's leading me to make a change. Around the time I was ready to talk with the senior pastor, a major immorality problem rocked the church. Hurt and confused members began choosing sides. The long, involved process of resolving this situation required much energy from several key leaders in the church as well as from the senior pastor.

When the problem surfaced, I knew that the time was not right for me to announce my departure. To do so would cause further chaos in the church. So I delayed. That delay became a year, but I knew that the church needed more stability before I could leave. Once things settled down and I felt that God's calling for me was the same, I announced my departure and left with a clean conscience. Sometimes being part of a team means that you make personal sacrifices for the good of the team.

Written Principles

Anytime you bring a group of individuals together, especially independent-minded single adults, you can expect differences of opinion. That's OK. People need to have a forum for discussing their differences. But to function as a ministry team, you need to operate by a set of team rules that avoids putting an individual in the position of enforcer. The best way to accomplish that is for the team to create a set of operating principles with which everyone agrees. These operating principles become the standard of quality and performance by which team members measure themselves. When problems arise, the team works together on solutions for realigning with the principles agreed on. This approach allows team members to unite to find a solution.

The value of written principles is in preventing the team from developing a top-down mind-set. If a member violates established rules the team agreed on, the team can refer to the list and say: "This list is something you agreed to; yet you are violating our rules. How can we work together to overcome this problem?" Using this approach prevents disagreements from becoming personal. It's not Bill or Sandy who doesn't like what Jim did. The team rules become the enforcer.

The traditional approach to problem solving is to make the member who violated something feel left out of the team, as if left out in the cold. Such an approach never builds unity; it tears it down. It pits one member against the team. That creates isolation, not unity. If a member is not being responsible, keep in mind the goal of improving the individual's actions. The goal is not retribution. It is not to solicit remorse, fear, or shame. It is to encourage a change in behavior or attitude. Focusing on the established principles keeps everyone's focus on the solution rather than on the problem.

Unity is promoted when team members commit themselves to be on the same side of an issue and to resolve problems together rather than to attack one another. As a team, write a set of operating principles. Add to them or revise them as your work progresses. But always keep the principles at the forefront. Their visibility reminds every member of his or her role and responsibilities.

Common Problems on Teams

Just as common elements blend to make a healthy, unified team, common problems occur in team building. From time to time each of the following problems can reoccur. Although these obstacles may vary in intensity and duration, the majority of teams will encounter them at some point. If you know what to look for, you will recognize them when they surface. Then the team can begin the process of mending the breach so that it can move forward.

Poor Communication

Perhaps the most significant problem that occurs on a team, especially in the formative stage, is communication. It can be easy to assume that because a group is talking, it is communicating. But there is a major difference. Talking is a physical function that affects the auditory senses of someone else; he hears what you say. But communicating means that another person receives a message and interprets it accurately.

For example, you can say, "I love you" yet communicate many different meanings. If you say it in the form of a question with the emphasis on the word *you*, you communicate the remote likelihood that you actually love the person. Saying these words as a statement and emphasizing the word *I* communicates that regardless of others, you love this person. Verbal emphasis on the word *love* says, "I don't just like you; I love you." The same words communicate three different meanings.

Genuine communication is a skill that is developed through practice and continual learning. In the beginning a team's work may involve a lot of talking, but the communication level may be minimal. One factor that affects the team's level of communication is the communication style of each personality type. Mels Carbonell's work, presented in strategy 2, provides valuable insight into how to communicate with different personality types. By using this information, team members can learn the best way to relate to one another. Here are some communication characteristics unique to each personality type.

- Instead of telling *D*'s to complete a task immediately, give them the choice between completing the task now or by a certain time. They will usually choose the latter, but at least they have a choice.
- *I*'s need to learn that they will have more friends when they make others look good. Praise them when they do well. Emphasize that their poor behavior makes them look bad when they underachieve. These especially need to guard against pleasing everyone.
- The natural submissiveness of *S*'s causes others to take advantage of them. *S*'s need to learn how to overcome their reluctance to be bold and assertive. Saying no can be frightening yet powerful. Accepting chances and

risks to take charge can be very rewarding.

- Provide *C*'s with happy, positive atmospheres. They tend to be naturally pessimistic and moody. Music can be encouraging. Especially avoid being constantly negative and critical with these personality types.

The personality types communicate differently. *D*'s and *I*'s primarily communicate verbally. But *S* and *C* personalities are not as well equipped to express themselves verbally. They communicate best by writing. When a disagreement or a discussion begins or stalls in a team meeting, the verbal personalities tend to dominate the conversations because they are naturally verbal. But to communicate best, someone needs to find a way to include the *S*'s and *C*'s. That is accomplished by allowing them to express their concerns, observations, and insights in written form. This way both verbal and nonverbal types have equal opportunities to express themselves, and communication improves greatly.

Here's a look at a fictitious team, consisting of the four personality types previously described, that talked instead of communicated in a team meeting. First, *D* would verbalize what needed to be done and why—but only in broad strokes. Because *D* is sure of himself, he would be persuasive, and confidence is contagious. *D*'s bold statement would be "I say we need to do _____ to reach our goals, and we need to do it tomorrow!" *D* seeks to communicate by focusing on results.

I would also jump in verbally, but her interests would not be so much on getting results. She would be more interested in the process and the relationships built in the process. *I*'s can be network kings and queens. *I*'s bold statement would be "I don't care so much about when we start or finish. I want to know what other persons we need to involve to make this happen!" *I* would seek to communicate through building relationships and having fun along the way.

Left as it is, *D* and *I* could dominate a team meeting with their verbal skills. But *S* and *C*, who are not as verbal, would also need to speak up. *S* and *C* often want time to think things through before making a decision, while *D*'s motto is "Act first; think later." *S* would tend to be intimidated, partially because of *D*'s forcefulness but also because these actions would mean change, which *S* doesn't like. Therefore, *S* would be more likely to question the need to move in the direction proposed by *D*. But not being as verbally skilled, perhaps *S* would speak up but without the confidence of *D*. *S*'s timid statement might be "Uh, excuse me. Can I say something? Are you sure we need to do this?" Unless the other team members recognized this personality type, the lack of confidence in S's verbal communication could be interpreted by other team members as a poor suggestion. Timidity breeds a lack of confidence. D and I, viewing timidity as weakness, would dismiss S's concern as fear. But S can communicate better on paper than he can verbally. If given time to draft a document, he could explain his concerns in a way that might prove invaluable to the team.

C is also less skilled verbally than D and I. C would also resist change, though not as much as S. As soon as D said, "I say we need to do _____ to reach our goals, and we need to do it tomorrow!" C would immediately begin to think about all of the systems and details needed to make this happen. Recognizing the enormous number of details D could be oblivious to, C would also timidly insert her concerns about the direction being offered by D. But C might be a bit more forceful than S. C's mild statement might be "I'd like to say something here if I could. If we're going to do this, a lot of work needs to be done first. I think we need to think about it before we jump in without thinking." If D felt that C was challenging his idea, he would verbally go on the defensive and ask C to explain himself. However, C, feeling intimidated by D and not being as verbally skilled, would tend to withdraw since she doesn't have all of the details D is asking for. Being a personality type that likes thoroughness, C would prefer not to present anything until all details are prepared. Like S, if given time, C too could draft all of the precise details needed to make the goal a reality. But again, unless the team allows for written communication, S and C could be ignored.

The detriment of this process is that S and C begin to feel that they are not being heard and that their ideas are not being taken seriously. When this happens enough, they begin to feel that they are not team members; they are privates in General D's army. Communication will break down after a while because S and C will stop offering their suggestions. Although talking will continue, communication will be lost.

A valuable tool to help all personality types communicate better is the practice of restating. When a team member says something in a meeting, another member can respond by saying, "What I hear you saying is ..." and restate the other person's message in terms that she believes say the same thing. If the original speaker doesn't agree with this interpretation, communication hasn't occurred. If both sides take time to restate, terms will be used that allow each person to clarify what he or she meant.

start a revolution

A final tool for communicating and building team unity is to discuss feelings openly. In team meetings someone can say something that arouses certain feelings in you. These feelings then become a filter through which you assess all the person says. But feelings can be inaccurate indicators of what is being said. A healthy team learns to say: "Wait a minute. When you said _____, it made me feel _____. Is that what you meant by what you said?" Often, it is not. By stating your feelings, you give the other person an opportunity to correct the misunderstanding. This requires mutual respect for all parties involved. There are no right and wrong feelings, although the assumptions they lead to can be right or wrong. These thoughts need to be admitted when emotions enter the communication process. "I'm feeling attacked." "That makes me feel that I'm not needed." Phrases like these help other team members understand what you are feeling. Then the team can provide further information to dispel those feelings. Open communication of feelings builds greater unity.

Bonding and Personality Traits

In addition to having different communication styles, the personality types have different relational and bonding styles. These must also be considered to build unity in a team.

We will use a fictitious team with the same four personality types previously described to illustrate the impact of personality traits on relational and bonding styles. *D* assumed the position as the team leader, but his tendency is to be the driver rather than a team player. He would be the commander-in-chief if the team would let him. *S* would easily accept *D*'s domineering role because it allows him to remain passive in his role. *S* would sort of melt into the woodwork. This arrangement would be OK as long as everyone was happy with it. But *C*, deciding that the project was doomed from the beginning, would adopt a defeatist attitude and would probably sulk. An independent-minded team such as this struggles at best.

To remedy this situation, *D* would need to acknowledge his tendency to take charge of the team—that although taking charge is sometimes helpful, at other times more thoughtful planning and processing are needed. *D*'s are not good at such details. But *C* is great at details. When a task is being developed that would demand details, let *C* assume the role as leader. This way the details stand a better chance of being communicated.

If the task at hand involves the need for people skills, the person to call on to lead would be *I*. *I* can walk into a roomful of strangers and within 10 minutes have lunch plans with half of them for the next week. *I*'s people skills are amazing. Learn from her strength on the team. She can best communicate to the others what is needed.

When you need someone to keep the routine elements on track, *S* is the person you need. *S* is methodical and stable, preferring consistency, stability, and security. *S* is not excited when change occurs, in contrast to *D*, who thrives on it. So when the team needs to handle ongoing maintenance, *S* is the person to help lead the team. *S* best remembers systems, routines, procedures, rules, and regulations because he thrives in that kind of environment.

Loss of Motivation

A third problem common among teams is the occasional loss of motivation. It can strike one team member or several. It can come suddenly or gradually. But eventually, it strikes most teams.

Understand that persons lose motivation for numerous reasons. Often, it is related to personality. While a high *D* finds an enormous challenge motivating, a high *C* quickly becomes discouraged because the goal seems far away in light of the countless details that need to be handled to reach the desired result. Different personalities respond differently to life's situations.

Conversely, while a high *C* finds motivation by delving into the finer details of a project, those same details can drive *D* into despair. *D* wants to move, move, move. Details just get in the way. Slowing down a *D* too much with details causes him to become discouraged and to lose motivation.

Stress, lack of rest, physical illness, ambiguity, and a host of other causes can result in a loss of motivation. To find the right cure, you must make the accurate diagnosis. A doctor can give excellent medicine to a patient, but if the medicine is not intended for the patient's problem, it does the patient no good. Neither can you use a general motivation builder as the cure-all for a team member's discouragement. You must find out where the defeat is coming from and then prescribe a solution.

If a team member is discouraged because of work overload, the other team members need to help lighten the load. But it is also good for the team to assess why this has happened. Did the overloaded member volunteer for too much? Did she allow others to volunteer her without protest? Does the stressed-out member have a hard time saying no? Part of re-instilling motivation may be to recognize a pattern if one exists, reveal it to the member, and commit the team to helping that member overcome that tendency.

When this approach is taken, it not only solves the immediate crisis but also communicates to the member that the other members are not just interested in producing the work. They are truly interested in helping each member improve her character by helping her overcome any faults that surface in the course of her ministry. When a team member knows that her weaknesses will not cause the other team members to ostracize her but rather to lift her up, she has hope for a better tomorrow. And that builds motivation.

Sometimes a loss of motivation comes from uncertainty of direction. People live by measurements. We measure life by years, months, weeks, days, hours, minutes, seconds, and fractions of a second. We measure salaries, vacation days, perks, bonuses, and titles at work. We measure status, wealth, value, and other social standards through our clothes, our cars, and our homes. And we measure success by progress. So when we cannot see that progress is being made, the tendency is to assume that it isn't. And if a team member does not think the team is going anywhere, he can become discouraged.

A helpful solution to a loss of motivation that is caused by a perceived lack of progress is to establish small, measurable goals for each major task in the ministry. Write them either on paper in notebook form or on a poster to display on a wall. As each step is completed, cross off that step. This practice visually shows progress as the team moves in a certain direction. One glance at the chart tells any team member whether the team is ⅓, ½, or ¾ completed.

If the *C* member of the team handles the details, she may want to work with the team to set deadlines for incremental goals. Setting deadlines keeps team members accountable to fulfill their responsibilities by certain dates. If a date is reached ahead of time, the team can celebrate being ahead of schedule. If it is behind, it can focus on what is needed to catch up. If the team is behind because one member is slowing the process, the team can come to his rescue. An awareness of the team's support motivates the team member to continue.

Incompetence

The term *incompetence* does not mean that a person is dull or stupid. *Webster's* defines it simply as "not legally qualified; inadequate to or unsuitable for a particular purpose; lacking the qualities needed for effective action."[2] Incompetent persons may be able to become competent, and many may be willing to do what it takes to gain competency. But in the meantime the team member may lose motivation because he can't do what is required at that time. Someone once said that the true test of a leader is not her ability to hire; anyone can do that. A real leader knows how to fire when needed. Of course, there is no boss on a self-directed team. If a change needs to be made, it needs to be addressed by the team rather than by an individual.

It may seem odd to talk about overcoming a team member's loss of motivation by removing him from something he agreed to do, but it can be done in a way that builds new motivation. Releasing a member from a responsibility may not necessitate releasing him from the team. If the work and the member are not a good match, help the member find work that is a better match. The goal is not to disrupt team unity but to build it. If a member is released from the team for not being able to handle a responsibility, other members could be discouraged from tackling future tasks, for if the new task proved to be too much, they too could be released from the team. That is not the message the team wants to give. The message is "We want you to be involved where you can best use your strengths, where you can accomplish the most, where you can succeed the greatest. Your present position does not allow you to do that. We want to help you find a place that does."

Many times a well-meaning member believes that a certain task would suit him, then discovers that it doesn't. If the team environment encourages each member to find the best place suited for him, having a task taken away need not be seen as a failure. It was a success for the team member because he identified an area that does not fit him. He will be able to make a wiser decision next time.

Make sure that the issue is truly a poor match rather than a lack of training. If the necessary education would not be too lengthy, the team can provide training for the member. Even if it slows progress, it can build the team. The other members will see that the team will respond to them the same way if they are in a similar position.

When motivation is lost, it can be regained. The keys are to find the genuine cause and to address it in a way that reinforces the team's desire to help each member grow while continuing the team's work in the area that is lacking.

When you use this approach, both the discouraged member and the team as a whole come out as winners.

The Rule of 33

In creating and uniting a ministry team, it helps to understand a group dynamic called the Rule of 33. When a corporation adds a new product line or a new product, downsizes or rightsizes, reorganizes, or goes through any other substantive change, three groups can be identified in the corporation. One-third of the employees are the initiators, the change agents themselves, who applaud the changes or additions enthusiastically. Having long recognized the need for change, they find encouragement and renewed energy from the coming changes.

Another third of the employees are weather vanes, who shift to whatever direction the wind blows. If the shift is to downsize, they go with the flow. If the shift is to diversify, they go with the flow. They quietly go along with any change like children of the Pied Piper.

The last third of the employees are terrorists. If a company brings change, a new product line, or an alteration from the way they feel comfortable, they not only dislike it but also do whatever they can to prevent it. They disrupt the process, question the directions, bicker, complain, and drag their corporate feet as the company adopts a new way of doing business. Unfortunately, many companies make the mistake of spending too much time coddling the terrorists, so much time that they often discourage the initiators by exhibiting inconsistent leadership patterns. A wise corporate sage once said, "In a company treat every person fairly, but never treat everyone equally." Of course, a company should try for a while to win over the terrorists. But after a fair amount of time, if the terrorists do not change their perspective, it is time for them to move somewhere else.

The Rule of 33 applies to the larger circle of single adults you associate with. When you begin a ministry team to reach a certain ministry goal, some single adults will enthusiastically support you, offering all the encouragement they can. They may financially contribute to your cause, volunteer to work, promote your cause, or ask to become team members.

Others will be somewhat indifferent to your ministry. Some you may have thought would be very supportive prove to be weather vanes, giving only halfhearted support. Whether the ministry is performed really doesn't matter to them. Don't be offended by their indifference. Apparently, God is not calling them to participate in your ministry. Be sure you have enthusiastic supporters to balance the weather vanes.

The last third consists of persons who hear about your ministry, do not like it, and take personal responsibility for discouraging you. I am not referring to the godly counsel of wise persons you have approached for insight. I mean single adults or others who don't want change. Why would anybody oppose a new ministry? Some might feel convicted if you begin a ministry they have avoided because they lack the commitment to do so. Others may not see you as a minister. After all, you're just Bill or Susan or the baby brother or a single adult! As Jesus said, " 'No prophet is accepted in his hometown' " (Luke 4:24).

Your church as a whole could also respond according to the Rule of 33. It may be overjoyed by your commitment to ministry and may become a major resource for all you want to do. Your church may be somewhat indifferent, letting you do what you want without genuinely supporting you. Or your church may resist your involvement in ministry. Your concept of ministry, in which single adults are empowered to act on their dreams and pursue them, might appear threatening to your church leaders. Some might question your qualifications for ministry if you have not attended seminary.

You need to be willing to accept any limitations your church establishes. If your church does not help you or helps only in limited ways, do not develop an adversarial role with your church. Instead, recognize that the church's dreams and your dreams may not be compatible at this time. Then go forward with God's leading in your life, with or without the church's assistance.

In building a ministry team, some will support you, some will be indifferent, and some will oppose you. Never lose sight of God's calling in your life. Share your vision, but let God bring other single adults to you to join the team and the dream. Live with the reality that some very good persons may oppose you. Do not be discouraged. Listen to the words of the writer of the Book of Hebrews. After listing an array of people through the years who had followed God's calling in their lives and had accomplished things most people considered impossible, the writer concluded by saying, "Since we are surrounded by such a great cloud of witnesses, let us throw off everything that hinders and the sin that so easily entangles, and let us run with perseverance the race marked out for us. Let us fix our eyes on Jesus, the author and perfecter of our faith, who for the joy set before him endured the cross, scorning its shame, and sat down at the right hand of the throne of God" (Heb. 12:1-2).

Toward Success!

You can expect your team to progress through stages of learning as you work together. Educators identify four stages in a learning process:

Unconscious competence. Team members do not know, and they do not even know that they do not know. You could call it ignorant ignorance. They are ignorant and don't realize it. Albert Einstein once said, "Everyone is ignorant, only in different areas." Imagine the consternation you would see on a rocket scientist's face if you asked him or her to milk a dairy cow. But ignorance is not the inability to learn; it is simply the lack of knowledge.

Conscious incompetence. At this stage team members are confronted with the knowledge that they do not know. They are still unable to perform, but they know that they do not know. Learning begins with the admission that you do not know something.

Conscious competence. When a musician first sits before a piece of music, she knows that she doesn't know it. So she begins to practice. Note by note, bar by bar she practices and practices. She studies every detail and every dynamic to digest the music mentally. As she does, she begins to be consciously competent. She can play the piece to some degree, but every note must be considered with conscious effort. At the level of conscious competence team members have progressed to the state of knowing and of knowing that they know.

Subconscious competence. As the musician practices for hours and days, something begins to happen. Little by little some of those notes and chord patterns begin to reside in her subconscious, allowing her to play them without consciously thinking about them. She has moved to a level at which she doesn't have to stop and think before she acts; her playing comes from her subconscious.

As you develop into a team, you will become aware of how much team building you do not know. Do not be discouraged by your ignorance. Recognizing your lack of knowledge is the first step toward overcoming it. You may begin assembling your team believing that it will be a fairly simple process. Sometimes it begins that way; rarely does it stay that way. As cracks begin to surface in the team, view them as opportunities to learn as a team how to deal with them. Recognize the stage of conscious incompetence. You know that you don't know.

But in time you will begin to get past some of the early issues. Your communication skills will improve. You will have a better understanding of each member's different personality traits. In the course of working together, at first you will have to think consciously about how to respond or not to respond to each member, as all team members will. This is the developmental process of becoming consciously competent.

Like the musician, you and each team member will gradually move into areas of subconscious competence. You won't have to stop and think before you act or respond to a team member; you'll do it without thinking. This is the level of subconscious competence. When you reach this level as a team, you can shift your focus from your relational needs to the ministry before you. When you reach that point, you will function as a well-groomed, highly effective team with a common goal, a clear perspective, and a precise understanding of each person's role in making it all happen. That's when the success will begin to show—not only in the ministry but also in your individual lives.

With these processes in place and your ministry dreams before you, you are now ready to begin the exciting, though sometimes frustrating, process of developing persons into a team. To be a successful team, persons must work together closely enough and honestly enough to resolve their problems on the way to attaining their commonly shared dream. You may not particularly like someone on your team, but a team is not a clique or a friendship circle. As you work toward your mutual goals, it is hoped that you can learn to care for one another and to love one another in Christ. Team members always respect one another, listen to and communicate with one another, and reveal Christ's character in their actions and attitudes toward one another as they pursue the vision God has given them.

---

[1] Aesop, "Four Oxen and the Lion," as quoted by John Bartlett in *Familiar Quotations* (Boston: Little, Brown and Co., 1942), 962.
[2] *Webster's Ninth New Collegiate Dictionary* (Springfield, Mass.: Merriam-Webster, 1991), 610.

strategy ⑥

define
your vision

the principle of clarity

> The very essence of leadership is [that] you have to have a vision. It's got to be a vision you articulate clearly and forcefully on every occasion. You can't blow an uncertain trumpet.[1]
>
> —Father Theodore Hesburgh

After discovering your primary personality traits, your spiritual gifts, and the way a self-directed ministry team works, you might be tempted to begin blazing trails with this newfound information. But before you begin, you need to clarify your final destination. When you prepare to travel a long distance, you first get a map and plan your route. You could begin driving without knowing how to reach your destination, but planning your route saves time and effort. The same is true of your ministry efforts. What do you specifically want to accomplish? Do you have a clear set of goals with measurable objectives? To make a difference in your world, the knowledge you have gained thus far will be needed, but you also need to clarify your vision and to set goals for attaining it.

By vision I do not mean that you are awakened in the middle of the night by a deep voice that issues you an exotic challenge. Too much pizza can cause that. Rather, a vision is much like a dream but clearer. For example, you may have a dream to accomplish great things someday. That is a dream. But you formulate a vision when you decide that the way you want to accomplish your dream is to become a godly medical doctor or schoolteacher. Or you may decide that the way to fulfill your dream is to reach out to persons in your apartment complex and to share God's love with them. Dreams and visions are related but distinct. Many people go through life with dreams but never acquire visions. Consequently, they rarely fulfill their dreams.

In addition to dreams and visions, you need goals. Once you decide to become a doctor, you need to set incremental goals to accomplish your vision. You will need a lot of education. That means money, so you must work and begin saving early in life. It also means making good grades. Actions like these are measurable goals that will help you accomplish your dreams and visions.

Someone once said, "Aim at nothing, and you'll hit it every time." If you don't know where you're going in life or what you want to accomplish in Christian ministry, how do you know that your current course is headed in the right direction? Until you define your dreams in terms of measurable goals, you will live your life with a vague feeling of wandering—hoping that at some point you will stumble onto God's course for your life.

God has a better approach. The purpose of this strategy is to help you set goals that clarify your dreams and chart the direction God wants you to go. By grasping the purpose, plan, and power of effective goals, you can set a course in life that has purpose, honors God, and brings personal fulfillment.

Defining your vision and setting measurable goals should not be confused with a name-it-and-claim-it theology that is fraught with a misguided use of Scripture. Nor is it a read-your-palm-and-tell-your-future approach. Such practices violate scriptural principles. This process is also not associated with the secular teachings of wealth or with achieving your ambitions through the sheer power of your mind and determination. Rather, you consider your God-given desires, personality, gifts, talents, and faith to identify a general course in life, which you more narrowly define by setting goals. The course you choose gives you a deep sense of fulfillment and belonging.

Earlier in this book I referred to a person who found that he had the gift of evangelism but the personality of an introvert. If he pursued a dream of evangelism by setting goals suited to an extrovert, he would not find fulfillment. If he found a style of evangelism that suited both his spiritual gift and his personality, he would feel that he had found his niche.

Perhaps you already have a vision for ministry. If not, consider some of the ideas beginning on page 235 in this book. Remember that pursuing your vision by setting goals can involve trial and error. You may set a course in life only to find that it does not bring deep spiritual fulfillment. Keep in mind that more than one way is available to fulfill your dreams.

Ingredients of Success

For a Christian, setting goals is much more effective if the foundation for the goals rests on scriptural principles. Any method is faulty that fails to recognize parameters established in Scripture. God wants you to succeed in life by His definition of *success*. In seminars I have often asked the question, How many of you hope one day to be a total failure, an absolute reject, a bona fide loser at anything that remotely smacks of being successful? I have never had any takers.

How do you define *success*? The way you define it determines the way you approach life. As a Christian single adult, you have been gifted by God to succeed in life. But God's criteria for success are not the same as secular society's.

Four primary ingredients in God's view of success include personal relationship, responsive action, active faith, and quality. When combined, these ingredients form a solid foundation on which to build personal goals.

Personal Relationship

God's definition of *success* begins with a relationship. Jesus identified the basis on which God the Father rewards people with eternal life:

> "Not everyone who says to me, 'Lord, Lord,' will enter the kingdom of heaven, but only he who does the will of my Father who is in heaven. Many will say to me on that day, 'Lord, Lord, did we not prophesy in your name, and in your name drive out demons and perform many miracles?' Then I will tell them plainly, 'I never knew you. Away from me, you evildoers!'
>
> "Therefore everyone who hears these words of mine and puts them into practice is like a wise man who built his house on the rock. The rain came down, the streams rose, and the winds blew and beat against that house; yet it did not fall, because it had its foundation on the rock. But everyone who hears these words of mine and does not put them into practice is like a foolish man who built his house on sand. The rain came down, the streams rose, and the winds blew and beat against that house, and it fell with a great crash" (Matt. 7:21-27).

The basis for entering heaven and for receiving a reward is a personal relationship with Jesus Christ. Those who do the Father's will, Jesus said, will enter heaven. And what is the Father's will? Jesus said it is not prophesying in His name or proclaiming His gospel like an evangelist or a preacher. It is also not practicing the ministry of exorcism, casting out demons, as a Christian leader or counselor might do. Nor is the basis for entering heaven determined by performing many miracles like a flamboyant healer. Going to heaven is not determined by being good or by doing good things. All of these things are noble and good but not good enough by themselves to succeed in life, according to God's definition.

Jesus said that the basis on which someone would be turned away from heaven is "I never knew you." His rejection is based on the absence of a personal relationship with Him, so the criterion for entering heaven is to have a personal relationship with Jesus Christ. To know Him and to be known by Him guarantee that God sees you as an eternal success, for through that relationship you have been granted access into heaven when you die and the means through Him to live a totally fulfilled life while on earth.

Responsive Action

Using the analogy of building a house, Jesus differentiated between a wise person and a foolish person. The difference has to do with their responses to Jesus' words. The wise person heard Jesus' words and acted on them; the foolish person heard and did not act. In both instances the persons heard Jesus' words. The need to act presupposes that His words demanded a response. They were commands. In the immediate context of Matthew 7, Jesus' challenge is for people to believe in Him as Savior. But in a larger context His challenge is for every Christian to respond to His leading with action.

Even Christians can hear Jesus' words yet choose not to act. Such a response is characteristic of a foolish person, Jesus says. What is the way to succeed in life? Hear the words of Jesus and act on them, regardless of whether they seem logical to you. Jesus gave no indication that His words necessarily fit your logic. At times they may seem quite logical; at other times they may not. The basis for responding to God is not your understanding; it is your obedience. Simple obedience is a mark of wisdom and a mark of success in God's eyes.

Active Faith

Peter demonstrated the ingredient of faith when He walked on water, as recorded in Matthew 14:22-33. After fighting a storm most of the night, the disciples feared for their lives. The last person they expected to see was Jesus, especially calmly walking across the lake. These men were frantically fighting for their lives, but in the midst of this storm Jesus called out to them: " 'Take courage! It is I. Don't be afraid' " (v. 27).

Peter's words reflected one of his desires, one of his goals: " 'Lord, if it's you,' " Peter replied, " 'tell me to come to you on the water' " (v. 28). Peter made it clear what he wanted to do; he wanted to walk on water. It was a clearly defined, measurable goal. But Peter did not begin to pursue his desire until he knew that it was God's will. And he knew this when Jesus called out to him. The simplest definition of *faith* is responding to God's word, whether it comes from the Bible, the Holy Spirit, or one of His servants. For inherent in that word is the element of faith.

Faith is a gift from God: "It is by grace you have been saved, through faith—and this not from yourselves, it is the gift of God" (Eph. 2:8). Faith must be in something. If your faith is in your own wishes, the substance of your faith is wrong. If faith is a gift, there must be something God gives you that enables you to have faith. What He gives you is His word. Paul said, "Faith comes from hearing the message, and the message is heard through the word of Christ" (Rom. 10:17). Literally, the verse says, "Faith comes through hearing, and hearing by the word of Christ." *Word* here is not the Greek word *logos,* which refers to the written Word. It is *rhema,* referring to God's spoken word. When God speaks to you through His Holy Spirit, you have something to place your faith in. You have His words. That's why Jesus said, " 'Blessed rather are those who hear the word of God and obey it' " (Luke 11:28).

That's exactly what Peter did; he waited until Jesus spoke to him; then he acted on Jesus' words. " 'Come,' " Jesus said to Peter. And with that one, simple word from Jesus, Peter heard all he needed to have faith that he could do what Jesus told him to do. He had something to put his faith in: Jesus' word to him. Peter got out of the boat, walked on the water, and came toward Jesus (see Matt. 14:28-29).

Peter is often remembered for sinking. It's true. But it's also true that you never succeed at walking on water if you stay in the boat. We may use Peter's moment of sinking to excuse ourselves from following God outside our comfort zone. But if you want to succeed in life by God's definition of *success,* you must obey Him in whatever He leads you to do. You'll never succeed at your goals if you seek direction from God, then fail to act on it. Sometimes following Jesus in faith requires that you get out of the boat, leave your comfortable surroundings, and risk sinking. After all, anyone can float in a boat.

Paul discussed a problem in the church at Rome that was ultimately an issue of faith (see Rom. 14). Some Christians were buying meat that had been sacrificed at pagan temples. Such meat was often sold in the market at reduced prices after pagan services. Some Christians saw this as a way to be frugal. Perhaps they were using the savings to support missionary causes. But other Christians in Rome saw buying such meat as evil, as supporting a pagan religion. Paul wrote to settle the disagreement:

> As one who is in the Lord Jesus, I am fully convinced that no food is unclean in itself. But if anyone regards something as unclean, then for him it is unclean. So whatever you believe about these things keep between yourself and God. Blessed is the man who does not condemn himself by what he approves. But the man who has doubts is condemned if he eats, because his eating is not from faith; and everything that does not come from faith is sin (Rom. 14:14,22-23).

Eating meat or abstaining was not God's concern. God evaluated whether the decision was made with faith. You have great freedom in decision making. When God does not clearly direct you through the Bible, prayer, or wise counsel, you must make a choice by faith. God views your using your limited but God-given knowledge in faith as a successful choice—even if He later redirects you.

Christians often view faith as a success-or-failure proposition. Either you make it, or you don't. You either succeed or fail. But when Peter walked on water and then sank, he was not a failure because he began to sink. He was a success because, to the best of his ability, he was doing all he could possibly do to believe and respond to God's calling in his life at that time. Jesus said, "Come," and Peter went. None of the other disciples ever walked on water. But then, none of them were told to come; Peter was.

Just as God's concept of success is not the same as the world's, His view of failure is very different from the world's. When Christians act in faith with a desire to please God, they are in a win-win situation. If Christians act in obedience, God views them as successful, regardless of the outcome. When you adopt this understanding of success, you will find freedom to pursue the dreams God gives you; you will see success not only in the final destination but also in the journey.

While I was in college, some of my professors promoted one seminary so much that I decided one day: *They think it's the only seminary that exists, but there are other excellent seminaries. If I ever go to seminary, it won't be that one. I'll choose my own path in life, thank you very much.* My senior year was split between the spring and fall semesters; I was to complete my requirements for graduation in December. The first semester of my senior year, I reviewed catalogs, prayed, considered various schools, and decided to attend a good seminary in my hometown. But during the summer God began to speak to me about the basis for my decisions. I came to realize that much of my decision was based on finances. Living at home would be financially advantageous. God began to challenge me, and by the end of the summer I agreed with the Lord that I would review those catalogs.

Earlier I had looked at the catalog for the rejected seminary but had ruled it out because it was too expensive. When I reviewed other schools to be more open to God, I returned to that catalog. Much to my surprise, the college I was attending was more expensive than this seminary, and God had met my needs for that. I began to realize that I wasn't being truly open to God's leadership. I stopped and prayed: "Lord, I truly want to be open to attend wherever You want me to. Just show me Your choice."

I was still mulling this over several days later when a friend at college was hurt in an accident. Her car was hit by a train one morning as she was in route to a prayer breakfast. While visiting her at the hospital, I met her dad and was very impressed with his commitment to God. Later I found out that he was an influential leader at the seminary I had determined not to attend. I had no idea that my friend even knew about that school. With her father's encouragement I agreed to apply to the school of my nonchoice. I felt, however, that my chances of being accepted were slim; this was a highly selective school. But sensing the Lord's leading, I began the application process, which was so involved that I turned my application in one month past the deadline. Still, I felt that if I scored well on the Graduate Record Examination, perhaps my missing the application deadline would be overlooked. My GRE scores set a new record, I believe. I doubt that anyone has ever scored lower. This was not looking good.

My last hope was my grade point average. If I could improve it, perhaps that would make up for the two strikes against me. But try as I might, I could not raise my GPA to the level I believed they expected. Strike 3. Nothing I had done was going to impress those people. Looking at my performance at that point, even I wouldn't have admitted me to the seminary.

But God had a plan that was not based on my ability to impress others; it was based on my obedience to His leadership in my life. I was doing what I believed He wanted me to do. The following spring I received papers indicating that I had been accepted to attend that fall. I was not accepted because of the timeliness of my application. I was not accepted because of my impressive GRE scores or my exceptional GPA. I was accepted because I was obedient to God.

During seasons of discouragement over the following months, I reflected on God's handiwork and remained true to His calling for my education. Had I thought I had gotten there on my own merits, I would have grown discouraged and would have given up before finishing. As the apostle Paul said, "By the grace of God I am what I am, and his grace to me was not without effect" (1 Cor. 15:10). I was where I was because God had told me to go there. Where else would I go but where I knew He wanted me to be?

Did this mean that this seminary was the best seminary around? No. It meant that it was the best seminary for me because it was where God told me to go. I could have gone to one of several other excellent seminaries, and I would have received an excellent education at any of them. But I would have had to do so outside God's revealed will for me. When a person willingly disobeys God, he limits his ability to be used effectively in service.

Quality

Jesus revealed several elements of God's definition of *success*. Romans 14 discusses the ingredient of faith. But the apostle Paul provided further insight in 1 Corinthians 3:12-15 by examining God's value of quality. In discussing the fact that God will one day judge Christians to assign rewards, Paul revealed ad-

start a revolution

ditional criteria for what God considers to be characteristics of a successful person: "If any man builds on this foundation using gold, silver, costly stones, wood, hay or straw, his work will be shown for what it is, because the Day will bring it to light. It will be revealed with fire, and the fire will test the quality of each man's work. If what he has built survives, he will receive his reward. If it is burned up, he will suffer loss; he himself will be saved, but only as one escaping through the flames."

Jesus spoke in Matthew 7 about succeeding eternally by having a personal relationship with Him. But Paul spoke in 1 Corinthians 3 of believers, not people in general. The relationship issue of salvation has already been settled. Paul was dealing with accountability before God for the kind of life you have lived on earth. Using an analogy of building, he mentioned several possible materials a person could use: gold, silver, costly stones, wood, hay, or straw. The implication is not that a person always chooses one element but that a person sometimes uses one element and sometimes another. What is the issue here? It is found in the verse "It [a person's work] will be revealed with fire, and the fire will test the quality of each man's work." What is God looking for to determine the basis for a reward? What is His criterion for success? It is quality. The fire tests the quality of your work. God is looking for quality. Not quantity. Not numbers. Not the accolades of others. Quality will stand the test of fire. Mediocrity will not.

Both Matthew 7 and 1 Corinthians 3 use the analogy of building when discussing eternal rewards. This analogy reveals the value of clarifying your vision and setting goals in life. If you begin to build a house, you first need a clear picture of what the house will look like when it is finished—a vision of what the finished product will look like. Without such a vision you would never know if the builders are going in the right direction. They may start putting a patio where a bedroom is supposed to be or a skylight where a chimney is supposed to be. The vision provides parameters for the building process, telling you what to do and what not to do. It provides direction and sets limits.

Also, when you begin to build a house, you must take incremental steps to achieve the finished product. You don't just build a house. You first prepare the ground for a foundation, then lay a foundation. Then you build the framework. Then you install the plumbing and electrical work, then the air conditioning and utility units. Meanwhile, the external framing has continued. With the roof laid and the external walls completed, the interior can be finished. Finally, the finishing touches are added before you move in. This is not a process with one big step. It is a process that requires many calculated steps, some big and some small. Combined, they help accomplish the vision. These steps represent incremental, measurable goals required to accomplish the bigger vision of completing the house.

Similarly, you must set incremental, measurable goals to accomplish your dreams or visions for life. As you establish your goals, keep in mind that God will not define your success by whether you reach them. That may or may not happen. If He wants you to reach them, you will. His purpose for you may be accomplished through what the pursuit of the goal does to your character rather than what the achievement of the goal may mean. God will consider your goals and your efforts to reach them successful if—

- you believe that they are the goals God has given you;
- your actions in pursuing those goals are acts of faith and obedience to His words to you;
- the effort you put into every incremental step is done with the best quality you can achieve.

Keep in mind that the pursuit of your goals in ministry is a team effort. Part of your task in defining your goals is to find persons who have the same ones. As you work together as a ministry team, a common bond will grow from each member's internal drive to reach the same goals for the glory of God.

Taking Healthy Risks

To set personal goals, you need to understand that faith in God is not a passive activity on your part. It requires that you accept the risk of failure in order to succeed.

Some Christians think that faith means doing nothing spiritually and letting God do it all. An equally erroneous idea is that you have to pull yourself up by your bootstraps, even spiritually. Both of these concepts are false. The truth lies somewhere between the two. Scripture teaches that accomplishing goals demands total dependence on God, as well as 100 percent of a person's effort. Total dependence on God is not passive; it is highly active. It is demonstrated by a person's actions, not by nonaction. Failing to act when God calls for action is not faith; it is religious cowardice. It is a convenient way to excuse yourself from becoming uncomfortable in following God by pretending to have faith. Actually, such a posture attempts to force God's hand to do what He wants you to do—and that is something He will never honor.

The account of Gideon in Judges 6–7 shows that God can do mighty things through a person who sets aside personal fears and doubts to obey God. Although the passage begins comically, it later reveals a person who acts in faith to pursue the goals God gives him. We first see Gideon hiding inside a winepress, threshing wheat. He is hiding because if the Midianites see him, they will take his wheat. This isn't exactly the picture of a valiant man of God. But the angel of the Lord approached Gideon and addressed him by saying, " 'The Lord is with you, mighty warrior' " (Judg. 6:12). Gideon probably thought so little of himself that when he heard those words, he looked around to see where the mighty warrior was. After all, it certainly wasn't he. Imagine Gideon's surprise when he realized that the angel of the Lord was addressing him! God saw something in Gideon that Gideon didn't see in himself. Gideon saw a fearful, insignificant man, but God saw a mighty warrior.

For Gideon to become what God saw, Gideon would have to act in faith on God's words and not rely on his own estimation. When the angel of the Lord first told Gideon to lead the children of Israel out of the Midianites' bondage, Gideon was skeptical. He reminded the angel that he was from the tribe of Benjamin, the weakest tribe in all Israel. And he was the smallest person in his family. Gideon apparently saw himself as the most insignificant person in the entire nation of Israel. Yet Gideon was willing to ask God for further confirmation of His will. And God provided it in the miracle of the fleeces.

Gideon chose to obey God even against his own logic. He obeyed in spite of his own perspective. The rest of the story in the Book of Judges reveals his willingness to act in faith; to follow God despite all logic; and in so doing, to prove himself the mighty warrior God saw from the beginning. When God told Gideon he had assembled too many men, Gideon remained obedient. He had every reason to believe he would fail when God eventually reduced the force to only three hundred. But he was willing to risk failure, as the world defines *failure*, in order to succeed, as the Lord defines *success*. And he did succeed because he did not remain passive to God's calling. He acted on his faith, totally depending on God while giving 100 percent of his own abilities.

God requires the same kind of active faith when you pursue the vision He gives you. When God began telling me He wanted me to pursue Christian ministry, I so feared making the wrong decision that I wouldn't make any decision at all. I feared moving forward if it was not truly His will, and I feared holding back if it was. Finally, after months of struggle I made a decision. It was the easy one, the safe one, but I was to learn that it was not the best one. But by making that decision, I acted, and God further directed me from there. And because He is willing to work with us wherever we are, I could later view it not as the wrong choice but simply as not the best choice. Because I acted instead of refusing to move, God began directing me along the path He desired.

As you pursue your goals, God focuses more on whether your heart is right and whether you are acting in good faith toward Him than on the decision you actually make. In my struggles about Christian ministry I decided that God did not want me in Christian work. After making that decision, I felt free to begin pursuing other things I believed He wanted. But as I pursued those things, God then redirected me. When I moved, then God moved.

On the other hand, your decisions are not to be flippant. God may provide insight into your decision through the counsel of godly, wise Christians. Prayer is also an avenue by which God may provide greater insight. He said in Jeremiah 33:3, " ' "Call to me and I will answer you and tell you great and unsearchable things you do not know." ' " God answers prayer. Before you make a decision, it is also wise to give God ample time to speak to you through the Bible. Through the Holy Spirit, God sometimes provides insight into Scripture that relates to the decision you need to make. If you receive "coincidental" insights at a moment you are looking for direction from God, accept those occurrences as His leading and act on them. If the choice is still not clear, make a decision in faith that He will superintend your choice in accordance with His plan for your life.

If God wanted, He could write His will across the sky. He could give you a million insights to help you make a decision. Sometimes He does; but other times He gives you only three. His purpose is not to frustrate you; it is to mature you. If God never gave you the freedom to make poor decisions, you would never mature to know how to make right ones. Hebrews 5:14 says, "Solid food is for the mature, who by constant use have trained themselves to distinguish good from evil." Maturity comes from practice. And practice comes from making choices. So when you begin setting goals, it is entirely consistent with

God's ways for Him sometimes to place before you two good options to choose from. If you choose one when He desires the other for you, He is more than able to alter the circumstances of your life to redirect you.

Faith is not a passive activity. It is an act of moving forward with the understanding you have, trusting God to guide your steps along the way. This is an important scriptural principle to remember when setting and pursuing your ministry goals.

The Need for Flexible Goals

Often, you will set a goal and begin pursuing it, but the goal may be altered while you are in process. You may begin with one result in mind but may end with an entirely different one. God's goals for your life are dynamic. They may stay the same from conception to completion. On the other hand, they may change once you are in process. The key is to remain flexible to God's leadership as you pursue your goals.

You may set goals in light of your dream or vision, but God may have other means in mind for reaching it. Be open to His sovereign plan for your life. God's altering the course of your life in the midst of your pursuit does not mean that you have failed. If you have pursued your goal in faith, God was using the goal to move you in a direction for a purpose; the final goal was not necessary for His purposes to be accomplished. If it had been, He would have enabled you to reach that goal.

Genesis 24 reflects the need to be flexible in pursuing the goals God has given you. Abraham told his servant to find a wife for his son, Isaac. The servant was instructed not to take a wife from among the Canaanites but to return to Abraham's home country. The servant was told, " 'The Lord ... will send his angel before you so that you can get a wife for my son' " (Gen. 24:7).

It is important to note what the servant did not do. He did not return to his tent to pray: "Lord, tell me who she is, and I'll go get her. Just let me know what You want, and I'll do it." Such a prayer would sound very much like an act of faith, but it would actually be an act of cowardice. It would be a religious response from fear rather than an affirmative step of faith. If the Lord through Abraham had told the servant to wait in the tent until He told him whom to choose, then the servant should have waited. To have done otherwise would have been presumptuous. But the servant did what his master, Abraham, told him to do: he went. When faith requires action, nothing else will suffice.

The servant did not begin with all the information he needed. Abraham had given him certain guidelines to follow. The woman was not to be a Canaanite but a woman from Abraham's homeland. And if God should not provide, the servant was free from his commitment to find a wife for Isaac. He needed more information than that to make a wise choice, but he knew enough to begin pursuing his goal of finding a wife for Isaac. By acting on faith, he knew that God would reveal more as he went. In the process he remained sensitive to God's leading and flexible to divine directives he might receive along the way.

After the servant discovered the bride for Isaac, he said, " 'As for me, the Lord has led me on the journey' " (Gen. 24:27). "On the journey the Lord led me," not "as I waited in my tent, the Lord led me," not "after I had all of the details, I began to pursue my goal." He said that God showed him the way while he was on the journey. In this case the goal was realized. Abraham's dream was to have a godly lineage through Isaac. His vision was to initiate this by finding Isaac a wife from his homeland. His goal was to send his servant to make this vision a reality. And the servant was open to God's leadership while he was in route. The result was success for Abraham and glory for God.

The Value of Goals

In his book *First Things First* Stephen Covey writes:

> Vision is the best manifestation of creative imagination and the primary motivation of human action. It's the ability to see beyond our present reality, to create, to invent what does not yet exist, to become what we not yet are. It gives us the capacity to live out of our imagination instead of our memory. … We all have some vision of ourselves and our future. And that vision creates consequences. More than any other factor, vision affects the choices we make and the way we spend our time.[2]

Covey is right. Power and motivation germinate in you when you set clear goals.

When motivational speaker Zig Ziglar talks about the importance of goals, he tells the tongue-in-cheek story of what would have happened if Sir Edmund Hillary, the first man to ascend to the summit of Mount Everest, had not had

start a revolution

clear goals when he began his journey. After he reached the top of the highest mountain in the world, reporters would have asked him, "Sir Edmund, how did you ever manage to climb the highest mountain in the world?" Sir Edmund would have replied: "I don't know. I just went out walking one day for a stroll, got carried away and before I knew it, there I was standing on top of the world!" What a ridiculous story, says Ziglar.[3] Sir Edmund Hillary scaled the highest mountain in the world because he had a vision, and he clarified that vision by establishing tangible goals that would allow him to get there.

The value of goals is that they enable you to go beyond the world of imagination into the world of actuality. Goals put feet to your dreams, allowing you to pursue them in realistic ways that make your dreams realities. For Christians, setting goals has a spiritual dimension.

Goals Reflect God's Will

God leads believers with visions He places inside their hearts and minds. Psalm 37:4 reveals how God often works in Christians who desire to pursue His will:

> Delight yourself in the Lord
> and he will give you the desires of your heart.

This verse is not a blank check from God; it's a conditional promise. If you delight yourself in Him, He will give you the desires of your heart. But carefully note what God gives you. He gives you desires. It does not say, "Delight yourself in God, conceive your own desires, and bring them to God to make them come true." That would make God merely a Santa Claus. When you truly delight in God, your love for Him creates in you the desire to have nothing in your life that does not please Him. And it creates in you the desire to cultivate in your life everything that pleases Him. When you truly delight in God, He lets you know what pleases Him by giving you internal desires.

Those desires, once realized, begin to translate in your mind and heart into a goal. It is not an overnight process. Some desires from God enter your heart as suddenly as a camera flash; others come like the rising sun. Both are valid and valuable for the same reason: they reflect God's will for your life.

It is crucial to recognize that desires are not to be automatically assumed to be God's will. The major prerequisites to your desires are your love for and commitment to God. Only when these elements live in your heart can you move with more confidence toward your desires. Otherwise, what you value may not truly be what God wants you to value. Stephen Covey recognized the importance of having the right values in life when he wrote:

> There are plenty of people … who tell us that achieving what they valued did not bring them quality of life. Consciously or unconsciously, these people acted on values that seemed very important at the time. They set goals and focused powerful effort to achieve their priorities. But when they got what they wanted, they found it didn't bring the results they expected. The fact that we may value something at any particular time in our lives does not necessarily mean that achieving it will bring lasting happiness. History is filled with examples of individuals and societies that got what they valued—and it didn't bring "success" or happiness. Sometimes, in fact, it destroyed them.[4]

Goals Motivate You to Achieve

When your desires lead you to set goals, these goals motivate you to take action. When you are in action, God can more easily direct you in the course He has planned.

The greatest motivation to achieve anything comes from the internal desires of your heart. This is why God places such desires inside you. But He does that only when the focus of your heart and mind is to love Him and please Him (see Ps. 37:4). Pursuing your desires is the most natural thing in the world for you. So if God places His desires in you, your pursuit of them will become your pursuit of God. Thus, another value of setting goals is that it becomes a tangible target that motivates you from within to achieve God's will for your life and to do so in a way that brings Him glory.

Goals Clarify Direction

Having clear goals helps you clarify the direction of your life. You could get involved in a number of worthwhile pursuits. But sometimes the greatest enemy of excellence is that which is merely good. You can do a lot of things with competence, or you can do a few things with excellence. Deep-seated, personal goals move you beyond being a generalist to a person with a passionate thirst for excellence. By pursuing those goals, you begin to define your life, determining the course you take each day. Clear goals don't discount difficulties or make the path of life smoother, but they can eliminate aimless wandering as you try to find a purpose for life. When your goals in life are clear, you can view every circumstance as either impeding or advancing your progress toward your dream.

Goals Strengthen Your Character

Defining your goals helps shape the character of your life. Zig Ziglar aptly says, "What you will get from reaching your objective is not nearly as important as what you will become by reaching that objective."[5] Single adults who discover their dreams and begin to pursue them will mature in their walks with God and will adjust their priorities to enable them to achieve their goals. Often, the focus of goal setting is on doing something. But before you can do something, you have to be something. And being is much harder than doing.

Personal character is vital to pursuing and achieving your goals (see Ps. 37:4). Before God gives you the desires of your heart, your number one focus must be loving God. That focus is character. It's what you are and who you are. Your character—who you are—influences the goals you set. But setting and pursuing those goals mentally and emotionally support your perception of who you are.

When the apostle Paul wrote his first letter to the church at Corinth, he addressed a group of Christians who were far from demonstrating a godly lifestyle. Paul addressed such issues in the church as divisions over heroes, jealousy, strife, arrogance, sexual immorality, lawsuits among believers, debates about diet, getting drunk at the Lord's Supper, abusing spiritual gifts, self-exaltation, and questioning Christ's resurrection. These people had problems! Yet Paul addressed them as "the church of God which is at Corinth, to those who have been sanctified in Christ Jesus, saints by calling" (1 Cor. 1:3). Literally, the word *saints* means *holy ones*. Was he serious? Why would he call these people holy? Why would he say that they are sanctified—set apart as holy? Had I been writing that letter, I would have said, "To you bunch of godless, pagan-minded, heathen people: What in the world do you think you're doing?"

But Paul knew that seeing themselves as holy because of Jesus Christ would affect their character, which would affect their goals or pursuits in life, which would affect their actions, which would reinforce their view of themselves as holy children of God.

You live from your belief system. Your values and actions are based on what you believe about yourself. That is why God calls you holy even when you don't necessarily feel or act holy. If you begin to believe the Bible's message for believers in Christ—that you are truly holy—your actions will begin to change to agree with your belief. When you sin, your response will not be "Well, after all, I'm just a sinner." The natural response of persons who see their essence as sinful is to sin. All children of God sin, and their sins are covered by God's grace. But for believers, sinning is not natural. The most natural thing for newly created believers in Christ to do is to be godly and holy, for that is what they are.

Examine your goals. They may reflect your character and reveal how you see or feel about yourself. When you let God give you desires that come from Him and when He raises your sights for loftier goals in life, your aspirations for achieving those goals will force you to evaluate your sense of worthiness to achieve them. The result will be a stronger character.

God never gives you success in reaching a goal because you deserve it; He does so because He is a gracious God who lovingly gives good gifts to His children. Your worthiness to achieve your goals is solely because of the work He has done in your life through Jesus Christ. That understanding allows you to give Him the honor and glory when each goal is achieved.

Hearing God's Voice

What if you don't have any desires, at least any you are aware of? What if you don't have any visions or dreams? Does this mean that you do not love God or that He does not love you? No, it simply means that you have not stopped long enough to hear the calling of your heart and the calling of God. He may place desires in your heart, but they may not come to the surface until you begin to conceptualize them through more concrete thinking.

Learning how to recognize God's voice is very important, but it is not simple. That is by God's design. Human nature usually doesn't appreciate things acquired relatively easily, not even relationships. That includes our relationship with God. But the result is more than worth the effort.

The way to learn to recognize God's leading in your life is to get to know Him in a deeply personal way. Personal relationships take time, trial, sacrifice, and compromise. You might have a hard time recognizing the voice of some-

start a revolution

one who calls you only once a year, especially if you're not expecting the call. But the person you talk with every week by phone could call you at 3:00 a.m., and you would immediately recognize her voice. Because you have spent time with her, a bond has developed that allows you to know each other in ways not possible with casual acquaintances.

The same is true with God. Do you want to hear His calling in your life? Spend time with Him and listen. Pursue what you believe is His calling, and He will direct you otherwise if it is not. Sometimes you will be correct; other times you will not. But through that process you will learn.

A young mother once took her three-year-old daughter to the state fair. The noise was deafening. People screamed on the roller coaster. Barkers yelled through bullhorns to entice people to their booths. Boom boxes blared everywhere. People laughed, yelled, and talked above the noise as best they could. But this mother and her little girl were having fun. For security the mother held her daughter's hand. But at one point, for about one minute, the mother became so enamored with something that her grip loosened on her little girl. The girl, attracted by a giant teddy bear at another booth, wandered from her mother. When her mother regained her concentration, she looked down and realized that her daughter was gone. Panic struck her! Had her little girl been kidnapped? This would be a perfect place with all the noise and confusion. She quickly combed the immediate area, hoping to find her little girl behind someone standing there. But she was gone.

At that moment the frightened mother began to call her daughter's name as loudly as she could. Somehow she was able mentally to block out the roller coaster, the barkers, the boom boxes, and the noises of the crowd to listen for and hear the voice of the one little girl she knew was hers. Within a couple of minutes the mother found her daughter because their bond enabled her to recognize the girl's voice in the midst of the chaos.

Spiritually, that is what happens to you every day. You live in a chaotic world. Everywhere you turn, voices and noises scream at you. You need to develop a bond with God so that in the midst of the noise you can recognize His voice when He calls to you. That bond comes by spending time with Him, learning from wrong choices, and communing with Him as a person rather than just as an authority figure. As you develop this relationship, you enhance your ability to hear His calling in your life.

Characteristics of Good Goals

You cannot have as your goal to be a better person or a better Christian. That is not a goal. It may be a genuine desire or a general life principle, but it is not a goal. Goals have certain elements that define them as either good or vague. Five primary elements are essential to every goal worth pursuing. Good goals are challenging, specific, attainable, measurable, and adaptable.

All five elements are necessary. If a goal is challenging, attainable, and measurable but not specific enough for you to know what you are trying to achieve, you will not know the best path to take to reach it. If your goal is specific, attainable, and measurable but not personally challenging, you will lack motivation. If it is challenging, specific, and measurable but not attainable, you will never know whether you reach your goal. If you set a goal that is challenging, specific, and attainable, but you can't measure your progress, you will never know whether you reach all of your goal on time, some of your goal late, or something in between. If your goal is not adaptable, you will miss excellent opportunities God sends along the way because you are unable to adjust your perception of your goals over time. Good goals must be challenging, specific, attainable, measurable, and adaptable.

Good Goals Are Challenging

God has always challenged His people to achieve things they previously thought they could not accomplish. He challenged Abram (later known as Abraham) and Sarah to believe Him when He said she would give birth in her old age. He challenged Moses to lead the children of Israel when Moses had no confidence in his leadership abilities. He challenged Gideon to lead Israel in battle when he saw himself as insignificant. He challenged Peter to walk on water on a night when he had been afraid of drowning. And God still challenges you and me today.

Goals should force you to move outside your comfort zone. When God sets your goals, you will be challenged. As you listen to Him and follow, you grow. And with every step of growth you begin to perceive yourself as succeeding in life, not because you have arrived but because you have learned to pursue life's goals with God's perspective.

Ask God to help you dream big! After all, He is a big God. He has said,

"No eye has seen,
    no ear has heard,
no mind has conceived
    what God has prepared for those who love him—
but God has revealed it to us by his Spirit" (1 Cor. 2:9-10).

God has great plans for your life. He wants you to listen to Him and to let Him help you establish challenging goals.

Good Goals Are Specific

You can't reach a goal you don't have. You must be specific when you set goals. If a single guy asked an entire roomful of single women if they would like to get married, all might say yes. But if he asked a particular woman in that room to marry him, she would probably say no! That's the difference between a general idea and a specific goal. Specific goals are narrow and clearly defined.

Having specific goals allows you to make better decisions that could influence your life. If you set as a specific goal to be out of debt by a certain time, and a great deal on a car comes your way that would place you deeper in debt, remembering your specific goal of achieving financial freedom could help you avoid an impulsive purchase.

Good Goals Are Attainable

Saying that a goal is attainable doesn't mean that you necessarily know how it will be attained. Sometimes God leads you to pursue a goal, but you do not know how you will attain it. You know only that it could happen.

When God called Abram to go to the land of Canaan, He did not tell Abram where to go to; He told him only from where to go: " 'Leave your country, your people and your father's household and go to the land I will show you' " (Gen. 12:1). Abram did not know how God was going to bless him, but he knew that goal was attainable.

Later, when God said He would allow Sarah to give birth in her old age, Abram initially questioned whether that goal could be attained, for this went beyond logic and experience (see Gen. 15:2). But in Hebrews 9:11 he is called the father of our faith because even when he could not see how God could attain such a miracle, he believed that God would keep His word. God gave a vision to Abram about the blessing He was to give to him:

> After this, the word of the Lord came to Abram in a vision:
> "Do not be afraid, Abram.
>> I am your shield,
>> your very great reward."
> He took him outside and said, "Look up at the heavens and
> count the stars–if indeed you can count them." Then he said
> to him, "So shall your offspring be." Abram believed the Lord,
> and he credited it to him as righteousness" (Gen. 15:1,5-6).

God told Abram to think big! Abram did think big, and he chose to believe all God said He was going to do. God placed in him the desire to be a blessing to the world. Abram believed, and through him one day that blessing came: Christ the Lord. When Abram believed, God honored him for it and began to make the dream a reality.

Good Goals Are Measurable

Zig Ziglar tells a story that demonstrates the need for measurable goals. A team of basketball players came out to practice before the game and went through their dribbling routines. But when they approached the backboard to shoot, they discovered that no hoops (also known as goals) were on the backboards. Approaching the coaches and officials, they complained: "There are no goals up there! How do you expect us to win a game if we can't score points?" Ziglar says that the same is true of life. If you have no measurable goals in life, how do you know whether you are ahead or behind, winning or losing? You need measurable goals to track your progress or lack of it.[6]

Good Goals Are Adaptable

Often, a long-range goal must be adapted when you get close to reaching it. The fulfillment of a goal may not be the way you envisioned it at the beginning. More than one way exists to reach a destination.

No one grows up with aspirations of failing in life. And no Christian dreams of failing in ministry. For a Christian, failure is never final. By virtue of your faith alone, you are an eternal success from God's perspective. But in the day-to-day affairs of this life you have experiences that you and others might label as failures. In fact, they may be. But this doesn't mean that these failures define who you are. For example, many people do not know that Babe Ruth struck out at bat more than any other baseball player before his time. But Babe Ruth was considered a baseball success because of his home runs. Sometimes when you step up to bat, you strike out. Things will not go as you expect them to. But it is most important that you keep coming back, that you keep stepping up to the plate. It's true that if you stay away from the batter's box, you will never strike out again. But it's equally true that unless you step up to the batter's box, you will never get a hit. You cannot hit a home run sitting on the bench.

As a Christian, you have the presence of the Holy Spirit, who can help you overcome any temporary setback, any momentary lapse of moral judgment, any rebellion against God, or any sin. The best way to begin is to make the decision to take tangible steps to move forward with your life. Setting goals will help you do just that.

Your goals must be adaptable because God is at work in your life. His sovereignty supersedes even your greatest plans and actions. God is actively involved in carrying out His plan in your life. Your choices, actions, mental plans, and unexpected events can be governed by God. As a Christian pursuing the goals you believe are from God, you can rest in knowing that He is more interested in your succeeding than you are! In His own way and time He will lead you.

Joseph's story is a clear picture of God's sovereignty in a person's life (see Gen. 37–50). His life course was drastically altered when his brothers sold him into slavery. Over many years Joseph endured the life of a slave and was falsely accused of attempted rape, which led to his imprisonment for several years. But God was still working His sovereign will in Joseph's life, even though Joseph probably could not understand God's purpose in his circumstances.

In prison Joseph accurately interpreted the dreams of two of Pharaoh's servants. Several years later, when one of the servants had been returned to service, he spoke to Pharaoh about Joseph when the Pharaoh wanted to have some disturbing dreams interpreted. Joseph interpreted the dreams, and Pharaoh exalted him to the second most powerful position in Egypt.

When a drought hit Israel, Joseph's family came to Egypt to ask for food. After revealing his identity, Joseph made a statement to his brothers that reflected his awareness of God's sovereignty: " 'You intended to harm me, but God intended it for good to accomplish what is now being done, the saving of many lives' " (Gen. 50:20). Joseph had arrived—but not in a way anyone would have predicted.

Clarify your dreams. Write them down and verbalize them. Commit them to God. But also be aware that God's route to reach those goals may be different from yours. If God takes you along an unexpected path, trust His judgment. Even if you encounter pain and evil or your path takes an unexpected turn, acknowledge that God can use these events to bring about His intended purposes for your life.

Practical Guidelines for Setting Goals

The following guidelines can help you craft goals that can clarify your direction in life. Use them as a general guide rather than a regimented procedure.

Write Your Personal Life Goal

Just as corporations have vision statements, you need to have a written life goal to define who you see yourself to be. This statement says, "This is what I want my life to be all about."

My personal life goal is this: "I want to be used by God to make the biggest impact possible in His kingdom for His glory." When I have a decision to make, this is one filter through which I evaluate it. Which choice would allow me the greatest opportunity to achieve my personal life goal? If one option is clear, the decision is made. If choices seem equally balanced, I use more specific goals to help influence my decision. Of course, in making every decision, you should pray, search the Bible for insight, and seek godly counsel.

It is best to keep your statement small, but size is not as crucial as your understanding of your life goal. If it's clear to you, keep it. It will help you make some of life's major decisions.

Establish Major Objectives in Four Primary Areas

Luke 2:52 capsulizes about 20 years of Jesus' life this way: "Jesus grew in wisdom and stature, and in favor with God and men." This statement reflects four major areas of your life. Wisdom refers to your mental growth. Stature refers to your physical development. Being in favor with God addresses your spiritual relationship with God. And being in favor with others concerns your ability to develop healthy social and relational skills.

While your personal life goal encompasses every area of your life, these objectives categorize your goal in four areas. The objectives are also to be governed by the characteristics of good goals and can change occasionally during the course of your life. These four areas should help you evaluate all of your activities and priorities to help you determine whether your growth is balanced.

For example, if you become intensely involved in church activities, volunteering for every conceivable task, other persons might see such actions as spiritual. However, if you become involved in these activities to avoid developing genuine relationships, your life will never be fulfilling. Something will always be missing, and adding more religious functions to the calendar will not solve the problem. God wants you to grow in every area of life. To avoid one area and attempt to compensate by working twice as hard in another area will not solve your problem, just as putting an excessive amount of air in one good tire cannot compensate for a flat tire. Eventually, the good tire will explode from overuse.

God wants you to have balance in each area of life. After all, He created your mind, your body, your spirit, and your relationships. His desire is for you to establish objectives that let you have optimal impact in each area. Although setting objectives does not establish balance, it is a tool for reaching it.

Here are examples of objectives in each area.

Mental objective: I will seek opportunities to deepen the gift of knowledge God has given me and to expand my mental horizons in ways that enhance my usefulness to God. A mental objective might be to decide the level of education you want to achieve or to maintain proficiency in an area of knowledge. Today no one can keep up with every bit of information bombarding society. But you can choose to stay abreast of certain areas that enhance your other objectives and goals.

Physical objective: I will reach my optimal weight and will maintain a healthy body through regular exercise, healthful eating habits, and regular checkups. A physical objective might be physical fitness according to medical standards for weight, pulse rate, and blood pressure. Achieving this objective would require learning those standards and deciding how to change your lifestyle to achieve and maintain them.

Spiritual objective: I will deepen my personal devotion to God, will increase my un-

derstanding of His ways, and will broaden my personal ministry as He provides oppor-tunities. Setting spiritual objectives is what much of this book is about, for one spiritual objective is deciding in what area of life you want to become involved in ministry. You have been designed and called by God to contribute to the lives of other persons in ways that bring glory to Jesus Christ. Set a major spiritual objective that will become your initial filter for evaluating every opportunity that comes your way. Be sure that your spiritual objective includes your relationship with God.

One spiritual objective might be to share your faith with your neighbors. If you are as mobile as many single adults, your neighbors provide regular opportunities to invest in other persons' lives for the sake of Christ. You might need to learn how to take initiative to develop relationships. You might need to improve your cooking skills so that you can invite your neighbors over. Perhaps you need to learn how to share your faith.

Social objective: I will improve my communication skills. To pursue this objective, you might need to evaluate your current patterns of communicating to determine what is healthy and what is not. This might involve developing friendships with persons who can give you honest feedback. Communicating might also refer to public speaking. While both aspects of communicating could fit into a broad goal, the detailed objectives for fulfilling each area would be different.

List Your Current Activities

With your personal life statement completed and your four major objectives clarified, it is time to begin assessing your current activities in light of your objectives in life. This list should include every activity in your life, including work, recreation, church, and hobbies. Try to place each activity under one of the four major objectives. If something doesn't fit, create a fifth category called miscellaneous. Some items can belong to more than one category. If possible, determine which category is primary and which is secondary. For example, if you play basketball once a week at the community center, that event could belong to social or physical. Ask yourself why you play basketball. If your primary interest is a physical workout, place it under physical. Is your main interest to develop friendships? Then the activity would be a social objective. Or perhaps your reason for playing basketball is to gain opportunities to share Christ. Then place it in your spiritual-objective category.

The purpose of this exercise is to assess why you do what you do. Often, your activities reveal your personality and internal desires God has been building in you to accomplish a purpose in His kingdom. But they may also reveal an imbalance. If you list 15 regular activities under social and only 1 activity under spiritual, you may need to readjust your priorities to establish balance.

Prioritize Your Top 10 Activities

Examine all of your activities and decide which you would keep and which you would abandon if you could do only 10. Making this list forces you to examine each activity carefully and to determine why you value it over another. This process can reveal unspoken personal values—things you truly deem important in your life. Everyone lives with priorities that are based on values, but many people never bring those values into clear focus. This exercise helps you do that. With clear priorities and an understanding of the values behind them, you can learn how other activities can also help you achieve your objectives.

For example, if one of your spiritual objectives is to share the gospel with your neighbors and one of your social objectives is to become more assertive in relationships, you may choose to combine an activity that advances both. You could move outside your comfort zone by planning a backyard cookout and inviting your neighbors. This would build bridges to them, paving the way to share the gospel someday. The immediate effect would be to help you take more initiative in developing relationships.

Look at your top 10 priorities and notice which activities you give most of your time. If you are spending more time on an event that doesn't relate to your objectives, adjust your schedule to focus on your primary pursuits.

Clarify Your Values, Based on Your Priorities

You made value judgments to list your priorities. The values behind those decisions are keys to setting your specific objectives. Now clarify the values that determine the events and activities in your life.

We are value-based people. We do what we value, and we ignore or are inconsistent with everything else. If the activities in your life reveal a value base that is not what you believe God wants for you, this recognition could be a turning point, beginning a new journey toward God's fullness for you.

List Dreams You Have Not Pursued

Stop now and pray for God's guidance of your thoughts, asking Him to bring to memory dreams of long ago that you let die over the years. Remember, a dream encompasses not smaller events but major interests in life.

Sometimes we didn't pursue dreams because they seemed so remote that we didn't even try to make them realities. Some of those dreams are God-given desires that lie dormant. He may want you to awaken them and pursue them by His leading. Peter never thought he could walk on water, but when he followed Jesus' lead, he did it.

By listing these dreams, you begin to challenge your own belief system. Could God really be saying to me that I can pursue the dreams I once had? Dare I think they could become a reality? If it frightens you a little, you may be afraid to raise your level of hope. If so, ask God to direct you. Then be willing to proceed.

What are your dreams or aspirations? If you had unlimited resources, what would you like to do? What would you like to achieve? What has God placed in your heart to accomplish for His glory? What do you want to be remembered for one hundred years from now? The answers to these questions can reveal your values and inner dreams.

By writing down these dreams, you can better determine exactly what is and is not right for you. List your dreams as you did your current activities. Which is most important to you, more than all of the others? Which is least important? Prioritizing them will help you evaluate your current station in life—whether you are making progress, have plateaued, or are regressing.

When you have prioritized your dreams, compare them to your list of current activities in life. Are the activities that are filling up your days moving you closer to your dreams? If not, they are a deterrent. Don't want to give up your current agenda? Then you must determine what about those things is so important to you that you would rather pursue them than your dreams. By being honest with yourself, you can identify the unspoken fulfillment those activities satisfy. Adding these activities to the mix, refine your list of priorities until your dreams and activities are compatible.

Don't expect every aspect of your life to match perfectly your list of dreams. You may find that most of your present course in life coincides with one dream, while other dreams are not being pursued at all. You may have the dream of being a deeply committed Christian yet notice that your involvement at church or with other godly Christians is minimal. If so, something needs to change. You must decide either to be a mediocre Christian and keep your current course or to keep your dream and change your current path. Saying that you want the dream to become a reality but that you don't intend to change is being dishonest with yourself. Goals can keep you honest if you'll let them. And the clearer you make them, the easier it is to make progress toward accomplishing them.

Setting goals in light of your personality and spiritual gifts is a great start toward the dream of being greatly used by God. When you establish your spiritual goals, you can then find others who share them. Together you can form a ministry team whose work is based on each member's personality strengths and spiritual gifts. You will create a formidable team that has a clear vision and the means to accomplish your incremental goals, broader visions, and life dreams. Your unity will come from the common vision each of you shares for ministry.

Clarifying your vision and setting goals to achieve it is not magic. You must work. And God must still guide you if it is to become a reality according to His will. But this process is truly motivational, for your goals will become a road map for your life. God may change the route, but that is up to Him. In the meantime, setting measurable goals in pursuit of your vision will tell you whether you are on course, have taken a detour, or are driving in the wrong direction. Learning where you are today and where you want to be tomorrow is a great start toward getting there.

---

[1]Father Theodore Hesburgh, as quoted by Tom Peters in *Thriving on Chaos* (New York: Alfred A. Knopf, 1987), 399.
[2]Stephen R. Covey, A. Roger Merrill, and Rebecca R. Merrill, *First Things First* (New York: Simon & Schuster, 1994), 103–4.
[3]Zig Ziglar, *See You at the Top* (Gretna, La.: Pelican, 1977), 155.
[4]Covey, 325–26.
[5]Zig Ziglar, *Goals: How to Set Them, How to Reach Them,* listener's guide for audiotapes (Carrollton, Tex.: Zig Ziglar Corporation, 1988).
[6]Ziglar, *See You at the Top,* 152.

find a place to start

the principle of details

Three things are to be looked to in a building: that it stand on the right spot; that it be securely founded; that it be successfully executed.[1]

—Johann Wolfgang von Goethe

This stage in the process of starting your own revolution is one of the most crucial. It is usually at this stage that most people get off course. Unless you master this step, you may wander through life without realizing your dreams. Knowing your personality traits helps you realize your personal strengths and weaknesses. Discovering your spiritual gifts helps you know how God has enabled and gifted you to work in His kingdom. Clarifying your goals gives you a clearer picture of how you want to pursue that work in His kingdom. Clarifying your goals can also provide needed motivation to make changes in your life. But these changes don't happen automatically. Finding a place to start requires giving attention to the details that enable you to begin pursuing your dreams.

In strategy 6 I encouraged you to begin setting goals by thinking big. The next stage is translating your goals into smaller, achievable objectives, so now you will need to think small. Think of it as designing your own paint-by-number painting. First you must decide what you want the picture to look like when completed. Then you must sketch the painting on a canvas. Then you must paint the complete picture. After this you must painstakingly sketch every shade or nuance of color on a white canvas, list all colors used in the painting, assign a number to each paint, and designate the places it is used in the painting. After you finish, your painting is instantly achievable for almost anyone. The principle of details enables you to discover the power of setting small goals that, when combined, fuel the larger goal of fulfilling your vision.

God's View of the Small Things in Life

Taking time to define and attend to the smaller, seemingly insignificant things in life is not only common sense but also spiritually significant. It is one of the foundational principles through which God operates. In Luke 16 Jesus revealed one of the most overlooked principles of how God works in our lives. Within the Pharisees' hearing range, Jesus told the disciples the parable of the shrewd manager. This manager collected partial payments for his master to fulfill his obligation to collect the monies and, more importantly for him, to place those debtors in debt to him. In summarizing, Jesus stated a principle of God's kingdom: " 'Whoever can be trusted with very little can also be trusted with much, and whoever is dishonest with very little will also be dishonest with much. So if you have not been trustworthy in handling worldly wealth, who will trust you with true riches? And if you have not been trustworthy with someone else's property, who will give you property of your own?' " (Luke 16:10-12). Jesus revealed that God values what we may consider the small things in life. In addition, God does not value what we often consider important: " 'What is highly valued among men is detestable in God's sight' " (Luke 16:15), Jesus said.

Christians often cry, "O God, I want You to use me in a great way for Your glory!" and truly pray that prayer from the heart. But Scripture says that God tests the heart (see Prov. 17:3; 1 Thess. 2:4). When individuals or churches ask to be used in a great way, God tests them by giving them responsibilities they may consider small. It could be keeping records for a single-adult Bible-study group. It could be taking care of a sick family member. It could be financial responsibility. Many times these Christians reject small ministry tasks or responsibilities because they want to remain available to respond when God calls with a grand opportunity.

More often than not, that major opportunity never comes. Seeing irresponsibility with the small things, God knows that irresponsibility will be the response with bigger things. As Jesus asked, " 'If you have not been trustworthy in handling worldly wealth, who will trust you with true riches?' " (Luke 16:11). When God sees Christians neglecting their responsibilities with the smaller things in life, He is hesitant to entrust them with anything larger. If you let someone borrow one hundred dollars and he doesn't pay you back, do you loan him one thousand dollars? Neither does God.

One of the most difficult messages I've ever preached was to a church that was living in corporate irresponsibility, at the same time waiting for God to bless it suddenly and mightily. It's the only time I have not wanted to preach a message God had given me. That message, the principle of Luke 16:10-12, was also a lesson I was to learn myself.

Several years later, as I sensed God's leading me toward another ministry, an opportunity presented itself to join a ministry and work with a man of God I greatly admired. Because the position would not be available until the next year, I had to remain where I was at the time. During that interim period I corresponded and talked on the phone with the man I would be working with. About 10 months later, believing that God was leading me, I resigned my ministry position and moved to Nashville near the time when the ministry was to make the new position available. This was a dream I had had for years, and now it seemed to be coming true.

But two weeks after I resigned and relocated, the ministry's leadership closed the position. I was in emotional shock. I had been certain that God had led me to make the decisions I had made. Every step to that point had seemed to have God's blessing. But now I questioned my judgment. For several months every opportunity I pursued closed in front of me. Had I missed God's leading this much? Why were these doors closing? I searched my life for unconfessed sin but found none. Why would God lead me here, then close all of these doors? I struggled in my confusion.

Then God reminded me of the principle in that message I had preached—the principle of small things. In moving, I had mentally positioned myself to be mentored by this great man of God, but I had lost sight of the little things. I knew now that I needed to get a job and begin supporting myself.

The first job I found was as a video clerk. My boss was a high-school student who cursed like a sailor and couldn't have cared less that I was a Christian. At first I found myself thinking, *After seven years of college, five years of graduate school, and five years of full-time ministry, I have been reduced to taking orders from a high-school student with a foul mouth.* From my perspective that job as a video clerk was pretty small. But following the principle of small things, I decided that this job would make me either bitter or better. Whether or not I liked it, God had given me that job. So I decided to accept where God had placed me and to work with all my heart as for the Lord and not for people (see Col. 3:23).

In time my high-school-student boss moved on. A new person was brought in after I declined the job offer. I trained the new person, who was closer to my age, and had numerous opportunities to counsel her over spiritual struggles. I was also able to build many friendships with wonderful persons, some of whom are still friends. I was given opportunities to minister to many persons I would have never encountered if I had not chosen to be faithful in the little things.

The temptation when I first got this job was to be angry at God and not to take the job seriously. After all, a video clerk with a master's degree? Not exactly required in the job description. But any work is honorable—especially when you know that God has given you that job. To be irresponsible in that job would have been to reject the gift God had given me. James 1:17 says, "Every good and perfect gift is from above, coming down from the Father of the heavenly lights, who does not change like shifting shadows." Any job, any work, any responsibility God gives you is not to be taken lightly. It is a gift from God. Only when you are faithful with the little things God places in your hands will He entrust you with anything larger.

Discovering Where to Start

Because God values the little things in life, you must place high value on the little things as you pursue your life goals. The following steps will help you reduce your larger goals into smaller components. Although these apply to every area of your life goals, I will focus only on your ministry goal.

Suppose you wanted God to use you to minister to an indigent community in your city. You have driven through that area on your way home from work, and the needs of the people have captured your heart. You don't see them as inferior or especially sinful. You just know that these hurting people need tangible help and spiritual direction. You've considered helping before, but after all, you're not a trained minister. What can you do? So you let the dream drift—until now. You've decided that you truly want to start a revolution. You want to move the world with the message of Jesus. And right now the world encompasses those 15 or 20 blocks of hurting people. Where do you start?

Begin with the End in Mind

First, with your ministry goal in mind, ask yourself what you want to accomplish with this ministry. If it progresses and succeeds, what specifically do you want to see happen? What will it look like at the end? Answering this question will help you recognize what the ministry will include. Don't assume anything here. For example, the founders of a successful restaurant chain recently said they are not in the food business; they are in the image business. In other words, the restaurant is not the end; it is only a means to an end. Therefore, they plan to branch into several other types of businesses that have nothing to do with food but everything to do with the image they wish to sell. Understanding the result you want to achieve makes it easier to identify multiple ways to accomplish your goal. Beginning with the end in mind fosters creativity, a necessary ingredient for ministry.

A results orientation also enables you to communicate with others who join your team. Without a clear focus, team members can make wrong assumptions about the ministry. When you propose changes, you may clearly see that they support the goal you have in mind. But team members may not see this relationship if they do not share your understanding of what the ministry is about. Their response may be to resist, and you will have dissension in your ranks. That's a sure sign of a lack of clear direction.

Face Your Fear

It is common at this point in establishing your ministry to begin feeling a bit overwhelmed. After all, perhaps you have never actually led the formation of any kind of Christian work. You could easily begin telling yourself that you aren't sure that you have what it takes to be a real leader.

Contrary to what many may say, any person can be a leader. It doesn't take a certain personality. You don't need a certain amount of charisma or magnetism. You don't have to be flamboyant, excessive, loud, or any of the characteristics you may visualize when you think of a leader. Even though you learned in strategy 2 about each personality trait's strengths and weaknesses, that does not mean that only one or two personality types can lead. The key to finding your leadership style is to develop a style that fits your personality. If your personality is quiet by nature, you will never feel comfortable using a style that is flashy and loud. You will need to develop your style to fit you. But realize that if God calls you into a certain area of ministry, He has equipped you to use your gifts and your personality to lead in that ministry.

The apostle Paul's prayer for the Ephesian Christians reveals that God empowers every Christian to dream God's dreams and to fulfill them through

Him. Paul wrote, "To him who is able to do immeasurably more than all we ask or imagine, according to his power that is at work within us ..." (Eph. 3:20). Your prayer and your imagination are at work, but God's power is also working within you to accomplish more than you can imagine! When you move out of your comfort zone with the prayer for God to use you in ministry, something powerful begins to happen: God begins to move through you to affect the lives of others. That is the essence of leadership. Every Christian has all of the resources of God Himself to accomplish His will.

When you are afraid, acknowledge your fear to God, but keep moving forward. If God wants to alter your direction, He is more than powerful enough to do so. But don't let fear hinder your discovering the deep blessings God has in store for you when you obey His leading. Leadership is not the absence of fear or the accumulation of knowledge. It is obedience in spite of the presence of fear and in spite of the lack of knowledge you may have at the time. God honors obedience. If you obey, fear can dissipate, and knowledge can increase. Rarely does that happen before you obey. What do you need to begin the process of leadership? Only obedience.

Determine the Skills and Persons Required

What abilities and persons will be needed to launch and grow this ministry? At this point you begin thinking through some of the details that will come into play when the ministry begins. The more details you can anticipate in the beginning, the easier it will be to determine the types of team members needed to begin the ministry.

At the beginning you may not know all of the skills that will be needed. Some needs will become evident only when you get involved in the ministry. But you can determine some needs at first. For example, you know that you will need bilingual team members because some residents of this community do not speak English. You know that you will need someone who understands the lifestyle of the area, someone who can answer questions like: Are there gangs in the neighborhood? Is crime high? Will the people be receptive to someone of different ethnicity? You know that you will need to learn about specific needs for physical care. You will need someone who has worked in this area to join your team or to act as a consultant as you gain knowledge. These types of questions will help you determine who is needed to form the team.

Now you are ready to apply what you learned about the team concept to your specific ministry goal. At this point you have clarified your ministry goal enough for others to decide if they want to be involved. Often, God places the same desire in the hearts of several persons, wanting them to find one another and work together. This is what the concept of Christian body life is all about: people coming together with various strengths and weaknesses to achieve a common goal. The more effectively you can position persons according to their strengths, the more effectively you can launch your ministry.

When you've gathered your team members, they should study this book to determine their personality traits, discover their spiritual gifts, and understand the team concept.

Consider Practical Elements

Every ministry involves practical necessities. What will you call your ministry? If you decide to promote the ministry through a brochure or a handout, who will design your material? How will you be financially supported? Perhaps your church will help. Will the ministry have a physical facility in the community? If so, where? How will you pay for it? If not, where can people reach you or the ministry? If it is located in a home, will callers reach a recording, or will someone be there to answer the phone? Do you need an extra phone line besides your personal one?

Determine What Needs to Be Learned

Especially when you are beginning a ministry that is new to you, you can expect a lengthy learning curve. The amount of time required depends on the complexity of the ministry. You will need to list the kinds of knowledge that need to be acquired. Here are examples:
  • Language
  • Culture
  • Physical needs
  • Spiritual needs
  • Emotional needs
  • The most effective means to address needs
  • Financial accounting methods if required
  • Legal requirements if any

- Christian materials for the ministry
- Number of team members needed
- Principles of discipleship
- Safety precautions
- History of previous ministries in the community
- Knowledge of current ministries in the community if any
- The best time to launch the ministry
- The first kind of ministry to begin
- Measurement of progress

These are just a few areas to consider early in the process. This stage is the point at which many people quit. Choosing not to do the detailed work required to make their dreams a reality, they drift along as if one day the answer to their dreams will fall out of the sky. But a wise person has said that if you want your dreams to come true, you need to wake up and go after them! Many people dream of success, but fewer wake up and work hard to achieve it. Going through this process is not easy at first, but it will save you many headaches down the road. If you have a personality type that is not good with details, one of your first tasks should be finding someone who is.

Consult with Your Team Members

Assemble persons who are interested in working on this project and ask them to share any details or questions that haven't been addressed. They will think of questions and issues you didn't think of. They will raise concerns that escaped you. They will also think of innovations that will help. They will have networks of other persons and resources that you do not have. As you discuss these aspects of what is needed, seek to develop personal ownership by each member. Make members feel that their questions and comments count, that they are being heard, that they are contributing to the progress of the goal. They must recognize that they are fulfilling their dreams, just as you are fulfilling yours. By involving the team members at the formation stage, you allow them to shape the ministry. This early involvement is key to a successful ministry.

Assign Work Responsibilities

The better you understand team members' strengths, the easier it will be to help them find their niches in this ministry. You will need members with good people skills who can meet the public and can develop relationships easily. You will need creative members who can devise unique ways to communicate the message of Christ and the ministry you offer. You will need detail-oriented members who prefer to work behind the scenes to handle the day-to-day actions that are vital to any ministry. Work with the team to match members' strengths with the tasks that need to be done. If you have more than one person with the same strength, let these members work together as a subteam.

It is wise not to stop with just agreeing to various assignments. Set due dates for team members to report their findings to the team. This aspect of team accountability fosters responsibility. When every team member acts responsibly, progress proceeds at a steady pace.

Assemble Data and Make Action Plans

Now that each member is working to fulfill his or her responsibilities, schedule a meeting for reports to the team. The purpose is to be able to make more intelligent decisions based on knowledge instead of speculation. Perhaps a team member discovers that two major ethnic groups live in the community: Hispanic and Vietnamese. The team member speaks Spanish but not Vietnamese. The team must decide whether to bring someone into the team who speaks Vietnamese or to reach out only to the Hispanic part of the community until it is established, expanding the ministry to the Vietnamese people later.

If you discover that the community is largely illiterate, your publicity will be affected. What good are beautiful brochures if you give them to people who cannot read? Such knowledge is crucial to making action plans.

Don Richardson was a missionary with Wycliffe Bible Translators, living with a tribe that prided itself on its ability to deceive people. It took a long time for Don to learn the tribe's language, but finally, the day came when he gathered the tribal leaders and anxiously told them the story of Jesus. Much to his dismay, when he told them about Judas's betrayal, they laughed and admired Judas as the hero! They thought it was wonderful that he had successfully deceived Jesus.

For months Don struggled to find a way to reach these people. Then a war broke out with a neighboring tribe. After several persons had been killed on both sides, the chief of his tribe did something to end the fighting. The tribes in this country had a custom. To bring peace between two warring tribes, the chief of one tribe would give one of his babies to the chief of the other tribe to rear as his own. The child was called a peace child. In effect, the chief covenanted never to fight against the other tribe again because if they fought, he or one of his tribe members might kill his own son.

In this transaction Don saw the analogy of God the Father's giving us His Son in order to offer us His peace. Giving up the baby was difficult for the chief, for he loved his child. Once again, Don gathered the leaders and explained that Jesus was the Peace Child whom God the Father sent to end His war against us. Through the child Jesus we could have peace with God. The tribe understood that Jesus was God's Peace Child. And Jesus became their Savior.[2] It is crucial to find the best ways to communicate with the people you want to reach.

A team member may report that there are no gangs but a large number of young people in this community. There are also many single parents. Drugs are a problem but not as widespread as it seemed. If such knowledge was gained by talking with police officers who patrol the area, the team member might recommend that an officer come talk with the team about the neighborhood. You don't need to reinvent the wheel in gathering knowledge. If others have already collected it, take advantage of their expertise. Such knowledge can help you determine where to begin the ministry, what age group to target first, what kind of material or literature to use, what needs to address first, and so on.

If one team member reports that a printing company is willing to help with publicity, you can bring these experts into the circle as needed.

If you introduced your single-adult minister to your ministry plans and he was supportive, he might know other church members who could help financially or as resource persons. For example, if the ministry needs to be established as a nonprofit organization, you might have a church member who could outline the legal steps required. Or your single-adult minister may know someone with accounting skills who is looking for a place of ministry.

Your single-adult minister or pastor can be a great resource person. If you want the ministry to become a part of the church's single-adult ministry, be sure to involve your single-adult minister from the beginning. Sometimes your ministry may fit well within the framework of your local church's ministry. In other cases it may need to be broader. Your relationship with your church depends on your ministry's goals and scope.

Get It in Writing

Some persons do not pursue their dreams because they fear the disappointment that the attainment of their dreams will not measure up to their projections. For some, it's better simply to live with the dream than to risk making it a reality that they find disappointing. They live in a continual state of anticipation with no intention of ever reaching fulfillment. Such a life is a shallow existence. God wants you to pursue your dreams.

When you get to the stage of developing strategic actions for making your dream a reality, one of the most powerful tools you can use is a written plan. Writing your plan does not set it in stone. You can and will make changes along the way. But it gives you a road map to follow—a road map that has several advantages.

A written plan incorporates your whole mind. With the technology available today, the human brain has been analyzed, researched, probed, and mapped. Knowledge of the brain is astounding. Scientists know that thoughts are housed in one part of the brain, auditory messages in another, and stimuli leading to action in a third part. To increase your brain's ability to etch your goals in your mind, write them down and verbalize them so that you hear yourself saying them aloud. (That's a creative way to say it's OK to talk to yourself.)

When you both write and verbally communicate your goals, you engage three different parts of your mind in looking for ways to reach your goals. Your subconscious mind works on those goals even when you are consciously focusing on day-to-day matters. When opportunities or choices are presented to you, your subconscious can help either by raising those goals to your conscious level or by subconsciously influencing your decision. That's why sometimes you make a decision and later recognize that it is consistent with your pursuit of your goals. Your mind was working on three different levels.

A written plan increases the exactness of your goals. Sometimes when you write something and read it, you realize that what you see is not exactly what you feel or think. As you examine what you have written, you can sift through the nuances of each word. If something doesn't feel right or look right, your mind may be telling you to be more exact.

Maybe your goal in college is to make the dean's list. But when you look at that goal on paper, you can see that you haven't been precise enough. Your actual goal is not the dean's list but what you believe the dean's list will do for you: open doors for an academic scholarship into a master's program. By making your goal to secure a scholarship for a master's program, you open your mind to other ways that might be possible. An academic scholarship is only one kind among many. Perhaps by stating that succinctly at the beginning, you do not overlook other opportunities that might come your way over a four-year time frame.

Another value of being exact is that it helps others who join the team. The more exact you are in stating your goal, the less frequently you will have to clarify it for others. Being exact facilitates team communication.

A written plan reveals holes in your thinking. When you write your goals, your team's strengths and gifts, your primary objectives, and your plan of action, you can look at the whole picture at once and can spot holes in the process. If your plan of action includes printing brochures or pamphlets, you might find by looking at your written plan that a process for distributing the material is not included. Or you might realize that you don't have a plan to pay for printing the brochure. Writing down your work from beginning to end will help you find the cracks that might not otherwise surface until they have become crises. And crisis management is not a healthy way to conduct a ministry.

A written plan allows you to duplicate the process. Writing down your processes enables you to repeat them later if you want to begin another ministry or pursue other goals. Going through a process is a tremendous learning experience for you and other team members. Recording the team's input clarifies the team's initial intent. Even the little words are important. If you decide to minister *to* a certain group of people, that implies no integration with the team. But if you state that you are going to work *with* a certain group of people, that reveals your intention to win them to Christ, then bring them into your ministry as well. There is a big difference. Having records of these subtle differences may save time and effort if a similar ministry is discussed in the future. In addition, recording parts of the process that did not work can help you remember to change or avoid that mistake in the future.

You may want to keep a journal in addition to simply recording the team's goals, action plans, and discussions. In a journal you can process your thoughts and feelings, as well as the facts. When you need encouragement, you can read earlier entries that recount God's provision through difficult situations. The Scriptures can also serve that purpose: "Everything that was written in the past was written to teach us, so that through endurance and the encouragement of the Scriptures we might have hope" (Rom. 15:4). Read in the Bible about ordinary persons God used mightily because of their faith and in spite of their weaknesses. Your Bible and your journal will help you see that God is using you, too. When you realize what God has done in the past, you gain hope for the present and the future.

One of Beethoven's most beloved symphonies is his Ninth Symphony in D Minor, first performed in May 1824 in Vienna, Austria. Many admirers of this symphony do not know that Beethoven was deaf when he wrote this masterpiece. When the performance ended, someone turned him toward the audience to observe the tremendous response he was getting but could not hear.

Beethoven had a song in his head, a dream if you will. Being deaf, he could have kept the music to himself, playing it only within the confines of his mind. But he chose to write it down, and the world has never been the same . Writing something down can have powerful ramifications that can reach farther than you might ever imagine.

The Potential of Small Starts

Because a ministry begins small does not mean it will stay that way. If a generous friend offered you two options, which would you choose? Your friend offers to give you either $50,000.00 as a lump sum or one penny on the first day of the month, then double that amount each day for 30 days. Your choice? If you chose the large amount up front, you would have chosen the less lucrative option. A penny the first day, doubled every day for 30 days, would generate $5.12 in 10 days. In 15 days it would have become $163.84, not even close to the $50,000.00 you would have received up front. In 20 days that $163.84 would have grown to $5,242.88, about ¹/₁₀ of the money up front. But by the end of 30 days that single penny would have grown to $5,368,709.12! More than 5 million dollars! But it began as only one penny a day.

Some of the greatest accomplishments you make in life and ministry may have very small beginnings. Small beginnings have no bearing on the significance of the final product. Even a giant oak tree begins as just a small acorn.

Also, many great accomplishments in life take time to grow. In the illustration of the penny, even when the number of days was half completed, the total was still only $163.84. Similarly, your actions in pursuit of your goals may take time. If you begin a ministry that doesn't take off like a rocket, don't be discouraged. Remember the penny. Small, slow beginnings can be a blessing from God. They allow you to get your feet in the water, gain the knowledge you need, establish your presence in your ministry, and gather the persons you need. You will then have a healthy foundation to build on. Otherwise, you can become a victim of your own success. Some ministries that have gone up like a rocket have also come down like a rock. Give your work time to take root. God will take care of the increase in His good time.

As much as you might like to, you cannot do everything at the same time. You must decide, on the basis of your strategic plans, what to do first. Although you cannot do everything at the same time, you can do some tasks simultaneously. Here are some tips that can help you move forward realistically with your plans and recognize progress along the way.

Make an Assignment for Every Action

Don't just set an action plan of steps that need to be taken. As the team agrees on each step, a team member should accept responsibility for it. Also set a date for that person to report findings to the team. People are motivated by deadlines. Few people file their income taxes on January 2. Most wait until the deadline gets closer. If people had until the end of the year to file instead of April 15, most taxpayers would not file during the first part of the year. They would wait until closer to the deadline. It's human nature. By giving the responsible members a date to report, you provide them motivation, and you provide a system for monitoring progress.

Begin with Small Successes

If the first tasks team members accept are mammoth, they can easily become overwhelmed and feel discouraged. Start with small tasks or divide large tasks into manageable pieces and make each piece a separate task. It is important not to discourage your team or yourself by taking on too much in the beginning. You can't eat a steak with one giant bite. To try would choke you. Instead, you eat it a bit at the time. Eventually, you consume the entire steak, and you remain free to breathe along the way. Beginning a ministry is the same. Team members need to experience small victories early to help them see progress and success.

Celebrate Victories and Progress

Sometimes you can set your sight on the tasks at hand and not take time to celebrate. Periodically celebrate your progress. Posting a chart that lists your tasks and their completion dates can portray the team's progress. However, list only a few tasks at a time. Looking at all of the steps toward the goal can be discouraging. As the steps are completed and marked off, take time to celebrate their completion.

A big error many people make in pursuing their goals is not to think small enough. After allowing your mind to think big, expand your horizons, and set major goals based on your life's dreams, it can be challenging to go to the other extreme and think of practical details and endless minutiae. But that is a necessary part of making your goals effective. Thinking big allows you to set long-term directions in life; thinking small enables you to see how you can accomplish your big dreams.

In this book you began with small things: your personality traits and spiritual gifts. Then you placed these in the larger framework of your dreams and aspirations to picture ways you want to be used by God. You formed a team of other persons who share the same dream and began setting goals for achieving your dreams. That required setting aside your six-inch paint brush and using a three-inch one. In this strategy I have asked you to set aside your three-inch paintbrush and to fill in the spaces with a fine-line, detail brush.

Handle details, set plans, assign responsibilities, and set deadlines. Learn from your successes and your failures and write them down for future reference. Celebrate small victories and progress early in the process. As you move forward toward your dreams, you will repeat these steps again and again. Realize that they are the means for making your ministry a living reality that changes the lives of the persons you are reaching and your own life, as well.

---

[1] Johann Wolfgang von Goethe, *Elective Affinities*, as quoted by John Bartlett in *Familiar Quotations* (Boston: Little, Brown and Co., 1942), 1057.
[2] Don Richardson, *Eternity in Their Hearts* (Ventura, Calif.: Regal, 1981), 103–4.

b e
flexible

Acts 6:3
II Cor 4:1
Rom. 15:13
Eph. 4:12
Col. 4:17
II Tim. 4:5
Acts 6:4

the principle of innovation and dynamics

I Tim. 1:12

> Many ideas grow better when transplanted into another mind than in the one where they sprang up.[1]
>
> —Oliver Wendell Holmes, Jr.

As you begin to implement the principles and processes you have examined, you will be most likely to succeed if you can be innovative. Innovation is the ability to stimulate change by introducing a new element or a fresh approach. It is the ability to view existing frameworks from a new perspective.

At one time in the automobile-manufacturing industry, each car was made one at a time, using one group of workers for each car. The process was lethargic at best. Henry Ford had a better idea. He standardized assembly functions and spread them along a line of employees, introducing the automobile assembly line. This method not only brought Ford great success but also established a pattern of production that most manufacturers still use today. Ford exercised innovation by taking one idea, the assembly line, and applying it to automobile manufacturing. The results revolutionized the automobile industry. Other manufacturers had the option of changing or dying. Changes were coming. Their responses would be crucial to their futures.

Anytime you work with people to bring about change for the future, as with a ministry team, you can expect things to go differently than you had planned and for things to change along the way. Once you begin plotting your course, you also begin to recognize changes that should be initiated. Your ability to recognize change and to create it is crucial. If you miss these opportunities, you can be left behind in a crucial area of development. It happened to the nation of Israel when Jesus called people to a new way of knowing God: by grace through faith rather than by a priest through sacrifices. Changes were coming to Israel, but the leaders refused to accept them and even fought against them. That didn't stop the change; it only left them to follow the people they thought they were leading.

The earlier story about the Swiss watch manufacturers is another example. When an innovation came along, the leaders refused to accept it. Before they realized their mistake, it cost them the world's market share in the watch industry. They have never recovered it. When innovation happens, those who ride the wave of the future are the ones who learn to respond to change.

Discovering your personality traits and spiritual gifts, creating and building a team, and establishing major goals for ministry are worthy pursuits for your life and for your team members. But an important part of teamwork is to initiate or accept changes when they are called for or when they occur. Flexibility is an absolute necessity. Do all you can to develop this character trait.

Because the model of team ministry is not traditional, you will not find many role models to follow. You will be pioneers—leaders who forge a trail and leave a path for others to follow. Pioneers by definition do not have access to road maps. That is the price you pay to be the first. It is not an easy role, but it is rewarding.

The Characteristics of an Innovator

Innovation comes more easily for some personality types than for others. A high *D*, for example, finds change motivating. A growth edge for a high *D* is to learn not to make changes just for the sake of change. Change is good only if it is beneficial. A *D* is usually attracted to change but needs to learn not to pursue it always. On the other hand, *C*'s find being innovative very challenging. A common trait of *C*'s is a desire for constancy; they like for things to stay the way they are. Security is found not in the revolution of change but in the environment of the familiar.

Regardless of your personality trait, you can develop some of the necessary ingredients of an innovator. Never use your personality trait as an excuse not to grow in an area that may prove difficult. The Holy Spirit can strengthen qualities you need for effective ministry. You can also rely on other team members to help you grow. That's what teamwork is all about.

In *The Creative Corporation* Karl and Steven Albrecht list seven character traits of a person who has the groundwork to be an innovator.[2] All of the traits center on mental flexibility. When you are flexible in your thinking, you have laid the greatest foundation needed to be open to new ideas. Flexibility is the very fabric of innovation.

Tolerance for Ambiguity

Have you ever sat at a table across from someone who continually straightened the items on the table? If your conversation was fairly involved yet you recognized your friend's tendency, have you ever kept talking while slowly moving something out of place just to watch him put it back? Your friend probably wasn't aware that you were having fun with him. He just kept talking and fixing, talking and straightening, talking and putting things in a nice, neat, orderly arrangement.

You can do that with salt and pepper on a tablecloth, but life is more complicated. If you like to see the things around you nice and neat, meticulously placed in their proper places, you probably do not like living with ambiguity in ministry. Your tendency is to box every aspect of the ministry, close it up, and put a pretty ribbon on top. But if you do that with a ministry, you will kill it. Just as life constantly changes, so does ministry. Ambiguity is a natural part of team ministry. You must learn to live with it.

Opinion Flexibility

A ministry team has no manager, no director, no boss, no minister in charge of everything. Different team members take the lead in different areas of the team's work. The leader is the team. Therefore, it is vital that you be flexible enough genuinely to consider each member's opinions as valid.

This is especially difficult when another team member espouses a view that opposes yours. If you have a strong personality, it is easy to use your inherent strength to be intolerant of others' opinions. If you operate that way enough, in time only one view will be expressed on the team—yours. The other members will get the message that their opinions don't count and that yours is the only one that does. If this happens, you will lose valuable, creative minds that are needed to accomplish the team's ministry.

Allowing for various opinions fosters not only team unity but also team creativity. When team members truly believe that their opinions count, they express them more openly and frequently. This is easier for some members than for others. But given the right atmosphere, even the quietest members contribute ideas.

I once began teaching a Sunday-morning Bible-study group of adults in which the previous teacher had used lecture as the primary teaching method. Pure lecture can be good, but it is not my style. I prefer direct interaction with participants because God often shows others truths in a Scripture text that I had never seen. When they express their observations, I learn too.

When I first began teaching this group, I would ask a question and wait for a response. Nothing happened. I would ask the question a second time, thinking perhaps members hadn't realized that it was a question. Silence. I decided to restate the question. Perhaps they simply misunderstood. All I got was a roomful of blank stares. Their faces seemed to say: "What? Do you actually expect us to say something, to get involved, to offer our opinions?" Yes, I did! Because I can be comfortable with silence, I stared back. At first I mused how interesting it would look if someone walked in and saw a teacher and a group staring at each other in total silence. These adults had been led to believe that their opinions were not valuable. Perhaps they had offered them freely at first but in time realized that the leader didn't consider them important. So over time they quit responding at all.

However, I am not one to give up. After several bouts with silence I would call someone by name and ask him to respond. Then I would call on someone else and ask, "Do you agree with Bill?" "Yes," she would respond. "Why?" I asked. Looking a bit perplexed, she realized that I wasn't going to let her off with a simple yes or no. She would respond; then I would ask someone else. When I found someone who disagreed, I began a debate among the members by asking who agreed with each position.

As I complimented each person's response and delved into the implications, group members began offering answers more readily. The staring sessions came to an end, and within a few months group members began blurting out their observations before I could ask a question or in the middle of reading a Scripture text. "Great observation!" I would comment. "I hadn't noticed that before. What do you others think?" By the end of the year it was the most vocal group in the church. These members had learned that their opinions count.

The same is true for a ministry team. If you stifle opinions that differ from yours or that would require another approach or direction, in time you will receive no other input. When you ask for the team's thoughts, you will get blank stares that suggest, "Do you really want us to say something, to get involved, to offer our opinions?"

You must be flexible in accepting others' opinions. Sometimes these ideas will be inferior to your own. But you may be able to blend and refine two or three ideas to produce a solution that is more powerful and effective than any single idea. That's when teamwork works.

Semantic Flexibility

When you use terms that are rigid, that draw lines in the sand and say, "This is black or white; it's either my way or not at all," you are being semantically inflexible. "People who are semantically rigid in their thinking patterns and rigid in their means of expressing themselves often habitually rely on what linguists call *all-ness language forms*. These include expressions like '*Everybody* needs a computer,' '*Nobody* cares about that,' 'You *always* do such-and-such,' and 'That will *never* work.' Sometimes the all-ness term is fully warranted by the facts, but many times it just pops out as a symptom of an oversimplified, rigid habit of thought on the part of the speaker."[3] Communication such as this divides a team. When you use inflexible language, you close the door to creative thinking and prevent innovation from growing. Unless an issue attacks the foundational truths of God's Word, it can be negotiated and an alternative approach found.

In developing an innovator's mind-set, learn not to characterize everything in life as an absolute. God's Word is absolute truth. Most issues your team will deal with are not. Semantic flexibility is a communication tool that helps feed dialogue about the issues and methods vital to your ministry.

Positive Orientation

Some people see the glass half full; some see it half empty. Others not only see it half empty but also assume that the glass is used and dirty. Innovation is difficult to find when you have a negative frame of mind. After all, if something is going to fail before you begin, why begin at all? Zig Ziglar has said that some of the greatest accomplishments in life have been made by people who were too ignorant to realize that something couldn't be done. Before someone told them that what they wanted to do was impossible, they went out and did it! The great-est inventions in history began with an idea someone believed could be ful-filled. Propelled by a positive mind-set, the ideas eventually became realities.[4]

Adopt a positive outlook on life. Look at life's possibilities from a positive frame of mind. Referring to God's promises, Paul said, "No matter how many promises God has made, they are 'Yes' in Christ" (2 Cor. 1:20). God wants you to have a positive outlook on your team's ministry possibilities. With a positive outlook you can view ministry opportunities with the realization that, as a team, you can find solutions that will benefit lives for the Kingdom.

Sense of Humor

Jesus said, " 'The thief comes only to steal and kill and destroy; I have come that they may have life, and have it to the full' " (John 10:10). Jesus offers Christians a life of joy overflowing. Not a pie-in-the-sky, happy-face kind of joy. I mean genuine, deep joy that comes from knowing Him. Along with this joy comes a sense of humor.

The serious nature of our faith may prevent our seeing the abundant humor in the Bible that reflects an unspoken attribute of God. God is holy, omnipo-tent, and righteous; but He also has a sense of humor. I believe that God was having fun with Adam when, recognizing that Adam was alone, He paraded the animals in front of him. God declared, " 'It is not good for the man to be alone. I will make a helper suitable for him' " (Gen. 2:18). But the next verse says: "The Lord God had formed out of the ground all the beasts of the field and all the birds of the air. He brought them to the man to see what he would name them." I believe that God had fun watching Adam's face as each animal passed by. With each animal Adam wondered, *Could this be the one?* Genesis 2:20 tells us that Adam was looking, "but for Adam no suitable helper was found." God wasn't looking; He knew what He was going to do. But Adam didn't.

God's humor is seen when the angel approached fearful Gideon, who was hiding in the winepress threshing wheat, and called to him, " 'The Lord is with you, mighty warrior' " (Judg. 6:12). Warrior? No doubt God viewed the scene with humor, knowing the profound awareness Gideon would gain as he began to see himself as God saw him. When the angel of the Lord called out to Gideon, I believe that God had a smile on His face.

When Jesus told the disciples to feed the five thousand personally (see Matt.

14:16), I believe that He was smiling. When Moses threw down his rod and jumped back when it became a snake (see Ex. 4:3), I believe that God laughed— not in derision but in the joy of knowing the courage this fearful man would display. When the Lord responded to Habakkuk's cries for God to judge Israel, telling Habakkuk to watch because he wouldn't believe what He was about to do (see Hab. 1:1-5), I believe that God wore a wry smile. Habakkuk cried out because Israel was sinning, but God told Habakkuk that He would use the pagan Babylonians to come down and judge Israel. God knew that Habakkuk would soon learn a new attribute of God: His indisputable sovereignty, which complements His absolute righteousness and justice.

God has a sense of humor, and so do His children. When you can laugh, you can see a different perspective of a situation. Seeing one different perspective helps you see another. And that third perspective might be the solution you are looking for.

Investigative Orientation

Innovators are continual learners. They never think they have accumulated all knowledge needed to make an intelligent decision. Innovators seek new knowledge; they are never satisfied with the status quo. They may respect the status quo and admire it, but they seldom rest on it very long.

Innovators look at learning like walking the wrong direction on an escalator. If you are walking up an escalator that is going down, you continue to make progress as long as you keep moving. But the moment you stop, you begin to descend. The same is true of learning. When you stop, you regress. New knowledge is the fuel that feeds the fire that boosts you to the top.

When you find something that works well, be careful not to "stop on the escalator." Use what works, but always be on the lookout for ways to improve. Persons who continually seek to learn live in a state of humility. Knowing that information exists beyond their current intellect, they are open to it. Innovation is receiving new information.

Team members should strive to be continual learners. This way each team member can regularly bring to the team new information that could be invaluable at some point. New information expressed one day may appear to be just interesting information. But next week or next month that information may be the solution that meets a need.

Resistance to Enculturation

This resistance is the ability not to be driven and guided in life by the culture at hand. "The radical thinkers of history who have eventually had their ideas accepted have all had this characteristic of resistance to enculturation to a high degree. People like Martin Luther, Mohandas Gandhi, and Martin Luther King, Jr., stood firm in their beliefs against powerful establishments, coalitions of hatred, and tremendous social pressure to abandon them. Not only did they believe as they chose, but they acted fully on their beliefs and were willing to face the consequences."[5]

Christians are to have values established by God's Word. But sometimes traditions can become so ingrained in culture that good people can confuse them with scriptural teachings. Is Sunday the only day a church can worship God? Some think so. Some believe that if a church begins a Friday- or Saturday-night service, it has abandoned the faith. Traditions are difficult to overcome when people attach unfounded value to them.

As an innovator, you must distinguish between the values God wants you to have and traditions that no longer have value. Opposition does not always mean that you have made the wrong choice. Martin Luther, the father of the Protestant Reformation, faced great opposition by very religious people. His teachings seemed so far removed from what the Roman Catholic Church had taught for centuries that some would not accept them. Those who did found personal relationships with Christ that they had never known. From Luther's persistent efforts came today's Protestant Christians.

These characteristics, though not exhaustive, can help you develop the mental flexibility to be more innovative. They will guide you on some days and will rescue you on others. They will teach you sometimes and support you at other times. With the ever-abiding presence of the Holy Spirit and your openness to new ideas, God can build into the team an innovative mind-set. When you combine your efforts, God can accomplish much as your creativity blossoms with each new challenge.

How to Gain or Maintain Flexibility

Whenever God spoke of the Israelites' shortcomings, He often referred to them as stiffnecked. They were inflexible. They had become too rigid to be open to any change God brought their way. They wavered in the characteristics God wanted them to maintain, such as holiness. But they were closed to ways God wanted to change them.

It isn't enough just to say, "Be flexible." You can take some tangible steps to become flexible or, if you already are, to maintain flexibility. These suggestions can help you guard against becoming stiffnecked.

Recognize Your Habits

You are a creature of habit, whether or not you realize it. For instance, which of the following do you usually do the same way?

❑ Wake up at the same time
❑ Eat the same food for breakfast
❑ Drive the same route to work
❑ Go to lunch at the same time
❑ Groom yourself the same way
❑ Frequent the same circle of restaurants
❑ Sit in the same area in church

This list could be lengthened, but you probably get the point. You are a creature of habit. That is not necessarily bad. A good habit can be helpful and efficient. But if never reviewed, a habit can keep you from looking for a better way to do things. And you will seldom find what you are not looking for.

Here is a process for identifying and eliminating unnecessary habits.

• Over the next week write down all of your habits you can think of. Spend time praying and thinking about your habits, asking God to help you identify all of them. When He brings something to mind, write it down. Your goal is to find out how many habits you have. This is not a bad list, but it is a true list.

• Group the habits by similarities. You may want to group all of the morning habits, midday habits, and evening habits. Or you may want to group all of the personal habits, business habits, and religious habits. The way you group them doesn't matter. Your goal is to organize them so that you can examine them.

• Taking one group at a time, evaluate each habit. Consider how long you have had this habit. Try to recall how it began. Then try to recall what you did before you developed the habit. Is your life better because of the habit? Did the habit solve a problem, or did it just become simpler than having to think? Try to prioritize your habits within each group. An *A* habit is one you cannot live without. A *B* habit is very helpful but could be altered. And a *C* habit exists but is not crucial.

- Now compile a list of your *C* habits. Choose one or two to change. Set a strategy for changing these habits. If you need motivation, offer yourself a reward when you achieve it. Find a close friend, share what you are doing, and be accountable to your friend for making these changes. If your ministry team is in place, be accountable to the team for changing the habits.

When you recognize your tendency to build good and bad habits, you can better recognize the need to evaluate all of your habits periodically and to remove those that hinder your effectiveness and creativity. This process can push you out of your comfort zone in selected areas and can challenge you to do things in new, creative ways.

Try New Things

In all likelihood you have things in the back of your mind you have wanted to do for a long time but have never gotten around to. Perhaps you have delayed because of a lack of time, money, or information. Maybe you have delayed because of fear. Regardless of the reason, it often boils down to procrastination. If you are going to be flexible, you must sometimes force yourself to take initiative you will be grateful for afterward.

Decide to attend a new event—a play, a concert, a single-adult conference, or a college course. If you fear meeting new people or facing new challenges, find a friend to try new pursuits with you. There are two theories to pursuing a new event with a friend. Some persons select a friend who has a similar struggle, such as shyness. That way they can encourage each other to grow beyond their self-imposed barriers. This can be helpful if your friend is as committed to growing as you are. You are peers in the journey of life together. You can experience genuine comradery with this approach.

Others prefer to find someone who is their opposite, someone who is bold in trying new things. In this situation you assume the role of a learner, and your friend is your teacher. Make sure your friend understands and accepts this arrangement. Be careful not to see your friend as so advanced in certain skills that he or she becomes a visual source of discouragement. Be realistic. Even if you can't be as outgoing as your vivacious friend, you can still improve your social skills and become more extroverted. You are wise to be willing to learn from someone.

Get involved in a mission or join a civic organization. You will find structure as well as persons who reach out to you. Although you will face a learning curve and will have a few awkward moments as you learn how the organization functions, you will have a framework in which to operate. The framework provides security as the new experience helps you build flexibility.

Adopt a new hobby. Learn to play a musical instrument. Choose something that will stretch you, something new that will force you to do things you haven't done before. Music lessons also provide structure as you adjust to something new.

When you willingly choose new activities and make the adjustments to learn them, you develop greater flexibility.

Look for Role Models of Flexibility

You can learn from persons who were or are examples of flexibility. Read military biographies of the war generals of World War II. Notice that they made their battle plans, laid out their strategies, then received last-minute information that forced them to change everything. Often, their willingness to change saved thousands of lives and advanced their troops. Soldiers must be flexible if they hope to survive.

Read stories of great missionaries who adapted to adverse living conditions to reach people for Christ. Notice that these soldiers of the faith remained resolute in their faith yet flexible in conveying the gospel where they lived. Rees Howells, a missionary in Wales in the 19th century, was a great man of faith and prayer. Feeling burdened for the people of Wales, he sensed that God was leading him to intercede on their behalf for national spiritual renewal. A big man, Howells was accustomed to eating four large meals a day. He knew that many of the coal miners never knew such luxury. To identify more closely with the people, he chose to reduce his meals from four big meals a day to two small meals of bread, cheese, and soup—the same rations as most of the men in the mining camps. He maintained this diet for more than two years.[6] Howells learned to be flexible in order to be used mightily by God. And he was. The

Welsh Revival of the late 19th century is largely attributed to God's work through Howells.

You can also read modern-day stories of Christians who have overcome enormous difficulties. Joni Eareckson Tada was an athletic teenager when a diving accident paralyzed her from the neck down. Rather than give up, she chose to become flexible. Joni learned to draw with a brush held between her teeth. Developing her singing, speaking, and writing skills, she became an internationally recognized model of what God can do through a person who gives everything to God.

To become flexible, recognize the flexibility exhibited around you. Find it in the circumstances of life. Look for it in the events and activities you join. Search for positive role models who emulate a life of constancy with God and flexibility to accept His work and ways. Through the books you read, the friends you relate to, and the role models you study, you can become more flexible. Flexibility will be vital as you grow your ministry team.

The Three Phases of Change

Life is full of change, and everyone's response to change is unique. Yet people commonly respond to change in three major phases. Most people are not aware of these phases, even though they live through them all the time. (You are in at least one right now.) Each phase has hardships and benefits. Each phase has its own purpose. Whenever you encounter change or introduce change into your life, you begin this process. It has no set time frame, no stop-and-go points. You enter, you progress, and you exit. Understanding these stages enables you to identify where you are in the process. That understanding can sometimes be very encouraging.

Let me illustrate how change can affect you. The day I began seminary, I had just completed seven years in college. (I took the short route.) The first day of class in college was the time I had received a syllabus and a list of required textbooks; that was about all. The first day of class in seminary I received all of that, plus several homework assignments due at the next class meeting: materials to buy and read, papers to write, reports to hand in. I immediately realized that seminary was going to be a lot of work.

About halfway through the first semester, I began losing touch with my senses and doing strange things. For example, I went to the grocery store two blocks from my apartment to buy something, only to forget what I went there for. Sometimes I walked up and down the aisles hoping something would spark my memory. More than once I went home empty-handed. I was getting concerned. I thought I was losing my mind.

That semester I was taking pastoral psychology and counseling. Shortly after I began experiencing my problem, the professor taught us about the stress of change and had us take a stress test. A score of more than two hundred points was considered significant enough to affect your personality for up to one year. My test scored over eight hundred points! I had gone through an inordinate amount of change during the previous year.

Instead of becoming alarmed, I was wonderfully encouraged. Characteristically, I said to myself: *You're not going crazy after all. You're just temporarily out of balance. It's going to pass with time.* I found hope in knowing what was happening and where I was in the process of change.

In a similar way, the three phases of change can help you understand what happens when you encounter changes that inevitably occur in team ministry. The following phases indicate what kind of emotions you can anticipate and the processes you will encounter. By allowing you to chart the process of change, the three phases can offer you hope.

Each phase on the chart on the following page represents a different set of characteristics that affect your life as you encounter change. The chart is a general time line that is read from left to right. As you progress from one phase to another, you are growing, gaining valuable information, learning new systems, and getting a grasp on what is required for you to reach your goals. No specific time frame is set for entering the different phases. It varies with individuals; you can go through one change at one pace and through another at a different pace altogether. Also, a person does not always go through every phase.

Phase 1: Formative

When you encounter a major change, you enter phase 1. In this phase your role is that of a visionary leader. You begin to implement your visions, whether they are in ministry, career, relationships, or another area of your life. At the forefront of your mind is the result you are pursuing. In the formative phase you gain many pieces of information you need. Here you formulate rules for the game and develop your plan of action.

THREE PHASES OF CHANGE

1. Formative	2. Normative	3. Integrative
Visionary leader	**Manager**	**Leader/manager**
Good news:	**Good news:**	**Good news:**
Energy	Efficient	Collaboration
Exciting	Secure	Fresh ideas
Learning	Confident	New directions
New	Predictable	Intelligent vision
Experimental		
Bad news:	**Bad news:**	**Bad news:**
Ambiguous	Boredom	Chaos must occur to
Exhausting	No new learning	induce this phase;
Ignorant	Perceived as arrogant	it must get bad be-
Inefficient		fore it gets better
Expensive		New competition
Risky		Takeover

Phase 1 is often characterized by excitement, high energy, enthusiasm, dreams, visions, and experimentation. These positive elements and emotional drives propel you toward change. But you may also experience ambiguity, risk, exhaustion, and ignorance in phase 1. You lack efficiency. Depending on your venture, this phase can be expensive; it can cost you time, energy, and/or money.

Let me illustrate phase 1 from a business perspective. If the owner of a successful company approached you and offered you the position of executive vice-president, you would immediately enter phase 1 of the change process. You would probably be excited. Your mind would begin to race wildly. This would mean a new office, new responsibilities, and a huge pay increase! You could pay off your debts and buy that house, car, and sailboat you've wanted. You could be in a better position to offer financial assistance to various ministries that approached you. What a fantastic day this would be for your career.

At this phase you would experience excitement, high energy, enthusiasm, dreams, and visions as you realized the potential of this new career move. But at the same time you would have feelings of ambiguity, risk, and ignorance. Now that you've said yes to the offer, are you really up to the demand of the position? What if it's too much for you? What if you can't handle the workload? What if you're not really qualified? You don't know. Everything is ambiguous.

This stage is also exhausting. The first day you drive to your new office, you arrive one hour and 15 minutes early because you weren't sure how long the commute would be from your home to the new office. Over the next couple of weeks you will learn the commute time, the best route to and from work, your way around the building, where to park, where to eat lunch, where the restroom is, and many other details that are required to help you function.

Phase 1 is also characterized by new learning and dependency. To learn how to use the phone system, you have to ask someone. To find the restroom, you have to ask someone. To use the copier, you have to ask someone. Virtually everything you do at first depends on other persons. These elements of phase 1 can make you feel somewhat helpless, but this is normal.

Nevertheless, your new learning is driven by your excitement, dreams, and visions. As much as possible, you take in everything offered to you. It seems fast and furious, but it is fun. This is a wonderful opportunity, and you want to make the most of it.

Phase 1 also involves trial and error. It is a time of experimentation in the change process. Because you come into this phase ignorant, you must experiment to find the best way to accomplish your goals. You are not encumbered by traditions of the past, because you haven't been with the company long enough to establish any traditions or to learn those that already exist. This is a very favorable situation for flexibility and innovation.

During this phase you lay the foundation you will build on in the days ahead. In the beginning you seek to take all information that comes your way. You process it, then add it to your mental and emotional foundation for the future. You will find later that some of the information you accept is unnecessary to retain. Receiving more information than you need is part of the exhaustion associated with phase 1. But it is necessary to lay a good foundation.

As you and your team begin a new ministry, you will no doubt begin in phase 1 in the process of change. You and your team members will have a high degree of excitement. The team's dreams can be electric. The energy level of each member will be escalated. It's an exciting time in ministry.

The team will need to learn a lot. For the first several weeks or months information will be gained in every area of ministry—from internal communication to insight into the target group the team wants to reach. Some information will be extremely valuable. Some will not. In time you will learn to determine the usefulness of information.

In phase 1 of your ministry you will sometimes proceed in a direction and spend a lot of energy and effort, only to find it unproductive. Trial and error will be common. Someone once identified two extremes to avoid in the Christian life: ignorance on fire and knowledge on ice. If I had to choose, I would prefer ignorance on fire. It's easier to learn than to motivate.

Don't let the errors that follow the trials discourage you. This learning process occurs in every facet of life. If you never make mistakes, you never improve. Making mistakes means that you are sometimes pushing the edge of your comfort zone and losing. But pushing the edge allows you to improve, too. Otherwise, you plateau and never grow. That's true in ministry and in life. Accept the trials and the errors that occur in this phase of ministry. Learn from them; grow from them. When you do that, it's not a loss at all. It's an education.

Phase 2: Normative

For the past several months you have begun to establish yourself in your new role as vice-president. At first it was highly uncomfortable though exciting. You weren't accustomed to seeing yourself in such a high, honorable position. You felt awkward because everyone addressed you with respect, especially when you were so ignorant that you had to ask your administrative assistant how to use the phone.

But in time you learned the best route to work and the best time to leave home to get there. You settled into that new home and car. You're making plans for your new sailboat next spring. You have mastered all the equipment you need to accomplish your new job. And you have grasped the internal organizational structure of your new company.

About this time you enter phase 2. Phase 2 is called the normative phase because the chaotic changes of phase 1 begin to take on a degree of normalcy. The term that most accurately describes the nature of phase 2 is *routine*. When routine is the predominant emotional state of your life in a certain area, you are in phase 2. Phase 2 takes you from blind enthusiasm to calm confidence.

While phase 1 requires dependency, phase 2 allows more independence. You no longer have to ask how to do something or go somewhere. You have learned what you need to know. In this phase you can work independently.

Phase 2 is also a time of great efficiency. Because you have gained vital knowledge, learned the necessary systems, and built a rapport with persons who can help you achieve your goals, you have moved out of the phase of a high degree of new learning into the phase of applying your new knowledge. You can accomplish much because of your competency. You can time your drive to work by the minute. You can operate the phone without having to consult the manual. You know what to do with reports you are given. You know what to expect of the persons who work with you. You can be extremely efficient.

In phase 1 you had been the visionary leader, building new dreams, scaling new mountains of ignorance, and conquering the kingdoms of automation and organizational systems. In phase 2 you take on the role of a manager, managing the knowledge you've gained. Unlike phase 1, phase 2 doesn't happen like a camera flash. You don't wake up one morning, stretch, and say to yourself, *Oh, I've just entered phase 2!* Phase 2 is gradual, like a sunrise.

Phase 2 also has its problems. One is confidence in your way of doing things, which some may perceive as arrogance. Your self-assuredness can intimidate some people. When they approach you with a new idea, you may be quick to dismiss it because you already know of another approach that will accomplish what they propose: the one you learned when you first started. The predominant phrase that characterizes phase 2 is "If it ain't broke, don't fix it." Something can be said for routine. It can be helpful, but it can also be dangerous when it begins to restrict creative thinking. Learning one way to accomplish something does not mean that you have learned the best way. Unless you are willing to evaluate things regularly, you can become stagnant, closed to new growth that may truly be an improvement over older methods. Be careful in phase 2 that you do not become closed to new ideas. It is a common tendency at this stage.

A second potential problem with phase 2 is that you can become bored with the same process and routine. We are creatures of habit, and habits can become boring. When things become routine, energy and quality can wane. The drive to achieve can be lost. Routine is not beneficial if it robs you of quality, drive, and passion in what you do.

After you have worked with this company as vice-president for several years, although you have learned the processes and have excelled in this position, you begin to feel that you aren't challenged anymore. In time you lapse into doing the same things over and over. After a while you become bored with the same job that once made you wild with excitement. Same company. Same prestigious position. Same challenging work. Same pay level. But something has changed. It may not be the work; it may be you. In this environment you can stay for an indefinite amount of time—for years if the circumstances allow. But circumstances bring change. And that's what can affect your phase 2 position, as well.

In your ministry, phase 2 is often the most productive stage. After you and your team have truly bonded and you have identified your target group and goals for ministry, you can be very efficient in conducting your ministry. Your team has learned its individual strengths and weaknesses, it knows its abilities and limitations, it understands its mission, and it knows how to perform it. This phase can be the most effective because you have become proficient at your work. But if you are not careful, learning how to do something can keep you from being open to new ways of doing it. After all, "if it ain't broke, don't fix it." But people are always trying to invent a better mousetrap. And sometimes they do just that.

During this phase you and the team need to remain open to new ideas and new ways of doing things. Don't automatically adopt any change that comes down the pike, but don't automatically close the door, either. A ministry needs stability, and repetition helps build stability. At the same time, continually look for ways to improve the proficiency of the team or the ministry.

Phase 3: Integrative

Phase 3 is an optional phase. Like phase 1, it is usually encountered suddenly, like a camera flash.

The point of entry to phase 3 is conflict and chaos. Whenever routine is the order of your day, you are in a position that is ripe for phase 3. Although we learned that phase 2 can be boring, it can also be comfortable. You have a routine way of doing things, thinking, and seeing things from the same perspective.

But when you are comfortable, blind spots can prevent your seeing new opportunities or growing problems. For example, as vice-president for the past five years, you have introduced positive changes for your company. You have settled into a routine that works well for you. Quite comfortable in this position, you think that if all goes well, you may one day become president. Life could not be grander.

But one day you hear a fearful rumor. You hear that the owner may sell the company to a competitor. At first you think, *That's absurd.* But you are worried. You remember that the owner asked you a month ago what your long-range goals are. At the time you thought he was sizing you up for a promotion. Now you wonder if he was prompting you to set your house in order for some unexpected changes.

Two weeks after you first heard the rumor, the owner calls you into the head office to let you know that the rumor is true. The company is being sold to a competitor. At the time your position is secure. However, the present owner cannot honestly speculate about what the new owner may wish to do.

At this point you confront phase 3. Suddenly, your nice, comfortable, leisurely world has been attacked by conflicting chaos. Now your world is turning upside down. Update your résumé. Make some phone calls. Assess your current value to the company. Will the new owner want to keep you because of your insight, or will he want to release you because of your association with the former owner? It could go either way. All of these thoughts go through your head.

You must decide whether you will enter phase 3. At this juncture some people choose to avoid it and find a new phase 1. New résumés are sent, phone calls are made, networking begins, and positions are secured with new companies. New learning begins, including everything from the best route to work to the location of the bathroom. It's exhausting, but it provides new hope.

Phase 3 is different from a new phase 1. If you choose to enter phase 3 in the business scenario, you decide to stay with the old company. In your current position you have the advantage of being able to capitalize on the knowledge and experience you have already gained. You take the knowledge you've gained in phases 1 and 2 and find new ways to integrate it, adapt it, and profit from it. The essence of phase 3 is taking information already acquired and finding new perspectives and ways to use it. Actually, phase 3 is a modified phase 1. Suddenly, the old assumptions must be discarded. All of the old perspectives are placed under the microscope and reexamined. Nothing is sacred in phase 3. Anything and everything is up for change.

Interestingly, the high-energy level of phase 1 also characterizes phase 3. The risk factor is also present, but it differs from the risk in phase 1. Now the risk is not ignorant risk but intelligent risk. In phase 1 you risked but did not know whether it would work. In phase 3 a background of information helps govern the risk. In phase 1 you had dreams and visions but no way to know if they were achievable and, if so, how. But in phase 3 you have the ability to have intelligent visions. Not only can you begin to dream again, but with the knowledge you gained during phases 1 and 2, you can also fairly accurately predict the success or failure potential of a new direction. Uncertainty still exists but not as much as in phase 1. Rather, your new challenge can be highly motivating.

What do you do in this business scenario as a lame-duck vice-president? You choose to stay and trust the new owner to do what is best. But in the meantime you decide to evaluate the current work for ways to improve. You compare the new owner's processes in his existing companies to yours. You identify the similarities and the differences and document what you think the impact will be. You share with your coworkers areas in which the new owner's methods seem superior. In areas in which they aren't, you compile the benefits of maintaining your approach. Such work doesn't make your position secure, but it certainly places you in a valuable position for the new owner. Anyone with your insight into both systems can help make transitions smoother. That can be a big advantage for the new owner, as well as for yourself. Even if you are released, the knowledge you have gained will be highly valued by many other companies.

In ministry, chaos strikes in a variety of ways. A new team member may be a control freak. A key team member may be lost. Some people in the community may protest your work. Church members or leaders may be uncomfortable with your ministry because it is not traditional. When chaos strikes your ministry, you can choose whether to go through it or to go around it. You and your team may choose to let your ministry die and to try another ministry via a new phase 1. Or team members may choose to experience phase 3 by applying what you have learned to a new situation and by gaining renewed energy in the process.

You will continually experience these phases of change in life. You may be ready to enter phase 1 with a new ministry concept such as a ministry team. You may be in phase 2 in a personal relationship. You may be in phase 3 at work. Life is a process of continual change. Assessing where you are in that process may not provide all of the answers you need at the time, but it can help you understand and anticipate the dangers and benefits of each phase, both for your personal life and for your ministry team.

How to Stay Motivated

We have seen that as you pursue dreams and visions, remaining flexible is vital to dealing with the inevitable changes that occur. Flexibility is also needed to stay motivated in times of discouragement. Following God's will does not mean that you will not be discouraged occasionally. Scripture records numerous instances when great men and women of God were discouraged even while being used by Him in mighty ways.

A loss of motivation is a loss of desire to act. You don't want to move forward. You don't want to take risks. You don't want to do anything. You should consider two major factors whenever you feel discouraged:

1. Although you have emotions, you are not basically an emotional person. You are a spiritual person who has emotions. As such, you have the capacity to refuse to be led through life by your emotions.
2. You can take steps to renew your motivation to move forward in life and ministry. The three scriptural directives that follow can help get you get off dead center and begin moving in a positive direction.

Scriptural Principles of Motivation

God's message to the church at Ephesus, recorded in the Book of Revelation, reveals important teachings about staying motivated. The apostle John wrote this book late in life, about 60 years after Jesus' crucifixion. When the apostle Paul had written the Book of Ephesians, that church had been strong and vibrant, full of committed believers. When John addressed it, probably around A.D. 95, the church still had positive qualities. By today's standards it would seem to be a thriving, evangelical church that had remained true to God's Word. The Lord Himself addressed the church by saying: " 'I know your deeds, your hard work and your perseverance. I know that you cannot tolerate wicked men, that you have tested those who claim to be apostles but are not, and have found them false. You have persevered and have endured hardships for my name, and have not grown weary' " (Rev. 2:2-3). This was a group of doctrinally sound believers who knew scriptural truth and evaluated ministries and people on that basis.

But doctrinal soundness was not enough. Even though the church was biblically sound, it was spiritually bankrupt. It had lost its motivation. It had lost its love relationship with Jesus Christ. It was limited in its effectiveness for God's kingdom. The Lord said, "I hold this against you: You have forsaken your first love" (v. 4). Then He told these believers how to regain the fire they had lost, how to recapture the passion that once burned brightly in their hearts. Through this instruction you too can learn some principles of motivation.

The Lord told the believers in the church at Ephesus to do three things to regain their first love, their love for Christ. Interestingly, the steps to regain a relational, emotional position with Him were pragmatic ones: " 'Remember the height from which you have fallen! Repent and do the things you did at first' " (v. 5). Jesus' advice also contained a warning: " 'If you do not repent, I will come to you and remove your lampstand from its place.' " If they did not change, He would remove His blessing and power from them. Their effectiveness as a church would be nil.

You can do the same things to find new motivation. First, Jesus said to remember. At one time the church at Ephesus was thriving. The people were alive, truly alive. The love within the church, the passion for ministry, and the fire in their words and actions were vibrant. Jesus said to regain motivation, remember what life was like at a time when you had that motivation, that passion. Remembering helps reclaim the lost goal of a love for Him in ministry.

Jesus also said to repent. The word *repent* means *to have a change of mind.* Jesus told the believers at Ephesus to change their minds. About what? At some point the leaders must have made decisions that placed doctrinal soundness above everything else in the Christian life. But as crucial as biblical soundness is, it cannot survive unless it is balanced with a relational passion for Christ and His people. If you have lost your motivation, Jesus said to change your way of thinking. Your thinking processes, your judgment calls, and your values got you where you are. If you have lost your passion for the Christian life and for Christ Himself, something is out of focus. Spend time in prayer and evaluation, asking God to show you what area of thinking is out of place or out of balance.

When you find something, repent: change your mind about the value you placed on it. You need to raise the importance of something you have devalued. Or maybe you've overvalued something at the expense of other important areas.

For example, perhaps in your ministry team you place great value on operating the meetings with great efficiency to cover the business at hand. That can be good unless you communicate to the team members that sticking to the agenda is more important than addressing their needs and concerns. In this case your team could become demoralized. You would need to repent, to change your thinking about the value of efficiency at the expense of team ownership and participation.

Finally, Jesus told the church at Ephesus to do the things it did at first. When you start well and go astray, go back to the beginning. Return to the way you did things at first. The principle here is "Actions determine feelings." The world says, "If it feels good, do it"—in other words, let your feelings determine your actions. But God created you to do the opposite. Your actions are to determine your feelings. Therefore, if your feelings are out of place, find the actions in your life that are out of place. Change the actions, and your feelings will follow!

Changing your actions is the key to finding new motivation. Waiting for motivation to act opposes the way God designed you. Act, and the motivation will follow. As a Christian, you have the Holy Spirit and the principles in God's Word to help you rise above your emotions when necessary. When God leads you in one direction and your emotions oppose you, follow God. Your emotions will catch up. Trusting God's plans and principles more than your own ideas and emotions is the essence of walking by faith.

Motivating Your Ministry Team

Bruce Wilkinson, the founder and president of Walk Thru the Bible Ministries, researched ways God motivated people in Scripture. He found that God used three primary ways to motivate people in the Bible: fear of punishment, hope of reward, and love of relationship. As he traveled across the country conducting seminars on this subject, he asked audiences the way they thought God primarily motivated people in the Old Testament. Most people answered, "Fear of punishment." When asked to identify the primary way God motivate people in the New Testament, audiences answered, "Love of relationship." Imagine their surprise when Wilkinson revealed that in both the Old Testament and the New Testament God used hope of reward three to one over either of the other two means of motivation. When God sought to motivate someone, He offered the person a reward.

That insight has implications for ministry. For example, many churches' primary means of motivating members to become active in ministry is fear of punishment: "Please, Bill, we really need somebody to work with sixth graders. If you don't do it, no one is left we can call on." This approach, called guilt motivation, is a form of fear of punishment. It motivates from obligation, not from desire. This is the major reason churches have difficulty keeping volunteer positions filled. People don't want to work in an environment that uses guilt to motivate.

Some churches combine fear of punishment with love of relationship to entice people to accept volunteer positions: "If you really love the Lord, you'll take this class of four-year-olds." It is true that you need to do some things purely from your love for God, and God will lead you to do that. Sometimes He motivates you from fear of punishment. Hebrews 12:1-13 says that God disciplines His children. But three of four times God will seek to motivate you with hope of reward. Christians are wise to heed this scriptural pattern.

Hope of reward is not the same as bribery. Bribery is paying someone to do something he would not do otherwise. A person who is bribed is motivated not to do the work but to receive the bribe. Hope of reward offers the person a benefit. When people realize the benefit that could result from their actions, the motivation comes from within.

God's methods of motivation work. If your ministry team loses motivation, it helps to know what rewards motivate each member. If a person values recognition, occasionally place her in the spotlight by recognizing her valuable work for the team and the Kingdom. Others are motivated by accomplishing goals. Chart their progress on a poster in the team's meeting room and call attention to it as each goal is achieved. Others may value tangible rewards like trophies, plaques, or gifts. Choosing rewards that fit team members' personalities can be a powerful motivational tool.

Although the ultimate rewards for ministry are intangible, tangible expressions of recognition and appreciation can be highly motivating for your team. They enable team members to recognize goals that have been accomplished, to feel affirmed for their efforts for the Kingdom, and to receive a boost when they are down.

Team ministry demands flexibility because it always involves change. Learn to adapt, roll with the punches, and accept change as a part of the dynamic of life and ministry. Museums can freeze time. Cemeteries can preserve memories. But when your ministry reaches out to others, you must learn to expect, welcome, and grow wiser through the changes that come your way.

---

[1]Oliver Wendell Holmes, Jr., as quoted in *The Macmillan Dictionary of Quotations* (New York: Macmillan, 1989), 270.

[2]List of traits is from Karl Albrecht with Steven Albrecht, *The Creative Corporation* (Homewood, Ill: Dow Jones-Irwin, 1987), 74.

[3]Ibid., 77.

[4]Zig Ziglar, *See You at the Top* (Gretna, La.: Pelican, 1977), 334–40.

[5]Albrecht, *The Creative Corporation*, 83.

[6]Norman P. Grubb, *Rees Howells: Intercessor* (London: Lutterworth, 1952), 61–62.

set limits and
replace yourself

the principle of duplication

A man's reach should exceed his grasp,
Or what's a heaven for?[1]

—Robert Browning

Because of a desire to control or a feeling of insecurity, many ministry leaders do not allow anyone else to learn their leadership tasks. Consequently, when the leader leaves, the ministry dies. You can prevent that by practicing the principle of duplication, the concept of nurturing others who can take your place in ministry if God leads you elsewhere. The prophet Eli taught Samuel the ways of God. Elijah had Elisha. Jesus had the twelve disciples. Barnabas mentored Paul and then John Mark. Paul taught Silas and then Timothy. Through duplication the work continued after the leader was gone.

You need to bring others along with you in your ministry role not only to continue the ministry but also to share the workload. As a finite, limited human being, you cannot perform all of the ministry tasks yourself. In addition, when you begin pursuing a course toward ministry goals, you can expect spiritual opposition. The ministry team can be a source of strength, but so can an individual kindred spirit. To be an effective ministry leader, you need to set limits and to share the leadership with others.

It may seem unusual to talk about setting limits near the end of a book that is written to motivate you to active ministry. But limits do not restrict you from achieving. They actually allow you to achieve. Learn to do a few things well. Then pass on what you learn to others who can go farther than you. To learn to do some things well, you must learn to say no to other good things that come your way. Learning to say no is a skill that improves with use. Learning to give your skills and wisdom in ministry to others is a character trait that will enable you to grow and expand your ministry time and again.

Spiritual Opposition

Getting involved in ministry is not just a mental decision. It is a spiritual one. Whether or not you realize it, a war is being waged all around you. It is not, the apostle Paul said, a battle against human beings. It is a spiritual battle: "Our struggle is not against flesh and blood, but against the rulers, against the authorities, against the powers of this dark world and against the spiritual forces of evil in the heavenly realms" (Eph. 6:12). When you begin a ministry team with the dream of being used by God and of glorifying Him, you will encounter spiritual opposition.

Satan will oppose you by trying to get you off track in following God or by trying to throw off your timing. Slowing down will put you behind in pursuing God's will. Moving too fast will put you ahead of God's timing for His plans to unfold.

As you begin your ministry, Satan may try to get you off track by trying to convince you that you are not worthy to be active in ministry, that you have made too many mistakes to give others advice, or that you are not qualified. He may use your fear of the unknown to keep you from pursuing God's will for your life.

If these tactics don't work, Satan may try to get your timing out of sync with God's purposes. At this stage in the development of your ministry, he may try to get you to run too fast. Remember that for several weeks or months you will be in phase 1, which is characterized by high energy, enthusiasm, and excitement. Sometimes when you are highly charged, your judgment can be impaired. Satan may try to take advantage of this fact by influencing you to commit to too many things. If he can't cause your heart to turn cold, he may try to get you to burn out.

Running too fast does not mean that you should reject hard work, diligence, and faithfulness in your ministry. It means that you presume upon God in some way or accept more responsibility than God intended for you to carry. There are several ways to run too fast.

First, you can run too fast by making rash decisions instead of thinking matters through and spending time in prayer. Don't let the pressure of a moment force you into a long-term decision. Pray and seek counsel from wise men and women of God before making a decision. If Satan can get you into the habit of making rash decisions, in time the integrity of your ministry and your judgment as a leader will be questioned. Then the ministry will be severely limited.

Scripture warns about making rash vows. King Saul made a rash vow when he promised to kill whoever violated his command not to eat before victory was accomplished in battle (see 1 Sam. 14:24). His son Jonathan, who hadn't heard the command, ate some honey along the way. When it was discovered, it seemed at first that Saul would keep his promise. But he let the army leaders talk him out of it and no doubt lost their respect.

As a leader, be slow in making commitments but faithful to the ones you make. Solomon said: "When you make a vow to God, do not delay in fulfilling it. He has no pleasure in fools; fulfill your vow. It is better not to vow than to make a vow and not fulfill it" (Eccl. 5:4-5).

You can also run too fast by becoming overcommitted in ministry. Sometimes a great number of valuable, needed ministries present themselves. At first it can seem that God is opening many doors for you. Be sure these opportunities are consistent with God's will. Just because a need is legitimate does not mean that God wants you to address it. Jesus did not minister to many people whose needs were genuine and legitimate.

After you have begun your ministry, people may approach you with seemingly related requests. Some requests will easily fit into the team's goals. Some will not. Even if something fits, it does not mean that the team needs to commit to it. Besides compatibility, you also need to consider the team's time. What is the team's current time commitment? Who would be needed to work in this area? Do those persons have time to add a new project? If so, make them part of the decision-making process. If not, the decision is already made.

Another concern to consider before committing to additional responsibilities is skills. Does the team have the necessary skills or training this new project would require? If so, that would allow a smoother transition into the team's framework and processes. But if not, someone would have to acquire training.

Even though the team has ample time and skills to accept new responsibilities, it does not necessarily mean that you should say yes. Sometimes God directs you to say no without telling you why. If someone wants to know why, be honest and state that you don't know why but that as the team prayed about it, you felt that this was not the direction God wants you to take at this time. It's OK not to have all of the answers.

If you cannot learn to say no, you will be unable to accomplish anything completely and with quality. You will begin to feel harried and pulled from every direction. Feelings of fight or flight will emerge. You may begin to resent the pressures and demands placed on you. These feelings are understandable for a person who is running too fast. And when you run too fast, you will make poor decisions and will minister ineffectively.

The Land of Rest

Joy comes when you give of yourself in ministry. Single adults can easily build egocentric lives, with everything revolving around themselves. Jesus gave a principle that is foundational to all of life and especially to single-adult ministry: " 'Whoever wants to save his life will lose it, but whoever loses his life for me will save it' " (Luke 9:24). In this verse Jesus explained a principle of life that God established. If you focus your life entirely on yourself, always doing what is best for you, what appeals to you, and what will bring you pleasure, you will never find abundant life. However, if you choose not to put yourself in the center of your life, letting God be Lord of your life and devoting your life to following Jesus, you will find the abundant life you seek. When you offer life to others in Jesus' name, He gives life to you. The joy you find in ministry is a by-product, a gift God gives to those who seek to follow Him. Jesus said, " 'The thief comes only to steal and kill and destroy; I have come that they may have life, and have it to the full' " (John 10:10).

After you begin a ministry, it is easy to become stressed out. Pressures can build, demands can increase, and expectations can grow to be more than you can handle. Unless you learn to set limits, you can lose what Scripture calls God's rest, the ability to rest in God spiritually and emotionally in the midst of difficulty. To keep this rest, you must choose to say no to those things that would rob you of His rest. That sometimes means saying no to some very good things. But His rest is more important in the long run.

The Book of Hebrews gives an interesting promise and warning to Christians:

As the Holy Spirit says:
"Today, if you hear his voice,
    do not harden your hearts
as you did in the rebellion,
    during the time of testing in the desert,
where your fathers tested and tried me
    and for forty years saw what I did" (Heb. 3:7-9).

The writer of Hebrews primarily addressed Jewish people who were very familiar with the way their forefathers had rejected God's direction, even though they were eyewitnesses to His miraculous works for 40 years. But the Scripture goes on to say:

"That is why I was angry with that generation,
    and I said, 'Their hearts are always going astray,
    and they have not known my ways.'
So I declared on my oath in my anger,
'They shall never enter my rest' " (Heb. 3:10-11).

These people witnessed the mighty hand of God for 40 years. Yet they never entered God's rest because they chose not to believe and follow God. There is a major difference between seeing God's works and knowing His ways. This situation would be comparable to a person who becomes a Christian at age 10 and for the next 40 years faithfully attends church and often sees God work miraculously in the lives of other people. But at age 50 he still does not understand the ways of God in spite of having observed God's work for 40 years.

Rest refers not just to personal salvation but also to a familiarity with His ways. When you see His hand at work, you can rest in knowing that He is still in control.

The apostle Paul was resting in the ways of God when he wrote his second letter to Timothy, even though he was fairly certain that he was about to be executed: "I am already being poured out like a drink offering, and the time has come for my departure. I have fought the good fight, I have finished the race, I have kept the faith. Now there is in store for me the crown of righteousness, which the Lord, the righteous Judge, will award to me on that day—and not only to me, but also to all who have longed for his appearing" (2 Tim. 4:6-8). Because he understood the ways of his Lord, Paul could rest in God even when he faced a cruel death.

In ministry you will encounter many trials and difficulties. Such encounters are common. Some will be spiritual, some will be emotional, and some will be physical. Sometimes trials will come in small doses; other times they will come like a landslide. When you can trace the ways of God even in the midst of a storm, you can continue in His rest. You may not see His hand or know how He is working. But if you trust His ways, you can still rest.

This world is hectic. Ministry is difficult but rewarding. Don't let the difficulties rob you of the joy and rest that come when you follow Him in obedience. Keep your focus on His plan, His timing, and His activity. Build that kind of a relationship with Him. Isaiah 26:3-4 says:

> "You will keep in perfect peace
>   him whose mind is steadfast,
>   because he trusts in you.
> Trust in the Lord forever,
>   for the Lord, the Lord, is the Rock eternal."

Isaiah 30:21 describes the way God directs His people: "Whether you turn to the right or to the left, your ears will hear a voice behind you saying, 'This is the way, walk in it.' " God wants to direct you in the journey of ministry. As you and your team encounter difficulties, remind yourselves of His promises. His grace and power can see you through, and you will be able to maintain your rest in God.

It's OK to Say No

We have seen that sometimes in ministry it is necessary to say no to some things in order to say yes to others. Saying no is not wrong. To remain effective in your personal life and in ministry, you must learn to say no.

Jesus is a perfect role model of someone who understood the value of saying no. For the first 30 years of His life He said no. Jesus did not use His powers until the Father told Him to begin doing so. Although He could have taught the Bible (the Old Testament), served in the synagogue, or used His power to heal people, He waited on the Father's timing.

When Jesus began His ministry, Satan tried to get Him off track by tempting Him to pursue His ministry goal in a way that circumvented God's plan (see Matt. 4:5-6). It's a tactic he's used from the beginning. When Satan tempted Eve in the garden of Eden, he appealed to a godly desire within her but enticed her to fulfill that desire in an ungodly way. What was the desire Satan tapped into? It was Eve's desire to be like God, her Creator. Her desire was not to be God but to be like Him (see Gen. 3:5), the same desire He has placed in the heart of every believer (see 1 John 3:2). Inherent in the life of every child of God is the desire to be like Jesus in holiness, purity, and righteousness. Satan convinced Eve to to try to reach that goal in an unholy way.

Satan tried the same approach when he tempted Jesus in the wilderness. First he tempted Jesus to misuse His powers for personal gain rather than for God's glory (see Matt. 4:3). Jesus said no. Second, Satan tempted Jesus to test the veracity of God's Word (see Matt. 4:5-6). Satan even used Scripture, taking it out of context and distorting its application, just as he does today. But again Jesus said no.

Satan's last temptation was subtle. Satan knew that Jesus' mission was to gain the kingdoms of the world through their redemption, a redemption brought about by His own sacrifice. As he did with Eve, Satan appealed to Jesus' desires: "The devil took him to a very high mountain and showed him all the kingdoms of the world and their splendor. 'All this I will give you,' he said, 'if you will bow down and worship me' " (Matt. 4:8-9). Satan was appealing to Jesus' righteous desire to be established as Lord over all kingdoms of the world. But he was offering Jesus a shortcut: "Don't go through the agony and pain of a crucifixion, Jesus. Don't put up with all that ridicule. You are the Son of God. You deserve these kingdoms. If you'll just bow down before me one time, I will give them to you right now, and you won't have to go through all that suffering." But Jesus said no.

You and your team will face many of these same temptations in your ministry. As the team becomes more effective, it can easily abuse its power and influence. But the team must say no. It will be tempting sometimes to abuse God's Word to accomplish a desired end. But the team must say no. And at times Satan may appeal to a righteous desire of the team, tempting it to compromise its integrity to achieve the goal. The team must always say no. God doesn't take shortcuts.

Jesus also said no in Matthew 12:46-50 when His mother and brothers tried to convince Him to end His ministry and come home. But Jesus said no, explaining that His family was larger than flesh and blood: " 'Whoever does the will of my Father in heaven is my brother and sister and mother' " (Matt. 12:50). No doubt it was difficult saying no to His family, but Jesus was determined to fulfill God's will for His life.

In John 6:14-15 Jesus again said no to a prestigious honor: "After the people saw the miraculous sign that Jesus did, they began to say, 'Surely this is the Prophet who is to come into the world.' " The people rightfully acknowledged Jesus as the answer to their prayers for a Savior. Seeing the works of God through Jesus, they decided to act. But Jesus' response in backing away reveals that His actions were based on the ways of God the Father: "Jesus, knowing that they intended to come and make him king by force, withdrew again to a mountain by himself" (John 6:15). Although these people wanted to lift up Jesus as King of kings, their methods were not in line with God's plan and ways. Jesus said no. The end does not justify the means.

Many times throughout His life and ministry Jesus said no. Some things He rejected appeared to be good, worthwhile things. But He knew what He was called to do and what He was not called to do. Part of setting limits is defining your purpose so that you can recognize when even good things are not consistent with your mission.

Some people don't seem to have the word *no* in their vocabularies; they say yes to almost anything. Knowing this, others often take advantage of them. That's why it is so important for an individual to set and accept limits. It's OK to say no, even to good things when necessary. Howard Hendricks of Dallas Theological Seminary asserts that you should say no to something every day just to strengthen that ability. Even if you say no to something small or to yourself, this practice will help you develop a good habit in your relationships.

Neither you nor your team will always be popular. Sometimes people will disagree with you. They will tell you that you are wrong, and sometimes they will be right. Just make sure that the focus of your choices is not on others' opinions. It must be on the belief that you are doing what God wants you to do and rejecting what God does not want you to do. In the end, you will answer not to the populace but to God.

Learn Your Limitations

In addition to saying no to some things, you need to recognize both as an individual and as a team that you cannot do it all. Even with a completed team—with your combined skills, personality traits, spiritual gifts, and talents—you can't do everything. Therefore, the team must choose a few things and do them well.

You may find that the ministry team conducts a fantastic ministry to college students but is ineffective with high-school students. You may be able to work well in a housing project but poorly in the suburbs. You may not have a rapport with the elderly but are loved by children. You may have the ability to help single parents with their finances but are all thumbs at practical-help ministries. Whatever it is, you need to find your niche, both individually and as a team.

Finding your collective strengths and weaknesses is sometimes a trial-and-error process. If you begin an area of ministry and fail, be willing to concede that and move on. This experience does not mean that you are a failure or that the team is a failure. It simply means that something did not work out. Keep at it until you find what works. Thomas Edison experimented with thousands of light bulbs before finding one that worked. Every time he failed, he would conclude, "That's one more way I know it won't work." He knew that he could find a way to make it work. Finding it was simply a matter of time and perseverance.

Psychologists and family counselors know that a growth stage of development for children is learning boundaries. We use discipline to teach children limits. Children find security in knowing where the limits are. They find the limits by pushing to the edge. If a parent ignores the push, the child pushes harder and farther until the limits are reinforced. In a similar way, pushing boundaries takes place in ministry. When you begin, you have no idea how far God wants the ministry team to go. As you try various avenues of ministry, you may find that some things don't fit because of the nature of the project, timing, or a lack of resources. As you move forward, you must determine what things God is calling you to and what things He is not calling you to. By learning these limits, you can focus on the things you can do well.

The apostle Paul spoke of his ministry's mission in light of the reward of a resurrected life that would follow: "Brothers, I do not consider myself yet to have taken hold of it. But one thing I do: Forgetting what is behind and straining toward what is ahead, I press on toward the goal to win the prize for which

God has called me heavenward in Christ Jesus" (Phil. 3:13-14). Paul had a focused ministry. Several times in Scripture he referred to himself as the Apostle to the Gentiles. Therefore, he did not invest large segments of his life and energy pursuing the Jewish people. Others could do that better than he. God had called him to reach the Gentiles, and that is just what he did.

Passing the Torch

The most universal symbol of the Olympic Games is the torch runner. When one runner reaches a destination, that person passes the torch to another, who takes the torch and continues. In your ministry a time will come when you too will need to pass the torch. Perhaps you are transferred to a new job or experience another change in your life. Perhaps you begin to recognize certain limitations, such as time or ability. You need to be able to let go when the time is right.

When your team began, you accepted certain responsibilities and may now excel in those areas. On a team you need to have ownership in the areas of your responsibility. But in time someone else may have joined the team who can also do well in that area. Remember that while you are ministering to a particular target group, you are also ministering to your team members. Scripture calls the process of developing leaders discipleship. When you have mastered a skill, invite someone alongside you to teach. In time she may be able or may need to take your place.

It can be difficult to turn over an area of ministry into which you have poured a significant portion of your life. A new person will probably not handle that area exactly the way you have done it. You must define boundaries in this area, letting other persons minister. Encourage them and accept the fact that they will approach some elements differently.

The apostle Paul was a bold, brash, bulldog of a guy. His ministry was full of controversy and adventure. Yet he chose to pour his life into mild-mannered, shy young Timothy. Paul wrote to him more than once to encourage him to be bolder. Paul could sense that Timothy was not going to pursue ministry in the same manner as he did, but that was OK. The last letter Paul ever wrote was to his spiritually adopted son. The book is 2 Timothy. In the last chapter you can sense Paul's emotions as he turned over the reins of ministry to Timothy. Paul knew that his life was almost over, and he wanted the work to continue: "In the presence of God and of Christ Jesus, who will judge the living and the dead, and in view of his appearing and his kingdom, I give you this charge: Preach the Word; be prepared in season and out of season; correct, rebuke, and encourage— with great patience and careful investigation" (2 Tim. 4:1-2).

Sometimes God calls you to a new ministry dream. You must be obedient, but that doesn't mean you must let the earlier dream die. Build a ministry relationship with other committed Christian single adults who can continue the team's ministry. If you have brought others alongside you in ministry, they can continue toward the team's goals. When your race is completed with the torch God has placed in your hand, you can place it into the hand of another runner. And you will have the satisfaction of knowing that you have started a revolution.

---

[1]Robert Browning, "Andrea del Sarto," as quoted by John Bartlett in *Familiar Quotations* (Boston: Little, Brown and Co., 1942), 488.

conclusion

I grew up watching a weekly television series that opened with a recorded message that went something like this:

> Hello, Mr. Phelps. We assume that since you are listening to this message, you have agreed to accept this mission. In the envelope you will find photographs of a mansion nestled in the mountains of Central America. It is the home of John Valdez. The safe in his home contains documents that are vital to the security of the United States. Your mission, Mr. Phelps, is to secure those documents and to destroy them. Of course, as is our policy, should you or any member of your team be captured, we will disavow any knowledge of your existence. Good-bye, Mr. Phelps. This tape will self-destruct in five seconds.

With that, the tape would begin to smoke, the background music would swell, and I would once again be on the edge of my seat to watch an exciting episode of "Mission: Impossible." Each week this expert team faced what seemed to be insurmountable odds. Yet it always succeeded. Things rarely went as planned. The team always encountered problems it hadn't anticipated. But the team would adjust, compensate, and move forward.

When the team was assigned a mission, members were briefed on the details. After team members understood the primary objective, they devised and rehearsed a plan again and again until they got it right. Each team member had different skills needed to accomplish the task. Although the goal would change each week, the skills used to accomplish it were be the same. One team member was an explosives expert. One was an electronics wizard. One was a makeup professional with countless disguises. Each member choreographed his skill with the others in light of the mission at hand. The team was a success, and so was the series.

I leave you with a mission. This book is not about to self-destruct. Your life may not actually be placed in danger. Your mission is to discover God's calling for your life, to find others with the same calling, to blend together as a team, to formulate collective goals, and to implement your plans for ministry.

Like the team on "Mission: Impossible," your ministry team will encounter obstacles you hadn't planned on. But you have at your disposal a group of committed Christians whose skills, talents, and resources can overcome any surprises. And you have the abiding presence of the Holy Spirit to give you the insight and strength you need to succeed. He wants you to succeed at fulfilling God's mission.

I believe that more than anyone else, single adults have the capacity to start a revolution in this world. Committed single adults represent Christianity's greatest untapped resource for performing evangelism and ministry. The question is not whether the revolution can happen, because it can. The question is not whether single adults have the capacity to accomplish a worldwide revolution, because you do. The question is, Are you going to be a revolutionary? Will you let God take you out of your comfort zone and use you in His kingdom in ways you have never conceived?

You have the capacity to start a revolution. You may be the change agent that awakens other single adults to the challenge of changing the world for Christ. Our God is a mighty God. Dream big and trust a big God.

As I end this book, I want to leave you with these questions of eternal significance: Will this material make any difference? Who will take the content of this book, apply it in their Christian lives and ministries, and start a revolution where they live? I pray that those revolutionaries will be you and your team. Let the revolution begin! Meet you on the front lines.

ideas for ministry

- Write letters to your newspaper editor.
- Volunteer at social agencies to build relationships with unbelievers.
- Host barbeques or cookouts to build relationships with your neighbors.
- Volunteer for a short-term missions project.
- Plan ministry projects based on needs mentioned in the newspaper.
- Adopt a senior adult in your church or in a nursing home.
- Adopt a little brother or a little sister.
- Volunteer time at a children's home.
- Join an environmental organization that advocates a Christian position.
- Run for political office.
- Support a Christian candidate who is running for office.
- Write a book or a magazine article.
- Write a weekly newspaper column that reflects Christian values.
- Organize rallies or marches for Christian causes.
- Call talk shows to express Christian positions.
- Write letters commending companies that support Christian positions.
- Write letters challenging companies that promote unchristian values.
- Organize coworkers for Bible study, prayer, and accountability.
- Begin your own Christian radio program on a secular station.
- Volunteer at your local public-television or public-radio station.
- Start a private company that promotes Christian values or products.
- Buy billboard space and promote a Christian message.
- Join a civic club to build relationships.
- Establish a home page on the Internet to express Christian positions.
- Begin a class that teaches English as a second language.
- Minister to physically or mentally disabled persons.
- Hold a fellowship luncheon for single adults.
- Begin a Bible study in an apartment complex or neighborhood.
- Minister to persons with AIDS.

- Visit the homebound, providing spiritual guidance and practical ministry.
- Volunteer at a rescue mission.
- Volunteer at a crisis-pregnancy center.
- Volunteer at a shelter for abused women and children.
- Provide tutoring and companionship for children and youth.
- Offer support groups on grief recovery, chemical addiction, codependency, abuse, and eating disorders. Advertise the groups in the community.
- Provide care packets for new residents in the community.
- Begin a counseling-and-referral service for persons who seek employment.
- Begin a prayer ministry.
- Hold a weekly, community-wide prayer breakfast.
- Develop and implement a witnessing strategy.
- Begin a ministry to prisoners and their families.
- Provide food, clothing, money, and furniture for the needy.
- Help organize and work in a Christmas toy store.
- Assist the elderly and disabled with home and lawn care.
- Minister to hospital patients and their families.
- Read to persons who cannot read for themselves.
- Provide child care one or more days a week to allow a parents' day out.
- Provide baby-sitting for new parents.
- Sponsor parenting seminars, studies, and retreats.
- Visit in the home of new parents and give a pink or blue Bible.
- Provide premarital counseling and seminars.
- Provide temporary care for pregnant women who have no place to live.
- Deliver care packets to new mothers.
- Provide temporary shelter, food, and protection for children in crisis.
- Provide housing and care for displaced, endangered, or abused women.
- Provide practical help for single mothers and fathers, such as encouragement, fellowship, seminars, and emergency child care.
- Provide before- and after-school care for children.
- Provide Vacation Bible School for children.
- Organize neighborhood Backyard Bible Clubs for children.
- Provide literature, personal letters, and encouragement for students attending college away from home.
- Offer seminars on grandparenting and advertise in the community.

- Offer automobile repair for widows, elderly persons, and single mothers.
- Offer aerobics classes.
- Sponsor the Red Cross bloodmobile and advertise the hours to the community. Provide refreshments and Christian tracts.
- Sponsor an event such as a walk/run or a softball or golf tournament that allows opportunities to witness.
- Offer fellowship and a Christian witness through team sports.
- Prepare and distribute baskets of food to needy families during holidays and at other times.
- Offer help with debt, budgeting, and planning.
- Provide help with income-tax preparation during specific, advertised hours.
- Mail a sympathy note to the family of every person whose name appears in the obituary column of the newspaper.
- Provide facilities in which homeless persons can sleep on inclement nights.
- Provide Christian literature and fellowship for long-distance truck drivers.
- Provide meals for the homeless on holidays or at other times.
- Offer Bible study or worship services at a nearby resort.
- Witness and minister at special community events.
- Teach persons to read, in the process sharing Christ with them.
- Provide Christmas-gift wrapping in a mall. Distribute tracts and witness.
- Develop a library that includes audiotapes on biblical subjects, life issues, and music. Make the tapes available to believers to share with unchurched family members and friends.
- Send birthday greetings with Christian messages to unchurched persons.
- Provide a 24-hour crisis-counseling line. Advertise the number.
- Provide immediate support and practical help for rape victims.
- Provide immediate crisis-intervention counseling for persons in crisis.

Many of these ministry ideas are from *Meeting Needs, Sharing Christ,* a resource that equips believers to share their faith as they meet physical and emotional needs. This would be an excellent follow-up study to *Start a Revolution,* giving biblical, practical instruction single adults can use to make a difference for Christ. *Meeting Needs, Sharing Christ* is available from the Customer Service Center; 127 Ninth Avenue, North; Nashville, TN 37234-0113; 1-800-458-2772; email customerservice@lifeway.com; fax (615) 251-5933.

Generation X'ers — Making Life's Journey Count

Generation X. Who are they? What makes them tick? This generation, though in conflict with itself and others, is filled with great potential. An individualistic, in-your-face group, X'ers want their leaders to be authentic, credible, willing to share their own struggles and feelings, contemporary and humorous in their approach, concise with biblical texts, and ready to provide concrete examples for living the Christian life.

David Edwards, a gifted communicator, provides all of these in *Destination: Principles for Making Life's Journey Count*, a video-based study for young adults. Resources include the following:

- 4, 45-minute VHS videos - available separately for $19.95 each
  The Road Ahead (Item #0-7673-2663-6)
  Signs That You Don't Get It (Item #0-7673-2664-4)
  Enjoy the Ride (Item #0-7673-2665-2)
  Getting to Your Destination (Item #0-7673-2666-0)
- *Destination: Principles for Making Life's Journey Count Member Workbook* - $5.95
- *Destination: Principles for Making Life's Journey Count* Leader Kit (includes all four videos, the member workbook, and a leader guide) - $79.95

Destination can be used in a variety of settings such as a weekend retreat, a 4-week study, or an 8-week study. Destination is high-energy and con-temporary—guaranteed to appeal to Generation X'ers!

Destination: Principles for Making Life's Journey Count resources can be ordered in any of the following ways:

Write to Customer Service Center; 127 Ninth Avenue, North; Nashville, TN 37234-0113; fax (615) 251-5933; call toll free 1-800-458-2772; email custom-erservice@lifeway.com; order online at http://www.lifeway.com; or visit a Baptist Book Store or a LifeWay Christian Store.